PARIS

A D D R E S S B O O K

Staff Editor:	Barbara Jones
English Adaptation:	Suzanne Patterson
Design:	Flavia Cocchi
Photography:	Claude Huber
Cartography:	Falk-Verlag

We would like to express our thanks to the following for their invaluable help in the research and preparation of this guide: Isabelle Turin, Françoise Mabillard, Ariane Bondroit, Véronique Bondroit, Eileen Harr-Kyburz, Jacques Schmitt, Jack Altman, Philippe Turin, Richard Ackermann, Patrick Château and Claude Huber.

We have made every effort to ensure the accuracy of the information in this book. But Paris changes very quickly. A shop might close its doors, a museum undergo renovation, a nightclub lose its charm; prices, telephone numbers, addresses and circumstances in general are constantly subject to alteration. We cannot, therefore, take responsibility for any factual errors of this kind.

We'd be happy to hear from you if you find a change or new feature we should know about. A postcard would do. Be sure to include your name and address, since in appreciation for a useful suggestion, we'd like to send you a free travel guide.

3

Firmly—and fondly—rooted in the past, Paris is nevertheless the world's most fashionable, trend-setting capital, resolutely turned towards the future. It's always on the move; there's always something new to see. And the city's heart beats day and night.

This book was designed to complement the Berlitz Paris Travel Guide, to help you discover, at a glance, where it's all happening—whether your interests lie in the fields of art, architecture, music, cuisine or haute couture.

With particular emphasis on the new, the experimental, the exciting, we have collected hundreds of addresses, covering everything imaginable from venerable monuments to bistrots à la mode, from museums to galleries of visionary art, from ancient, never-changing quarters like Saint-Germain to the futuristic Villette and Défense districts. You need a hotel? We help you find one. Where to have dinner? More than one of the restaurants listed will entice you. What about nightlife? There's plenty to do after dark—concerts, theatre, cinema, jazz clubs, discos, nightclubs.... We even venture into the outskirts, to the leisure parks, the new towns, the royal châteaux—as far as the beaches at Honfleur and Deauville.

Each address is keyed to a large-scale street map; we have given the nearest métro station or, whenever valid, precise instructions from the railway station. You'll find information on public transport, along with other helpful guidelines, in a short section of Practical Information just before the maps. In each chapter, addresses are listed in alphabetical order, but to help you find sights quickly, there's a complete index at the back of the book.

No matter how long you stay in Paris, we sincerely hope this book helps you enjoy your visit even more.

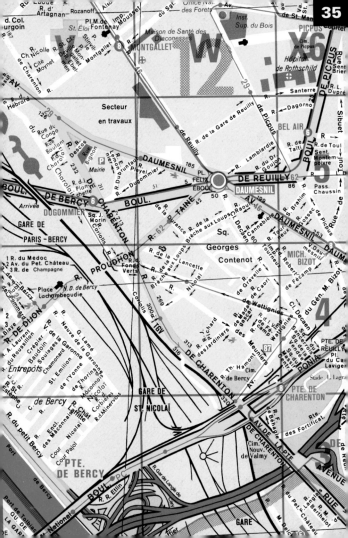

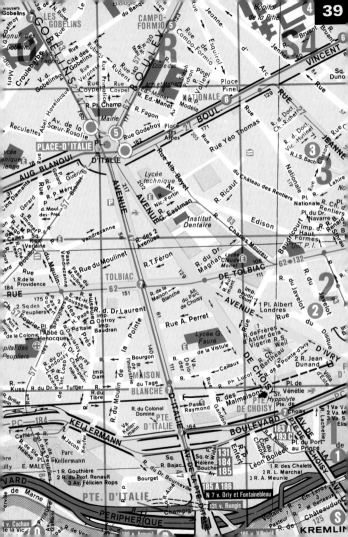

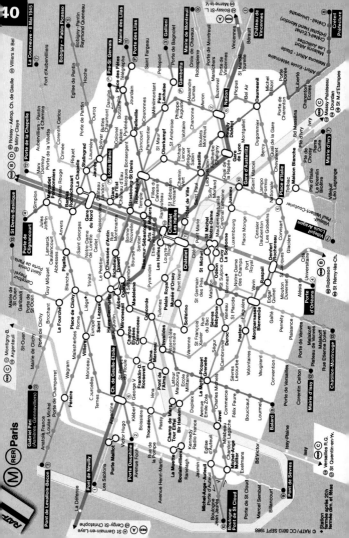

247

249

250

Until Julius Caesar appeared on the scene in 50 B.C., Paris was just a handful of Celtic fishermen living on an island in the middle of the Seine. The Romans called it Lutetia, and its inhabitants the *Parisii*. Because the right bank was unmanageably boggy, the Romans settled on the south side of the Seine, on the spot now known as the Latin Quarter.

Renamed Paris under Emperor Julian in A.D. 360, the town prospered. It became the capital of France when Hugues Capet, Duke of Paris, was crowned king in 987. The first great period of construction was under Capetian rule—while the monarchy built the Louvre fortress and the first stone city walls, Notre-Dame and the Sainte-Chapelle were erected on the Ile de la Cité, and the left bank became the domain of the clergy and scholars.

Commerce flourished, and by the 14th century, the merchants were almost as powerful as the king himself. Their provost, Etienne Marcel, ruled Paris briefly until he was assassinated. Paris gained status as a municipality, and the Hôtel de Ville (City Hall) was built on the Place de Grève. The population soon began to spread outside the walls. To the west, the new districts of faubourgs (lit: suburbs) Saint-Germain and Saint-Honoré went up; to the north and east, labourers and craftsmen took over faubourgs Saint-Denis, Saint-Martin and Saint-Antoine.

The Renaissance and the revival of Classicism inspired many elegant private mansions and public buildings. François I reconstructed the Louvre, but it was Henri IV who made Paris a truly royal capital. He built the splendid Place des Vosges and Place Dauphine, beautified the river banks and completed the grand Pont-Neuf. Even when Louis XIV abandoned Paris and took the court to Versailles, the city continued its expansion, at the same time becoming more salubrious.

At the end of the 18th century, Louis XVI agreed to the construction of a new city wall. However, this Mur des Fermiers Généraux was not intended to protect the population, but rather to facilitate the levy of a tax on merchandise entering Paris. It was hardly a popular move—the resulting rise in prices helped spark off the Revolution. It was no coincidence that one of the first targets of the rebels was the Bastille fortress, considered to symbolize royal despotism. Or that the new flag and cockade imposed on the king incorporated the colours of the town of Paris with the white of the royal banner. For the Revolution of 1789 was essentially the victory of the people, the craftsmen and

Who could resist soaking his feet after a long trek round the Louvre?

merchants, over the privileges of the aristocracy. The offending city wall was demolished and a circle of wide boulevards built on its site.

In the aftermath of the Revolution, Napoleon Bonaparte initiated a veritable building boom. Besides erecting prestigious monuments to celebrate his battles, he greatly improved Paris for the people with warehouses, food markets, slaughterhouses and bridges. Under Napoleon III, Baron Haussmann, the Prefect of the Seine district, gave Paris its airy look by ruthlessly razing old neighbourhoods to make way for wide, sweeping boulevards and avenues. He drew a new boundary round Paris, incorporating parts of the forests of Boulogne and Vincennes and peripheral townships such as Belleville, Montmartre, Passy and Auteuil, then divided the city into 20 administrative segments known as *arrondissements*. Paris underwent a frenzy of bourgeois construction—great stone apartment houses with expensive rents that banished most of the working-class population to the suburbs.

At the turn of the century, the Belle Epoque style surfaced during the World's Fairs held in Paris, leaving cast-iron buildings such as the Grand Palais and the Eiffel Tower as monuments to the Third Republic, which also began construction of the underground railway, the Métro.

Paris survived the two world wars virtually unscathed, and today it very much resembles the city as Haussmann left it. Recent presidents have added their share of monuments—such as Pompidou's cultural centre and Mitterrand's Pyramid in the Louvre. Other modern developments were attempts to relieve Paris of its heavy traffic and horrendous parking problems. A through road, the *voie sur berges*, was created along the banks of the Seine to enable traffic to cross the city rather than get caught up in the perpetual traffic jam of the *autoroute périphérique*, the circular motorway forming the modern city limits. In order to give the 2.5 million inhabitants some breathing space, a vast complex of office buildings, the Quartier de la Défense, was designed on the edge of the city—visible in the perspective of the Champs-Elysées as a hazy Manhattan on the horizon. New towns sprang up in clusters along the main railway lines radiating from Paris—Evry, Saint-Quentin-en-Yvelines, Cergy-Pontoise, Marne-la-Vallée—and the Métro was supplemented by the rapid RER line which transports thousands of commuters each day.

For 20 centuries Paris grew in concentric circles. But on contemporary maps, it looks more like an octopus, reaching its tentacles in every direction. With its populaton of 10 million, Paris and its *agglomération* form the largest metropolis in Europe. Who knows how far it will go....

We have listed below a selection of the most important historic buildings of the capital, set in alphabetical order. The churches are grouped together, then some of the finest town houses (*hôtels particuliers*), and finally the monuments. To avoid repetition, some entries are cross-referenced to other chapters. The coordinates refer to the map section, after page 206; map page numbers are indicated in **bold face**.

CHURCHES

LA MADELEINE   **15** M11   Ⓜ Madeleine
Place de la Madeleine (8th). With its Greek façade and Roman interior, the Madeleine looks more like a Greek temple than a church. The original idea was to match the National Assembly building on the other side of the Place de la Concorde, and Louis XV laid the first stone in 1764. But construction was halted with the Revolution, until Napoleon took over and put up the temple-like structure. He variously considered using it for a stock exchange, the Bank of France, a theatre or a library, and finally decided on a Temple of Glory dedicated to the soldiers of his Grande Armée. Then the architect persuaded him to build the Arc de Triomphe instead. After Waterloo, Louis XVIII reverted to the plan for a church, but with no transept, aisles or bell-tower, not even a cross on the roof. Today, it's a favourite place for celebrity weddings.

9

   Concerts are held here regularly. One of them, *Une heure de musique à la Madeleine* (An hour of music at the Madeleine) takes place once a month except August and September, on Tuesdays at 6.30 p.m. Information and booking on the spot, or phone 39.61.12.03.

Musical Churches
Concerts are held in many churches—too many to mention them all here. To find out what's going on when you're in Paris, call the tourist office, tel. 47.23.61.72, or consult the weekly magazines **L'Officiel des Spectacles**, **Pariscope** or **7 à Paris**, which give all details including seat prices. "Entrée libre" or "concert gratuit" means admission is free.

NOTRE-DAME DE PARIS   **25** Q8   Ⓜ Cité
Place du Parvis (4th). This 12th-century landmark was built to be awe-inspiring. The main part took 167 years to complete, and the

transition it represented from Romanesque to Gothic is said to be a perfect expression of medieval architecture. Given the cathedral's gigantic size, the balance of its proportions and the harmony of its façade are nothing short of miraculous. We can thank architect Viollet-le-Duc for the present structure with its majestic towers, spire and breathtaking flying buttresses. He painstakingly restored the edifice between 1845 and 1863, after Victor Hugo's novel *Notre-Dame de Paris* started a public outcry over pre-Revolutionary "improvements" and Revolutionary pillaging.

Look for the Gallery of Kings across the top of the three doorways. These 28 statues representing the kings of Judah and Israel were pulled down during the Revolution, because they were thought to be the kings of France. The original heads are on display in the Musée de Cluny (see page 43). Inside, stand in the middle of the transept and admire the two outsize rose windows that bathe the cathedral in a wonderful light. The blue north window dates from the 13th century, whereas the south window, mainly red, was largely restored.

Climb to the top of the north tower for a close-up view of the gargoyles and a beautiful panorama. There's a free guided tour of the cathedral at noon on weekdays, 2.30 p.m. on Saturdays and 2 p.m. Sundays, lasting about an hour. A free organ recital is held every Sunday at 5.45 p.m.

NOTRE-DAME-DES-VICTOIRES   16 O11   Ⓜ Bourse

Place des Petits-Pères (2nd). Pilgrims have left more than 30,000 votive offerings in this church, built by Louis XIII to celebrate his victory over the Protestants at La Rochelle. The tomb of Jean-Baptiste Lully, a 17th-century composer, served as hiding place for the church's treasures during the Revolution, but it was ransacked. Fortunately the looters didn't notice the seven Van Loo paintings hanging in the choir.

SACRÉ-CŒUR DE MONTMARTRE   8 P15   Ⓜ Abbesses/Anvers

37, rue Chevalier-de-la-Barre (18th). To save your legs, take the little funicular from the Anvers métro station exit.

The dazzling exterior of this Romano-Byzantine church derives from a variety of stone that whitens and hardens with age. It was erected from 1875 to 1914 as a symbol of penitence for the insurrection of the 1871 Commune and defeat in the war against the Prussians. With its over-ornate exterior and extravagant interior mosaics, the Sacré-Cœur enjoys a dubious reputation. Though it attracts thousands of tourists and pilgrims, for many its only redeeming feature is the view from the dome, which covers a radius of 30 miles on a clear day.

SAINT-AUGUSTIN   **15** L13   Ⓜ Saint-Augustin
Place Saint-Augustin (8th). This Italo-Byzantine church, built between 1860 and 1868, is capped by a 60-metre-high dome. The
framework holding up the vaults is cast iron—the architect Victor
Baltard was one of the first to use this material. His best-known
achievement in Paris, however, was Les Halles, the central food
market; the huge iron halls were regretfully demolished when the
market was transferred to Rungis in the suburbs in 1969. Some of
them were salvaged and reconstructed in the Parc Georges Brassens
(see page 171).

SAINT-ÉTIENNE-   **32** P6   Ⓡ (line B) Luxembourg
DU-MONT   Ⓜ Cardinal-Lemoine
1, place Sainte-Geneviève (5th). The shrine of Geneviève, the patron
saint of Paris, is kept here. Of Flamboyant Gothic style, with a
Renaissance façade, this is the only church in Paris that can boast its
original rood screen (1545).

11

SAINT-EUSTACHE   **24** P10   Ⓜ Les Halles
2, rue du Jour (1st). A monument of the Renaissance period (the
cornerstone was laid in 1532), but decidedly Flamboyant Gothic in
silhouette, Saint-Eustache is remarkable for its 17th-century stained-
glass windows over the choir, crafted according to medieval traditions. The church wasn't very noticeable until the neighbouring
Halles were demolished; the circular Place René-Cassin was designed in the gardens of the new Forum to set it off beautifully. The
strange sculpture of a huge head and hand reposing on the steps is
the work of Henri de Miller.
   Berlioz gave the first performance of his *Te Deum* in Saint-
Eustache, and Liszt his *Gran Mass*, and the church is still the venue of
excellent concerts. It's worth going to Sunday mass, at 11 a.m., to hear
the reputed choir, *les Chanteurs de Saint-Eustache.*

SAINT-GERMAIN-   **24** O9   Ⓜ Louvre–Rue de Rivoli
L'AUXERROIS   or Pont-Neuf
2, place du Louvre (1st). This used to be the parish church of the
French kings. Its untidy appearance stems from the fact that it shows
vestiges of various architectural styles from the 12th to the 17th
centuries. Linger in front of the porch, a marvellous example of
Flamboyant Gothic. The church was secularized during the Revolution, and until 1838, when it was reconsecrated, led a chequered
career as a saltpetre factory, a store for fodder, a printer's workshop
and a police station.

SAINT-GERMAIN-DE-CHARONNE

Ⓜ Porte de Bagnolet

4, place Saint-Blaise (20th). With all the greenery around, you might think you're out in the country. This is one of the last churches in Paris (with Saint-Pierre-de-Montmartre) to have retained its own cemetery.

The church was rebuilt in the 15th century. Inside, look for an unusual ornamental support (cul-de-lampe) sculpted with vine leaves and bunches of grapes, a reminder that Charonne was once a village surrounded by vineyards.

SAINT-GERMAIN-DES-PRÉS

23/24 N8   Ⓜ Saint-Germain-des-Prés

3, place Saint-Germain-des-Prés (6th). The church of Saint-Germain is all that remains of a huge Benedictine monastery founded in the 6th century by St Germanus of Paris. It was most influential in the 17th and 18th centuries. The oldest part is the tower, dating back almost 1,000 years, and the rest is a hybrid of Romanesque and Gothic. The interior was painted (some would say daubed) with murals in the 19th century. Grave slabs commemorate philosopher Descartes and critic Boileau.

SAINT-JULIEN-LE-PAUVRE

24 P7/8   Ⓜ Saint-Michel

1, rue Saint-Julien-le-Pauvre (5th). In the heart of the Latin Quarter, this is the most modest church in Paris but also the oldest. Like Notre-Dame, it represents an architectural transition from Romanesque to Gothic. The capitals of the choir are superb, intricately

---

Saint-Germain-des-Prés

The literary district par excellence, Saint-Germain-des-Prés is the home of the major French publishing houses, the Académie française, lots of bookshops, and the cafés where Jean-Paul Sartre, Simone de Beauvoir and their existentialist acolytes used to work and keep warm in the years following the Liberation. Existentialism has now had its day, and the smoky jazz cellars where Juliette Greco made her débuts singing Sartre, Camus and Queneau are replaced by discotheques. But the easy-going atmosphere of the pavement cafés lives on around the Place Saint-Germain-des-Prés. The Café Bonaparte, Brasserie Lipp, the Deux Magots and the Flore offer ringside seats for the street theatre of mimes, fire-eaters, jugglers and street musicians who pass round the hat—and for the neighbourhood eccentrics who offer their show for nothing.

sculpted with acanthus leaves and harpies. On Sundays, mass is said here in Greek or Arabic, for this is not a Roman Catholic church but Melchite, as can be seen from the rich iconostasis.

SAINT-LOUIS-EN-L'ÎLE   25 R7   Ⓜ Pont-Marie
19 bis, rue Saint-Louis-en-l'Île (4th). Appropriate to the stylish reputation of the Ile Saint-Louis, its church is as elegant as any of its great mansions, bright and airy with a golden light illuminating a veritable museum of Dutch, Flemish and Italian 16th- and 17th-century paintings and some splendid tapestries from the 12th century. The church itself, commenced by Le Vau in 1664 and completed by Le Duc and Doucet in 1725, is a superb example of 17th-century baroque. Numerous concerts are held here.

Below the tower, the clock swings from a bracket like an old shop sign.

SAINT-MÉDARD   33 Q5   Ⓜ Censier-Daubenton
141, rue Mouffetard (5th). This church bears traces of practically every **13** century since the 12th. A painting inside, *Le Christ mort*, is attributed to Philippe de Champaigne, a 17th-century Belgian artist of the Flemish school.

The little square next to the church was once the cemetery. Louis XV had it closed because of "the fits at Saint Médard"—the tomb of a Jansenist had brought about miracles and subsequent mass hysteria. He put up a notice on the door: "By order of the king, God is forbidden to perform miracles in this place!".

SAINT-MERRI   25 Q9   Ⓜ Châtelet
78, rue Saint-Martin (4th). Though it was built during the Renaissance, the church is a typical example of Flamboyant Gothic. One of the oldest bells in Paris still tolls in the left-hand tower. Apart from some beautiful 16th-century stained-glass windows, the church contains several interesting works of art—a Virgin and Child by Van Loo, a reredos by Simon Vouet, and a wonderful organ. Two of the many recitals given here are free: Saturdays at 9 p.m. and Sundays at 4 p.m., all year round.

SAINT-NICOLAS-   17/25 Q11   Ⓜ Réaumur-
DES-CHAMPS   Sébastopol
254, rue Saint-Martin (3rd). Though the Parisians pass it by, Saint-Nicolas-des-Champs is worth a visit for the 17th-century altarpiece with two paintings by Simon Vouet. The south doorway on Rue Cunin-Gridaine is a particularly graceful example of Renaissance architecture. The sun dial dates from 1666 and still tells the time.

Take time to wander through the little streets south of the church (Rue des Gravilliers, Rue Chapon), lined with ancient façades and old mansions. On Rue de Montmorency you'll see the House of the Big Gable (no. 51), built for the alchemist Nicolas Flamel in 1407 (see page 29).

SAINT-PIERRE-DE-MONTMARTRE   8 O15   Ⓜ Abbesses

2, rue du Mont-Cenis (18th). Just down the hill from the Sacré-Coeur, this church is unfairly neglected by visitors in favour of the basilica. Consecrated in 1147, 16 years before Saint-Germain-des-Prés, it represents a significant work of early Gothic art, belied by its 18th-century façade. It has the oldest Romanesque vaulted ceiling in Paris and green marble columns said to be the vestiges of a Roman temple dedicated to Mercury. The church was part of a significant abbey in the Middle Ages, but played a much less glorious role during the Revolution when a baker's oven was built in one of the apses.

Hooray Henri

At the end of the 16th century, future king Henri IV camped with his army on Montmartre hill to lay siege to Paris. The local abbey was a handy retreat. Henri, who already had quite a reputation as a womanizer, received a warm welcome from the abbess. So warm, in fact, that the fond encounter encouraged nuns and soldiers to follow suit. The news spread like wildfire, delighting the French, who have always been partial to a bawdy joke. Needless to say, the abbess was covered in shame. But Henri never lost the hearts of the people—except for that of Ravaillac, a Catholic zealot who stabbed him to death.

SAINT-ROCH   23 N10   Ⓜ Tuileries/Pyramides

296, rue Saint-Honoré (1st). Lots of concerts are held in this fine church, reputed for its acoustics. Built in pure Jesuit style, Saint-Roch is almost as spacious as Notre-Dame; three successive chapels behind the choir are an unusual feature, richly embellished with works of art. Louis XIV laid the foundation stone in 1653.

The cannonball craters on the façade stay as a reminder of the Royalist uprising of October 1795, crushed by Bonaparte whose soldiers melted down the organ pipes for bullets. Since then the organ case has been restored; it's now classified as part of the national heritage.

Information about the concerts can be obtained from the Service des concerts de Saint-Roch, tel. 42.61.93.26.

SAINT-SÉVERIN   24 P7/8   Ⓜ Saint-Michel
1, rue des Prêtres-Saint-Séverin (5th). This church combines two
architectural styles: 15th-century Flamboyant Gothic (look up at the
superb palm vaulting in the double ambulatory) and 18th-century
Gothic Revival. It calls up shades of J.-K. Huysmans, a Dutchman
"petrified with Parisianism", who wrote prolifically about the church
and neighbouring district.

The church organ is said to be one of the best in Europe. Saint-
Saëns liked its tone so much that he asked to be the honorary
organist of St-Séverin in 1897. Recitals are often given; admission is
free to two concerts a week from October to June: Saturdays at 9 p.m.
and the third Sunday of the month at 4.30 p.m.

SAINT-SULPICE   24/32 N7   Ⓜ Saint-Sulpice
Place Saint-Sulpice (6th). One of the largest churches in Paris. The
Saints-Anges chapel is decorated with frescoes by Delacroix, painted **15**
between 1853 and 1861, which apparently sent Baudelaire into rap-
tures.

If you visit the church at noon and it's a sunny day, look up at the
window in the middle of the transepts. A sun ray will shine through a
little hole in the window and fall on a bronze meridien linking the
north transept and a marble obelisk, the remains of an 18th-century
sun dial.

Saintly Saint-Sulpice
*Every other shop in the district around the church of Saint-Sulpice
is crammed with rosaries and crucifixes, holy pictures and statues
of saints. It's the domain of what the French call disparagingly
"l'imagerie sulpicienne", the insipid paraphernalia of excessive
piety. But the maze of little streets are worth investigation for the
many boutiques, restaurants and bars tucked between the con-
vents and religious bookshops. Some of the façades are architectural treasures, with sculpted porches, wrought-iron balconies and
unexpected surprises—Rue des Canettes, for example, got its
name from the little ducks waddling across the front of number 18,
a fine 18th-century apartment house. Rue des Ciseaux is not
"Scissors Street" but "Six O's Street", after a hostelry called the "Six
Golden O's". Rues Princesse, Guisarde and Mabillon also make a
pleasant stroll.*

Visitors to Paris soon find out than an *hôtel* is not always a home-from-home. *Hôtels particuliers*—private mansions or town houses—are sometimes the finest expression of a period's architecture. Many of the houses listed below may be visited.

HÔTEL DES AMBASSADEURS DE HOLLANDE **25** R9 Ⓜ Saint-Paul

47, rue Vieille-du-Temple (4th). Construction was completed in 1657. The celebrated playwright Beaumarchais spent 12 years of his life here, writing *The Marriage of Figaro* while earning his living in the arms trade selling cannon.

HÔTEL LAMBERT **25/33** R7 Ⓜ Sully-Morland

2, rue Saint-Louis-en-l'Ile (4th). The finest 17th-century town house in the city, designed by Le Vau, the architect of Versailles, is listed as a protected monument. Voltaire once enjoyed a tempestuous and lengthy love affair here with the lady of the house, the Marquise du Châtelet. The actress Michèle Morgan also lived here until members of the Rothschild family took up residence. Closed to the public.

HÔTEL DE LA ROCHEFOUCAULD-DOUDEAUVILLE **23** L8 Ⓜ Varenne

47, rue de Varene (7th). The Italian Embassy has been housed in this 18th-century building since 1938. The façades on courtyard and garden sides, the interior decoration and the staircase are listed as part of the national heritage. Closed to the public.

HÔTEL DE LAUZUN **25** R7 Ⓜ Sully-Morland

17, quai d'Anjou (4th). Built by Le Vau in the 1650s, the *hôtel* has been the property of the City of Paris since 1928; it is sometimes used for official receptions. Its opulently ornamental décor provided the perfect setting for Baudelaire's Club des Haschischins, co-founded with his friend Théophile Gautier when they resided here.

Guided tours every weekday, at 2.30 or 3 p.m. From Easter to November, tours are organized on Saturdays and Sundays at 10 a.m. and 5.30 p.m.

HÔTEL MATIGNON **23** L8 Ⓜ Varenne

57, rue de Varenne (7th). Talleyrand lived it up in this 18th-century mansion, now the official residence of the French prime minister. VIPs are received in the grand semicircular courtyard. The magnificent park is the biggest private garden in Paris. Closed to the public.

16

HÔTEL DE ROHAN   25 S10   Ⓜ Saint-Sébastien-Froissart
87, rue Vieille-du-Temple (3rd). Dating from the beginnning of the 18th
century, this edifice is connected to the Hôtel de Soubise by a garden
(not always open to the public). Look for Robert Le Lorrain's magnificent stone bas-relief, *Les Chevaux d'Apollon* (The Horses of Apollo),
over the doorway of the old stables in the second courtyard—it's
widely considered to be the most beautiful 18th-century sculpture in
France.

Visits are possible during temporary exhibitions, and guided tours
can be arranged through the Caisse des Monuments historiques (see
below).

Visiting Times
Whenever possible, we give precise details on the opening hours of
monuments and town houses. As this information is subject to
change, it's always best to check with the times given in the daily
newspapers or the weekly magazines *L'Officiel des Spectacles,
Pariscope,* and *7 à Paris,* issued on Wednesdays.

You can also obtain information from the following offices,
which can provide a useful blue leaflet listing all current events:
Affaires culturelles de la Ville de Paris: Hôtel d'Albret, 31, rue des
Francs-Bourgeois (4th), and Hôtel Coulanges, 37, rue des Francs-
Bourgeois; tel. 42.76.67.00 or 42.76.67.87. Map **25** R9; métro Saint-
Paul.
Centre d'accueil de l'Hôtel de Ville: 29, rue de Rivoli (4th); tel.
42.76.43.43. Map **25** R9; métro Hôtel-de-Ville.
Office de tourisme de Paris: 127, avenue des Champs-Elysées
(8th); tel. 47.23.61.72. Map **14** H12; métro Charles-de-Gaulle–Etoile.
There are several associations that organize guided tours,
sometimes with lectures, for individuals or groups, such as:
La Caisse des Monuments historiques: 62, rue Saint-Antoine
(4th). Map **25/26** S8, métro Saint-Paul. No information is given by
telephone.
Evasion Loisir Accueil: 119, boulevard Lefebvre (15th); tel.
45.31.68.46 or 45.32.61.20. Map **36** J3; métro Porte de Vanves (for
groups of minimum 10–15).
Paris et son théâtre: 82, rue Taitbout (9th); tel. 45.26.26.77. Map **16**
N3; métro Trinité/Saint-Georges.
A special pass, the Carte Musées et Monuments, gives access
to 60 museums and monuments for a single fee. For details, see
page 34.

HÔTEL DE SENS   **25** R8   Ⓜ Pont Marie

1, rue du Figuier (4th). A blend of Gothic and Renaissance style, it looks more like a military fortress than a town house. It's one of the oldest buildings in Paris, dating from 1475, and now houses a library. Closed to the public—but you can venture into the courtyard to look around.

HÔTEL DE SOUBISE   **25** R9   Ⓜ Rambuteau

60, rue des Francs-Bourgeois (3rd). The National Archives are kept in this magnificent 18th-century mansion which, like the Hôtel de Rohan next door, was designed by Pierre-Alexis Delamair. The horseshoe-shaped courtyard leads to an exquisite rococo world: the apartments of the Prince and Princess of Soubise, the high point of Louis XV décor, house the Musée de l'Histoire de France.

For guided tours of the royal apartments, enquire at the museum (tel. 42.77.11.30).

MONUMENTS

ARC DE TRIOMPHE   **23/24** N10   Ⓜ Palais-Royal
DU CARROUSEL

Jardin des Tuileries (1st). A lovely avenue leads to this monument erected by Napoleon in 1809 to celebrate the victories of his imperial armies. Its big brother at the Etoile is visible in a straight line beyond the Obelisk on the Place de la Concorde. This imposing effect was originally planned for Napoleon to see from his bedroom in the Louvre. The Grande Arche at the Défense on the horizon now forms the end of the longest perspective in the world.

ARC DE TRIOMPHE   **13/14** H12   Ⓜ Charles de Gaulle-Etoile
DE L'ÉTOILE

Place Charles-de-Gaulle (8th). Napoleon decided to build this triumphal arch, perhaps his most famous monument, after his return from Austerlitz. Jean-François Chalgrin's design was so complicated and difficult that it took 30 years to build and was not finished until long after Napoleon's demise. He only ever saw a life-size wood and canvas model. Louis-Philippe inaugurated the final version in 1836, complete with bas-reliefs and statuary celebrating victories of the Revolution and Napoleonic empire. The main sculpture, *Le Départ des volontaires de 1792* by François Rude, is more commonly known as *La Marseillaise*. The remains of the Unknown Soldier were buried under the arch in 1920, commemorating the victims of World War I. Three years later, the eternal flame was lit; it's revived by army veterans during a public ceremony every evening at 6.30 p.m. The Armistice Day ceremony takes place here on the 11th November.

At the foot of the arch the eternal traffic moves slowly round in circles or jams up—a fascinating sight from the top. From here you also get a good view of the 12-pointed star, formed by twelve avenues radiating from the arch in a tour de force of Haussman's town planning. The lift is in service every day from 10 a.m. to 6 p.m.

ARÈNES DE LUTÈCE   33 Q6   Ⓜ Jussieu
10, rue des Arènes (5th). This Roman amphitheatre—or rather, the ruins of it—is the oldest monument in Paris (not counting the Obelisk of Luxor, in the Place de la Concorde). The *arènes* are now a favourite playground for the neighbourhood children, and for their fathers who play *boules* in the middle.

BIBLIOTHÈQUE NATIONALE   16 O11   Ⓜ Bourse
58, rue de Richelieu (2nd). Part of the buildings of the National Library date from the 17th century; it has been expanding ever since to accommodate some 6 million books and periodicals, 12 million engravings and 2 million photographs. Not to mention the 250,000 ancient manuscripts, including the Dead Sea Scrolls and Charlemagne's *Evangéliaire*.

19

The reading rooms are closed to the public, but the Mansart and **Mazarine galleries** are sometimes opened for exhibitions. Details are published in the daily newspapers, or can be obtained from the reception desk, tel. 47.03.81.26.

Numismatists will be delighted to know that the **Cabinet des Médailles et des Antiques,** with a rich collection of coins, is open every day except Sunday, from 9 a.m. to 4.45 p.m.

BOURSE DU   24 O11   Ⓜ Louvre–Rue de Rivoli
COMMERCE   or Les Halles
2, rue de Viarmes (1st). This circular building dating from 1888 is the Commodity Exchange. You can learn how the prices of raw materials are fixed by participating in a guided tour or group visit (minimum 10 persons), which take place on weekdays. Information and booking on tel. 45.08.37.40. The Wednesday **Corn Exchange** (*Bourse du Grain*) is particularly lively and interesting.

Adjoining the building on the south side is an old corkscrew staircase of 147 steps, in a tower 3 metres in diameter and 27 metres high—all that's left of Henri II's palace, which stood on this site in the 16th century. The astrologers and cabbalists employed by his superstitious wife Catherine de Medicis used to toil up the stairs to read her future in the stars.

BOURSE DES VALEURS   **16** O11   Ⓜ Bourse
4, place de la Bourse (2nd). The French version of the Stock Exchange—an imposing building with Corinthian peristyle, constructed in 1808–25.

Visits (with commentary) possible from Monday to Friday from 11 a.m. to 1 p.m., every half hour and lasting 90 min. (From 1st July to 15th September, one visit only, at noon.) Entrance by the gate, Rue Vivienne; tel. 40.41.10.00.

CONCIERGERIE   **24** P9   Ⓜ Cité
1, quai de l'Horloge (1st). When it's lit up at night, the Conciergerie looks like something out of a fairytale. But it has rather a grim past—some of the most colourful characters of French history books spent their last hours in the dingy cells of this ancient prison: Ravaillac, the assassin of Henri IV; the Marquise de Brinvilliers, a famous 17th-century poisoner; the highwayman Cartouche; Marie-Antoinette; Danton and Robespierre. A few macabre mementoes are on display: a guillotine blade, the crucifix to which Marie-Antoinette prayed before execution, and the lock from Robespierre's cell. Look out on the Cour des Femmes and see where husbands, lovers, wives and mistresses were allowed one last tryst before the tumbrels came.

The Conciergerie is part of the **Palais de Justice,** the law courts, which was the Royal Palace before the kings of France moved to the Louvre. Three of its rooms still retain their 16th-century splendour. Open daily from 10 a.m. to 5 p.m. (the ticket office closes at 4 p.m.). Tel. 43.54.30.06. On the corner of the building, near the Pont au Change, you can see Paris's first public clock, very ornate in blue and gold.

EIFFEL TOWER   **21** H9   🚇 (line C) Champ-de-Mars
Champ-de-Mars (7th). Gustave Eiffel's contribution to the World's Fair of 1889 was greeted with derision and scorn by the critics. Guy de Maupassant signed a manifesto against "this vertiginously ridiculous tower", and Verlaine rerouted his daily walks to avoid seeing it. But the people loved it, and still do, especially since the end of 1985 when new spotlights were installed, illuminating the tower from *inside* and giving it a delicate, ethereal glow in the night sky. In 1889, two million visitors paid 5 francs each to climb up to the top. At the time, it was the highest construction in the world, and an astounding engineering achievement—15,000 pieces of metal joined together by 2,500,000 rivets, soaring 984 feet into the air on a base area of only 1,400 square feet. Ten thousand gas lamps lit it up at night.

Electric elevators now take you up to the third floor for the best possible bird's-eye view of Paris. On a clear day, you can see up to 40 miles around or more (best an hour before sunset). Gustave Eiffel had his private apartments up here, together with laboratories of astronomy, biology and meteorology.

Once you've admired the view you can dine in one of the tower's three restaurants: **Le Jules Verne**, **La Belle France**, and **Le Parisien**.

Visiting times: from 10 a.m. to 11 p.m. (midnight in July and August); tel. 45.55.91.11. Group visits can be arranged—phone 45.50.34.56.

FONTAINE SAINT-MICHEL 24 P8 Ⓜ Saint-Michel

Place Saint-Michel (5th). The heart of the Latin Quarter, this is where the youth of Paris hangs out, meets up, drops out, jumps in.... The atmosphere gets hotter as the evening wears on. It's quite fun between 4 and 8 a.m. The fountain was designed by Gabriel Davioud, the architect of the two theatres on the Place du Châtelet on the Right Bank.

21

Elysian Fields for Ever

The world's most celebrated avenue, the Champs-Elysées sweeps majestically up from the Place de la Concorde to the Etoile, flanked by chestnut trees all the way. It was Catherine de Medicis' idea to construct a wide avenue over the marshy fields in front of the Tuileries, for the king's daily constitutional. Louis XIV added a few decorative improvements, rich burghers built their mansions along it. As the avenue became an ever more popular venue for family outings, a host of cafés, bars and dance halls sprang up. Napoleon envisaged the Champs-Elysées as a vast Triumphal Way, culminating in the Arc de Triomphe; under the Directoire, the "Champs" was the chic place to be seen.

Today, from the Rond-Point to the Etoile, both sides of the avenue are lined with flashy shops and arcades, gleaming airline offices and car showrooms, cinemas and merciful café terraces to rest your feet and watch the people passing by. The best places are at the corner of the Avenue George-V on the shady side and at Rue du Colisée on the sunny side. Don't try to cross from one side to the other if you're of a nervous disposition. The steady stream of honking traffic only stops for special ceremonies, when the Champs-Elysées shows what a Triumphal Way it can be. On Bastille Day the regiments, tanks and artillery of the French army parade proudly for the President; and on the last day of the Tour de France, the whole city comes out to cheer the final lap of the bicycle cavalcade, up to the Arc de Triomphe and back again.

HÔTEL DES INVALIDES   **22** K8/9   Ⓜ Invalides
Esplanade des Invalides (7th). Beneath the monumental dome lies
Napoleon, encased in six tombs, one inside the other like a set of
Chinese boxes, which took Lodovico Visconti 20 years to complete.
Napoleon's tomb is probably the most visited in the world; it's in
Hardouin-Mansart's chapel, entrance on the south side. The **church
of St. Louis** (entrance on the north side) is bedecked with the
hundreds of flags taken from the enemy by the imperial armies.
Military ceremonies and high society weddings are held there.

The rest of the building is devoted to the **Musée de l'Armée** (see
page 46). The splendid north façade looks out over the wide Esplanade.

Visits every day except Saturdays, Christmas Day and New Year's
Day, from 10 a.m. to 7 p.m. in summer and to 5 p.m. in winter; tel.
45.55.92.30.

HÔTEL DE VILLE   **25** Q9   Ⓜ Hôtel de Ville
Place de l'Hôtel de Ville (4th). The present building, dating from 1873,
is a Renaissance-style reproduction of François I's original, burned
down during the Commune uprising in 1871.

The interior is grandiose, resplendent with thick carpets, crystal
chandeliers, tapestries, marble and gold leaf—a fitting setting for the
receptions held by the City of Paris.

Individual visits possible on Mondays at 10.30 a.m.; group visits
Monday–Friday; tel. 42.76.59.27 or 42.76.59.28. Entrance Rue Lobau.

Striking on the Strand
*Before it took the name "Place de l'Hôtel de Ville", the square in
front of the City Hall was known as "Place de Grève"—"Strand
Square"—from the gravelly bank of the Seine which served as a
port from the 12th century onwards. The square was at the centre
of Parisian life, the site of fun fairs and public executions, the place
everyone would stop for a gossip or a grumble. Men looking for
jobs would stand there waiting to be hired, hence anyone out of
work would be described as "en grève". Nowadays the unem-
ployed are "au chômage", and "faire la grève" has become the
watchword of the trade unions: to go on strike!*

INSTITUT DE FRANCE   **24** N/O9   Ⓜ Pont-Neuf
23, quai de Conti (6th). This building was designed by Louis Le Vau in
1668 to harmonize with the Louvre across the river. It began as a
school for the sons of provincial gentry, financed by a legacy of
Cardinal Mazarin. In 1805 the building was turned over to the Insti-

tut de France which comprises several academies: Belles Lettres, Sciences, Beaux Arts, Sciences Morales et Politiques, and the august body of the Académie française, the supreme arbiter of the French language.

Individual and group visits, generally the first Saturday of the month. Information can be obtained from the Institut (tel. 43.26.80.66), from the Caisse des Monuments historiques or the association Paris et son histoire (see page 17).

MOSQUE 33 Q5 Ⓜ Monge

Place du Puits-de-l'Ermite (5th). Part of the Muslim Institute. The Moorish-Hispanic architecture and decoration are attractively authentic-looking. Besides the Turkish baths *(hammam)*, there's a very pleasant café where you can drink mint tea and sample Arab pastries. Visits every day except Friday, from 9 a.m. to 1 p.m. and from 2 to 5 p.m.; tel. 45.35.97.33.

OBSERVATOIRE 32 N/O4 Ⓡ (line B) Port-Royal
DE PARIS Ⓜ Denfert-Rochereau

23

61, avenue de l'Observatoire (14th). Built under Louis XIV by Claude Perrault and François d'Orbay, the observatory is the oldest of its kind and has always served the same purpose: today it's the seat of the International Time Bureau. Its four sides were constructed facing the four points of the compass, and a copper wire set into the floor shows the north-south axis of Paris. The domes and wings were added in the 19th century.

An astronomer conducts individual visits on the first Saturday of every month at 2.30 p.m.; tel. 40.51.22.21. For group visits, write to the Observatoire.

OPÉRA DE PARIS–GARNIER 15 N12 Ⓜ Opéra

Place de l'Opéra (2nd). When Napoleon III's wife, Empress Eugénie, first saw this ornate neo-Baroque building, she exclaimed, "What an ugly duckling! It has no style!". "But Madame, it's pure Napoleon III!" promptly retorted the architect, Charles Garnier. Now many consider it the masterpiece of the Second Empire. Marble-clad, exuberantly sculpted and scrolled, it's less of an aesthetic joy than a proclamation of the prosperity of the French bourgeoisie. Though it takes honours as the world's largest theatre, it seats only 2,000 people, who crane their necks to see the extraordinary ceiling mural painted by Marc Chagall in 1964.

The Palais Garnier is reserved for ballet, while the National Opera Company has moved to Opéra-Bastille.

For tickets, see pages 138–139.

PALAIS BOURBON   **23** L10   Ⓜ Invalides/Assemblée Nationale
33, quai d'Orsay (7th). The seat of the National Assembly provides a
rather formidable riverside façade for the Left Bank's most stately
district. It was designed in the 18th century as a residence for a
daughter of Louis XIV; the Grecian columns echoing the Madeleine
on the other side of the Place de la Concorde were added by
Napoleon.

Individual visits on "open days"—every Saturday from the beginning of January to mid-March, and from the beginning of July to
mid-September, at 10 a.m., 2 and 3 p.m. To arrange visits for groups
(15 to 30 people) phone 40.63.63.08.

PALAIS DE CHAILLOT   **21** G10   Ⓜ Trocadéro
Place du Trocadéro (16th). Built in 1937, it houses several museums:
the Navy; Man (Anthropology); French monuments; Cinema. Its
paved terrace is the ideal place for photographing the Eiffel Tower.

24 **PALAIS DE**   **15** L12   Ⓜ Miromesnil
    L'ÉLYSÉE   or Champs-Elysées-Clémenceau
55, rue du Faubourg Saint-Honoré (8th). What have the Marquise de
Pompadour, Alfred de Vigny, Napoleon Bonaparte and Tsar Alexander got in common? They all lived in this magnificent town house,
before it became the official residence of the French head of state in
1873.

The watchful Republican Guard make sure that casual bystanders
don't get any nearer than the door of Louis Féraud's shop across the
street.

PALAIS DE JUSTICE (see *Sainte-Chapelle*, page 27)

PALAIS DU LOUVRE   **24** O9/10   Ⓜ Palais-Royal
Right bank of the Seine (1st). In 1190 Philippe Auguste built a stone
fortress to protect his capital from river attack by the Normans while
he was away on a crusade. Two hundred years later, Charles V
realised it was safer than his home on the Ile de la Cité and went to
live in it, transforming it into a turreted fairy-tale castle. His successors
were too lazy to improve the building, and it gradually declined, until
François I acceded to the throne. He was a great art lover, and
besides renovating and beautifying the Louvre itself, he began a
collection of masterpieces by acquiring four Raphaels, three Leonardo da Vincis and one Titian. Henri IV, Catherine de Medicis, Louis XIV
and Napoleon altered the palace until it took its present-day appearance under Napoleon III. In 1793, the leaders of the Revolution
declared the palace a national museum, at which time it contained

650 works of art. President Mitterrand's twinkling glass pyramid in the Cour Napoléon has completed eight centuries of construction. Designed by American-Chinese architect leoh Ming Pei, this controversial structure covers the new entrance. Beneath it, moving staircases lead to a series of rooms created for temporary exhibitions, restrooms, an auditorium, a superb bookshop, a restaurant and a café. Excavation of the Cour Napoléon was begun in 1981; besides thousands of ancient statuettes, vases, coins, jewellery and bones, the foundations of Philippe Auguste's fortress were revealed; they now form part of a fascinating archeological crypt.

The Louvre houses three of the world's greatest treasures: the winged *Victory of Samothrace*, a immense female figure discovered on the island of Samos, beautifully poised at the top of the Daru staircase; the admirable marble *Venus de Milo*; and Leonardo da Vinci's enigmatic *Mona Lisa*. A rundown of the collections and visiting times are given on pages 34–36.

PALAIS DU   **32** N/O7   Ⓜ Odéon **25**
LUXEMBOURG   Ⓡ (line B) Luxembourg
15, rue de Vaugirard (6th). If the building reminds you of the Pitti Palace in Florence, the birthplace of Marie de Medicis, you won't be mistaken. It was built in her honour in 1615–26, by Solomon de Brosse. Today it's the seat of the Senate. To visit, apply to the Caisse des Monuments historiques (see page 17).

PALAIS-ROYAL   **24** O10   Ⓜ Palais-Royal
Place du Palais-Royal (1st). There are few pleasanter places to dip into the history of Paris. Completed in 1639 for Cardinal Richelieu, this serene arcaded palace with its garden of limes and beeches and a pond where the young Louis XIV nearly drowned has always been a colourful centre of more or less respectable activity. It housed the first "Italian" theatre of Paris, where Corneille's *Le Cid* was performed. In the days of Philippe d'Orleans, regent of France during Louis XV's minority, the Palais-Royal was the scene of notorious orgies. To meet the family's extravagant debts, the ground-floor rooms were turned into boutiques—the last of which still sell old coins, medals, engravings and antiques—and cafés that attracted a fashionable society. But it soon took over from the Pont-Neuf as the meeting-place of artists, intellectuals, charlatans, prostitutes and pickpockets. It eventually became a respectable place for artists and writers to live (Colette, among others), and now the French Council of State and the Ministry of Culture occupy the front buildings, around a courtyard dotted with a contemporary series of 260 truncated black and white marble columns, much appreciated by children and dogs.

PALAIS DE L'UNESCO   30 J7   Ⓜ Ségur

9, place de Fontenoy (7th). A good example of mid-20th-century architecture, it boasts art works by Picasso, Miró and Calder. The ground floor is open for visits every day (except Saturdays, Sundays, and public holidays) from 9 a.m. to 5 p.m.

In 1958, Japan donated a superb zen garden to the UNESCO building. Recently restored by the original designer, the sculptor Isamu Nogushi, it is a microcosm of peace and quiet. Free admission from Monday to Friday, from 9 a.m. to 5 p.m.

PANTHÉON   32 P6   ⓇⒺⓇ (line B) Luxembourg

Place du Panthéon (5th). This gigantic, neoclassical building is the resting place of the nation's military, political and literary heroes. Originally designed as the church of Sainte-Geneviève for Louis XV (1755), it was secularized during the Revolution as a vast mausoleum with the inscription, "To our great men, the Fatherland's gratitude". But the Revolutionaries had a hard time deciding who deserved the honour. Mirabeau and then Marat were interred and subsequently expelled. Napoleon ended the controversy by turning the Panthéon back into a church. Throughout the 19th century it seesawed between secular and consecrated status, according to the regime's political colour. Finally, Victor Hugo's funeral in 1885, the biggest the capital had seen, settled the Panthéon's status as a secular mausoleum. Hugo was buried there, followed (retroactively) by Voltaire and Rousseau, and then prime minister Léon Gambetta, socialist leader Jean Jaurès, Emile Zola, Louis Braille, Resistance hero Jean Moulin, and, in 1988, Jean Monnet, founder of the EEC.

Open for visits every day from 10 a.m. to noon and from 2 to 5 p.m.; tel. 43.54.34.51.

PONT ALEXANDRE III   22 K10   Ⓜ Invalides

Cours la Reine (8th). Lovers love to stroll beneath the Belle-Epoque lanterns of Paris's most romantic bridge. Distinguished architecturally by its single steel arch, it was a gift from Tsar Alexander III, whose son Nicholas II laid the first stone in 1896. The melodramatic statues represent Fame and Pegasus.

PONT DES ARTS   24 O9   Ⓜ Pont-Neuf

Quai du Louvre (1st). This frail footbridge, built under Napoleon, was the first metal bridge constructed in France. Cross over it for one of the best views of Paris and the Ile de la Cité.

PONT-NEUF   24 O9   Ⓜ Pont-Neuf

Ile de la Cité (4th). The oldest standing bridge in Paris (though *neuf* means "new") was completed by Henri IV in 1606. It was built without houses: a novelty for the Parisians, who could see their river from the middle for the first time. It soon became a favourite spot for promenades, for street-singers, charlatans, amateur dentists, professional ladies, pickpockets and above all for the *bouquinistes* selling their old books and pamphlets out of boxes.

The provocative Bulgarian artist Christo amused most Parisians a few years ago when he wrapped the Pont-Neuf in gauze like a gigantic parcel.

PONT DE LA TOURNELLE   25/33 Q/R7   Ⓜ Pont-Marie

Quai de la Tournelle (5th). Constructed between 1614 and 1654, the bridge was widened in 1927 and adorned with Paul Landowski's statue of the patron saint of Paris, Geneviève.

PORTE SAINT-DENIS   17 Q/R11   Ⓜ Strasbourg-
AND PORTE SAINT-MARTIN   Saint-Denis

27

Boulevard Saint-Denis (10th). These two triumphal arches built to commemorate victories of Louis XIV were once gates to the city.

SAINTE-CHAPELLE   24 P8   Ⓜ Cité

4, boulevard du Palais (4th). A Gothic masterpiece, within the portals of the Palais de Justice. With its walls of stained glass and its harmonious proportions (nearly equal height and length), the chapel has an ethereal quality—in startling counterpoint to the ponderous surrounding palace. It was built in 1248 by the pious king Louis IX (known as St. Louis) for the relics obtained from the emperor of Constantinople. The 15 stained glass windows include 1,134 different pieces, depicting mainly Old Testament scenes.

Numerous concerts are held in the chapel. Open for visits every day except Christmas, New Year's Day, 1st May, 1st and 11th November, from 10 a.m. to 5 p.m. For information, phone 43.54.30.09.

SORBONNE   32 Q/P7   Ⓜ Cluny–La Sorbonne

Place de la Sorbonne (5th). Founded in 1253 as a college for poor theological students by Robert de Sorbon, Louis IX's chaplain, the university was taken in hand by Cardinal Richelieu, who financed its reconstruction (1624–42). His tomb is in the 17th-century chapel.

The Sorbonne is not open to the public, but you may manage to mingle with the students and sneak into the courtyard or even the Grand Amphitheatre. Try to imagine the scene in May 1968, when the hall was crammed with 4,000 students up in arms against antiquated teaching methods, bureaucracy and the very basis of the social system. When the police invaded the sanctuary—which for centuries had guaranteed student immunity—the revolt was on.

Visits to the chapel can be arranged through the Caisse des Monuments Historiques (see page 17).

THÉÂTRE-FRANÇAIS   24 N10   Ⓜ Palais-Royal
2, rue de Richelieu (1st). Better known as the "Comédie-Française", which in fact is the name of the group of actors working there, this institution was founded by Louis XIV. In 1680 he decided to merge three troupes of actors, including those of Molière, as the "Comédiens du Roi" which became the Comédie-Française under Napoleon. The theatre itself was inaugurated in 1790. The main corridor features a statue of Voltaire by Houdon and a line-up of busts of famous authors by equally famous sculptors, such as Dumas by Carpeaux and Hugo by Dalou. While you're waiting for the curtain to rise, look up at the ceiling and try to identify Molière, Racine, Corneille and Victor Hugo in Albert Besnard's 1913 fresco.

The original theatre burned down in 1900 and was restored the same year. The façade on the Place du Palais-Royal, however, dates from 1850.

To obtain tickets for a play, see pages 138–139. If you would like to join a group tour of the theatre, contact the Caisse des Monuments historiques, which organizes visits on the third Sunday of each month at 10.15 a.m. Tours can also be arranged for groups of at least 30 people through the Administration de la Comédie-Française, tel. 42.96.10.24.

TOUR MAINE-   31 L5   Ⓜ Montparnasse-
MONTPARNASSE   Bienvenüe
Place Raoul-Dautry (15th). The first skyscraper office block built within the city limits (1969–73) sticks out over the rooftops like a sore thumb. You can visit the 56th and 59th (terrace) floors for a breathtaking view of Paris and surroundings—as far as the Channel on a clear day, or so they say. Open from 10 a.m. to 10 pm. (ticket office closes at 9.30 p.m); tel. 45.38.52.56.

TOUR SAINT-JACQUES   24/25 P9   Ⓜ Châtelet
41, rue de Rivoli (1st). This old tower in a quiet little square on the Right Bank is a useful landmark, for you can see it from just about everywhere. It's all that's left of the church of Saint-Jacques-la-Boucherie, demolished during the Revolution, which was one of the halts on the pilgrimage to Santiago de Compostela. Blaise Pascal carried out scientific experiments on the tower, and today it serves as an atmospheric observatory. Closed to the public.

Who lived Where

From 1825 to 1827, **Honoré de Balzac**, author of *The Human Comedy*, lived at 17, rue Visconti (6th) in a small flat above his ground-floor printing press (map **24** N8; métro Saint-Germain-des-Prés).

The celebrated classical author **Pierre Corneille** spent the last two years of his life at 6, rue d'Argenteuil (1st). He died on 1st October 1684 (map **16/24** N11; métro Pyramides).

Eugène Delacroix painted some of his best works, including *The Entry of the Crusaders into Constantinople*, during the 8 years he spent at his second-floor studio at 17, rue Visconti (6th); he also lived for 6 years on the delightful little Place Furstenberg (6th) at number 6 (both addresses map **24** N8; métro Saint-Germain-des-Prés).

The "House of the Big Gable", 51, rue de Montmorency (3rd) was built in 1407 for **Nicholas Flamel**, the alchemist. He never lived there, but rented out the ground floor to merchants and the upstairs rooms to paupers in return for nothing but a paternoster or two (map **25** Q10; métro Arts-et-Métiers).

Marcel Proust, the author of *In Remembrance of Things Past*, lived at 102, boulevard Haussman (8th) from 1907 to 1919, but he died at 44, rue Hamelin (16th), as testified by a plaque on the wall (map **13** H11; métro Boissière).

Appointed historian to the king, playwright **Jean Racine** spent 7 years of his life at 24, rue Visconti (6th). He died there on the 21st April 1699 (map **24** N8; métro Saint-Germain-des-Prés).

Maximilien de Robespierre, the father of the French Revolution, lived at 398, rue Saint-Honoré (1st) until the 27th July 1794 when he was arrested. He was shot and guillotined the next day by the Revolutionary Tribunal (map **15** M11; métro Concorde).

29

CITY SQUARES

PLACE DE LA BASTILLE   **26** T8   Ⓜ Bastille

The prison was torn down during the Revolution, but the square remains. It evolved into what we see today in the second half of the 19th century, and has recently become the centre of a trendy district with renovated buildings, art galleries and artists' studios. Paving stones at the conjunction of Rue Saint-Antoine and Boulevard Henri-VI outline the spot where the prison stood. The column in the middle of the square commemorates the Revolution of 1830.

PLACE CHARLES-DE-GAULLE   **13/14** H12   Ⓜ Charles-de-Gaulle–Etoile

Everyone still prefers to call it by its former name, Place de l'Etoile ("Star Square"); from the top of the Arc de Triomphe looking down on it you can see why.

PLACE DU CHÂTELET   **24** P9   Ⓜ Châtelet

The square occupies the site of the Grand-Châtelet prison, demolished at the beginning of the 19th century. On one side is the Châtelet theatre and opposite it, the Théâtre de la Ville, formerly the Sarah-Bernhardt. The fountain in the centre is topped by a gilded statue of Fame.

PLACE DE LA CONCORDE   **23** L11   Ⓜ Concorde

More than 1,000 people were guillotined here during the Revolution, the drums rolling to drown out any incendiary words the condemned might utter. In 1934, it was the scene of bloody rioting against the government. Ten years later it was the Germans' last hold in Paris. Frantic with traffic in the daytime, the square is delightful at night, with floodlit fountains and elegant lamps. It was designed by Gabriel in 1753. Pavilions in the corners are topped by statues representing eight of France's most important towns: Brest, Rouen, Lille, Strasbourg, Lyon, Marseille, Bordeaux and Nantes. One fountain is named after the Rivers, the other after the Seas. Plumb in the middle is the oldest monument in Paris, the 75-foot pink granite obelisk of Luxor from the temple of Ramses II, dating from 1300 B.C. It was a gift from the viceroy of Egypt, Mohammed Ali, and erected here in 1836. The opening onto the Champs-Elysées is guarded by the *Horses of Marly*, sculpted by Guillaume Coustou.

PLACE DAUPHINE   **24** O9   Ⓜ Pont-Neuf

Baron Haussman was tempted to replace triangular Place Dauphine's gracious red-brick, gabled and arcaded architecture with a neo-Grecian colonnaded square. Fortunately, he was forced out of office for juggling his books before the wreckers could move in. The square was built in 1607 by Henri IV in honour of his son the dauphin, later Louis XIII. Sadly, only the houses at numbers 14 and 26 are still in their original state. Yves Montand lived here with Simone Signoret, but since her death he spends most of his time in the south of France.

PLACE DENFERT-ROCHEREAU   **37** N4   Ⓜ Denfert-Rochereau

The two bossed buildings on the square were built by Claude Nicolas Ledoux at the end of the 18th century. They served as tollhouses for the city gates in the wall of the Fermiers-Généraux. Now one of them leads to the Catacombs (see page 166).

The handsome *Lion of Belfort*, reclining in the centre of the square, is a replica of Bartholdi's original, sculpted in honour of Colonel Denfert-Rochereau and his regiment who heroically defended the city of Belfort in 1870–71.

PLACE DE FURSTENBERG   24 N8   Ⓜ Saint-Germain-des-Prés
This lovely little square, between rues de Furstenberg and de l'Abbaye (6th) is shaded by four magnolia trees and very romantically lit at night. Delacroix's studio on the square is now a museum dedicated to the artist.

PLACE DU TERTRE   8 O15   Ⓜ Abbesses
The old village square of Montmartre has retained its charm, and early in the morning—before the "artists" set up their easels and the tourists arrive—still has something of the atmosphere it had when Renoir, Van Gogh, Gauguin and Utrillo worked in the district.

PLACE VENDÔME   15 M/N11   Ⓜ Opéra
This airy, elegant octagon was designed by Jules Hardouin-Mansart to provide an imposing setting for a statue of Louis XIV. Only his financiers could afford the rents here, and 300 years later the situation has not changed: world-famous jewellers, banks, the Ministry of Justice and the Ritz Hotel encircle the column with which Napoleon replaced the Sun King. The spiral of bronze bas-reliefs depicting scenes from the Great Battles, topped by a statue of Napoleon himself, was cast from 1,250 cannons captured from the enemy at Austerlitz.

PLACE DES VICTOIRES   16 O11   Ⓜ Bourse
The façades of eleven houses surrounding an equestrian statue of Louis XIV form a harmonious classical ensemble.

PLACE DES VOSGES   26 S8   Ⓜ Chemin-Vert
Perhaps the city's most picturesque square. Its classical harmony is achieved by a subtle diversity of detail in the gables, windows and archways of its red-brick façades. When Henri IV had the square built in 1605, on the site of a horse market, it consisted of 36 houses, each encompassing four arches, nine on each side. But these have since been expanded or contracted according to the means of the owners. Victor Hugo lived at number 6, now a fascinating museum of his manuscripts and drawings. The gardens of the square, a peaceful playground for children, were once a favourite spot for duels and, after Louis XIII's wedding festivities here, the town's most fashionable promenade. From Place Royale, the name was changed to honour the Vosges, the first *département* to pay its taxes to the Revolutionary Government.

No longer does the word "museum" conjure up images of mustiness and boredom. In Paris the authorities have at last realized that a museum can, and should, be a lively place to learn and make exciting new discoveries, not just somewhere to take the children on a rainy day. Whether it's the venerable Louvre or the more recent Picasso, Orsay and Fashion museums, the reception and displays are refreshingly modern and pleasant, while at the same time respecting—or even enhancing—the artistic value of the works on show. Huge crowds queue up to enter the temporary exhibitions, which attract more enthusiasts than a Cup Final!

You could spend a good part of your life covering all of the city's museums. But don't be discouraged by the enormity of it all. Visiting just one or two of them will make any stay in Paris more worthwhile. The Louvre should come first. It's so huge that it sometimes frightens people away. But you can't visit Paris without seeing at least the *Mona Lisa*. Another must is the Centre Pompidou. And you shouldn't miss the Musée d'Orsay, in an old railway station, or the fascinating Cité des Sciences et de l'Industrie on the site of the old slaughter-houses.

33

After the great "classics", we have included in our list a selection of smaller museums, each based on specific themes as diverse as forgery and perfumes. Finally, we mention a few intimate museums in private homes, made famous by the exceptional people who lived there.

Lectures (in French) are organized in many museums, on a specific work of art or theme, on Wednesdays and Saturdays. You can obtain further information at the museum reception desks.

Musée d'Orsay: new look for an old railway station.

MUSÉE DU LOUVRE   **24** N/O10   Ⓜ Palais-Royal
Rue de Rivoli (1st); tel. 40.20.51.51. Daily except Tuesday, from 9 a.m. to 6 p.m. (late closing 9.45 p.m. Monday and Wednesday). Hall Napoléon: auditorium, History of the Louvre rooms and medieval foundations, restaurant and café 9 a.m.–10 p.m. Bookshop 9.30 a.m.–10 p.m. Temporary exhibitions noon–10 p.m. Free entry for anyone under 18.

Guided tours: 11.30 a.m. (in French), 3.30 p.m. (French and English).

Lectures on specific works of art: 12.30 and 1.30 p.m., admission free. The subject changes each month. Enquire at the reception desk for details.

Lectures on specific themes: Wednesday 2 p.m. and Saturday 10 a.m. and 2 p.m. Subject changes every two months.

Enter the Louvre through I.M. Pei's sparkling glass pyramid—kept clean by a squad of acrobatic rock climbers. Designed to take up the smallest possible place, it serves not only as the entrance, but also as a hub for other areas and activities not visible above ground—snack bar, restaurant, gift shop, auditorium, and so on. The construction of the pyramid was the first stage of a vast reorganization plan, intended to make the museum even bigger by liberating the rooms presently occupied by the Ministry of Finance, along the rue de Rivoli.

34

The exhibits are divided into several departments, so it's easy to plan your visit based on the sections that interest you. Don't try to see the whole museum in a day—if you did, you'd become allergic to museums for ever.

Museums Galore
A special pass, the *Carte Musées et Monuments,* grants unlimited access to around 60 museums and monuments in Paris and the suburbs. It can be obtained from the ticket offices of the métro or the museums themselves, at the tourist office, or, if you live in the US and want to buy it before your trip, from

Marketing Challenges Inc., 10E 21st Street, Suite 600, New York, N.Y. 100 10.

The pass is valid for one day (50F), three consecutive days (100F) or five consecutive days (150F). You validate it yourself by writing in the date of your first visit in ink.

Egyptian antiquities: sculptures, such as the *Scribe accroupi*, and monumental statuary, from prehistory to the Arab conquest, as well as collections of small articles—statuettes, domestic and funerary objects, jewellery (Rameses II's pectoral, Amenhotep's signet ring).

Oriental antiquities: important collections from the birth of civilization in Mesopotamia, Iran and the Levant (note particularly the statues of Gudea, the Code of Hammurabi, the magnificent winged bulls that once defended the gates of Sargon's palace at Khorsabad).

Etruscan collections: from pre-Roman Italy, sarcophagi with reclining figures, beautiful filigrane jewellery.

Greco-Roman antiquities: besides the *Venus de Milo* and the *Victory of Samothrace*, numerous ceramics, mirrors, gold jewellery, and a splendid series of terracotta tanagras.

Islamic arts: superb collections tracing the evolution of Islam, from the 7th to the 17th centuries.

Objets d'art: jewellery, furniture, porcelain, enamels, from prehistory to the 19th century (note particularly the splendid furniture of Riesner and Boulle).

35

Sculpture: impressive collection from the Middle Ages, the Renaissance and the 18th and 19th centuries (equestrian statue of Louis XIV by Girardon; Coysevox's *Horses at the Drinking Trough)*.

Drawings: a vast collection in the Cabinet des Dessins, partly presented as temporary exhibitions.

Royal collections: the treasures of the rulers of France are displayed in the Apollo gallery: the Treasure of St-Denis; Charlemagne's sword; Louis XIV's gems; the Crown diamonds; the jewels of the queens of France; the crowns of Louis XV and Napoleon.

But maybe you came just to see the *Mona Lisa*? The main part of the Louvre is devoted to painting, with thousands of masterpieces representing all the European schools, from the Middle Ages to the 19th century, with a heavy accent on the French.

Spanish painting, especially from the 15th century onwards: El Greco, his disciple Luis Tristan, de Ribera, Herrera, Zurbarán, Velasquez (portraits of the royal family).

Flemish and Dutch schools: Van Dyck, Van Eyck, Bosch, Holbein, Rembrandt and Vermeer, to name but a few. And, of course, Rubens, incontestably the master of 17th-century Flemish art. His set of 21 canvases depicting the history of Marie de Medicis was commissioned for the Luxembourg palace (1622–1625).

Italian painting: the *Mona Lisa*, of course, if you can see it over the heads of the crowd of admirers (it's known to the French as *La Joconde*). And more works of Leonardo da Vinci, as well as Cimabue, Giotto, Fra Angelico, Uccello, Botticelli, Correggio, Titian, Veronese.

French painting: there's so much of this it's easier tackled by period.

16th century—Jean Clouet *(Portrait of François I)*; François Clouet *(Pierre Outhe)*; the first and second Fontainebleau schools (*Diane de Poitiers* as the goddess of hunting, and *Gabrielle d'Estrées and her Sister*).

17th century—Philippe de Champaigne, Claude Lorrain, Georges de la Tour, Nicolas Poussin, Hyacinthe Rigaud, Simon Vouet, Charles Le Brun, the brothers Le Nain and Mignard.

18th century—Watteau (*Embarkation for Cythera* and *Gilles*), Boucher, Quentin de La Tour, Mme Vigée-Lebrun, Fragonard, Greuze and Chardin, and the landscapes of Joseph Vernet and Hubert Robert, precursors of Romanticism.

19th century—the immense historical tableaux of David *(Coronation of Napoleon)*—where the life-size cardinal and witnesses look suitably surprised at Napoleon crowning himself emperor; Géricault *(Raft of the Medusa)*; Delacroix *(Liberty Guiding the People)*; Ingres.

An hour for the Love of Art

At lunchtime from 12.30 to 1.30 p.m., some of the great museums offer visits with lectures (in French) on specific works of art. Details are published in a brochure that you can obtain from the information desk of all the national museums.

Once you have made your choice, all you have to do is turn up fifteen minutes before the start of the lecture (which is free, but you have to pay the museum entry fee).

Cluny: *"Une heure, une œuvre"* Monday, Wednesday, Thursday and Friday. Map **32** P7; métro Cluny–La Sorbonne.

Louvre: *"Les midis du Louvre"* Monday, Wednesday, Thursday, Friday. Map **24** N–O10; métro Palais-Royal.

Orsay: *"Une œuvre à voir"* Tuesday to Friday. Map **23** M9; métro Solférino.

BEAUBOURG (CENTRE NATIONAL D'ART ET DE CULTURE GEORGES-POMPIDOU)   25 Q10   Ⓜ Châtelet

19, rue Beaubourg (4th); tel. 42.77.12.33 (information about weekly programmes: 42.77.11.12). Daily except Tuesday noon–10 p.m.; Saturday, Sunday and holidays 10 a.m.–10 p.m.

Admission free, except to the exhibitions and museum where there's so much to see that it's worth investing in a day pass.

The Georges Pompidou National Centre of Art and Culture, usually called ''Beaubourg'', opened its doors in 1977. President Pompidou had always wanted the capital to have a real cultural centre—not just a museum, but a place where things would *happen*, a place to kindle contemporary artistic creation in every domain.

The extraordinary building contrasts violently with the surrounding 17th- and 18th-century façades. To leave the maximum of space inside, architects Renzo Piano and Richard Rogers designed it deliberately inside-out, leaving the underpinnings and various ducts and pipes visible and colour-coded: red for the transportation, green for the water pipes, blue for the air-conditioning and heating, yellow for the electrical system. As the building went up, so did a hue and cry similar to that inspired by the Eiffel Tower. But now most people have grown accustomed to the construction's resemblance to an oil refinery. They just shrug their shoulders and take the escalator in its clear glass tube to watch Paris unfold before their eyes (the best view is from the fourth floor).

37

Musée national d'Art moderne (National Museum of Modern Art): exhibits depict all the artistic trends of the 20th century—from 1905 to 1965 on the 4th floor, and from 1965 to the present day on the 3rd.

The collections, comprising 4,000 paintings, 2,000 sculptures, more than 8,000 drawings, and so on, are partly presented as permanent displays and partly in rotation. To mention just a few of the artists represented: Bonnard, Braque, Chirico, Dali, Delaunay, Dufy, Ernst, Gris, Hartung, Kandinsky, Klee, Léger, Matisse, Miró, Modigliani, Mondrian, Picasso, Soutine, Van Dongen, Vasarely, Vlaminck.

La Grande Galerie, on the 5th floor, shows 20th-century works.

Institut de recherche et de coordination acoustique-musique (IRCAM): an experimental laboratory of acoustics, where Pierre Boulez directs an orchestra of sophisticated synthesizers and computers. It is closed to the public, but if you like contemporary electronic music, you can listen to tapes in the foyer, or attend a concert by the resident *Ensemble intercontemporain.*

Bibliothèque publique d'information (BPI): a public library on three levels, containing numerous written documents, videodisks, films and videos (to be watched on the spot), as well as data banks (accessible for a fee). There's also a language laboratory, a record library (you can listen, but not borrow), as well as a microfilm copying system.

Centre de création industrielle (CCI): exhibitions and debates on any subject within the realm of industrial design, architecture, town planning and environment.

Salle d'actualité: a popular reference library, with all the latest records, books, and French and foreign newspapers.

Logithèque: a lending library of educational and professional software, with a large assortment of computer magazines and video-cassettes.

Librairie Flammarion 4: books, posters and postcards on sale.

Atelier des enfants: a children's workshop, for kids from the age of five (see page 176).

Bibliothèque des enfants: children's library.

La salle Garance: a cinema for film addicts.

38 The plaza outside is Place Igor Stravinsky, a favourite hang-out for freelance street performers—jugglers, conjurors, flame-swallowers and would-be Houdinis, who all give it a merry carnival atmosphere. Tinguely's "animated fountain" is adorned with colourful statues by his wife Niki de Saint-Phalle. The clock in front of Beaubourg, known as the *Génitron*, is ticking away the seconds to the year 2000.

MUSÉE D'ORSAY   **23** M9   Ⓜ Solférino
1, rue de Bellechasse (7th); entrance place Henry-de-Montherlant for the temporary exhibitions; tel. 40.49.48.14. Answering machine (in French): 45.49.11.11. Groups: 45.49.49.49. Open Tuesday, Wednesday, Friday and Saturday 10 a.m.–6 p.m., Sunday 9 a.m.–6 p.m., Thursday 10 a.m.–9.45 p.m.

The Orsay museum, opened in December 1986, has a rather unusual history. The building was originally a railway station, erected in 1898 on the ruins of a palace destroyed during the Commune uprising of 1871. People were not too enthralled by the idea of a cast-iron station right opposite the Louvre, so the architect, Victor Laloux, hid the metallic skeleton behind a stone façade along the river bank. When the station was abandoned in 1939, the building was used as a film set (for Orson Welles' *Trial*), then it became the seat of the Renaud-Barrault theatre company. There was talk of demolishing it, but the public was already so outraged at the destruction of Les Halles that it was decided to convert the station to house the city's collection of Impressionist paintings.

The architects retained all the main glass and metal structures of the building, and Italian architect Gae Aulenti designed the interior as separate spaces on several floors, paying special attention to the lighting. The effect as you enter is breathtaking. But pick up a floor-plan at the main door, for it isn't easy to find your way round at first.

The exciting displays cover French creativity in all domains—including advertising and photography—from 1848 to 1914. You'll see paintings by Cézanne, Courbet, Daumier, Millet, Moreau, Puvis de Chavannes, the great Impressionist foursome Degas, Manet, Monet and Renoir, as well as Bonnard, Douanier Rousseau, Gaugin, Van Gogh, and so on. Sculpture is mainly represented by Bourdelle, Carpeaux, Maillol and Rodin.

Some of the bronze statues on the esplanade symbolize the continents, others represent animals. They were specially commissioned for the World's Fair of 1878.

39

CITÉ DES SCIENCES   **11** V6   Ⓜ Porte de la Villette
ET DE L'INDUSTRIE
Parc de la Villette, 30, avenue Corentin-Cariou (19th); tel. 40.05.70.00. Answering machine (in French): 46.42.13.13). Minitel 36 15 VILLETTE. Open Tuesday, Thursday and Friday 10 a.m.–6 p.m., Wednesday noon–9 p.m., Saturday, Sunday and public holidays noon–8 p.m.

The **reception desks** are in the main hall, levels 0, S1, S2 and Explora. Here you can hire a cordless headphone, which provides a running commentary (available in English) to guide you while you walk around. Reserve one in advance by writing to the Agence Sycomore, 9, rue des Métiers, 95120 Ermont, or call 40.05.76.23 during the museum opening hours.

Guided tours of 2½–4 hours are organized for the permanent and temporary exhibitions. There is also a series of guided circuits which last from 3 to 7 hours depending on the itinerary chosen. To book, call 40.05.70.70 (10 a.m.–4 p.m., at least 10 days in advance).
All the Cité's brochures are available in English.

The downtrodden district of the slaughterhouses on the north-eastern fringe of Paris has become the capital's window on the 21st century. It was the idea of President Giscard d'Estaing to use an abattoir building for a "City of Science and Techniques"—a hand's-on science museum where the accent is on public participation in all phases of space technology, computers, astronomy and marine biology. Though it's four times bigger than Beaubourg, it's only a part of the vast Villette complex, which also contains the Zénith rock concert hall, the Géode sphere, the "City of Music", the "Grand Hall"—and it isn't finished yet.

Designed by Adrien Fainsilber, the glass and steel Cité des Sciences is divided into several sections:

Explora: a permanent exhibition, aimed at the discovery and exploration of the evolution of mankind. It has four main themes: From Earth to the Universe; the Adventure of Life; Matter and Human Labour; Language and Communication. It may sound overwhelming, but you're sure to enjoy it. You can feel what it's like to travel in space, watch the continents drift apart, design a car, talk to a robot, pilot a plane, see what happens inside an eye, and play on the computers to your heart's content.

Planetarium: a voyage in time and space, with live images relayed directly from the greatest observatories in the world. *Daily except Monday, at 11.45 a.m., 1.15, 2.30, 3.45 and 5 p.m; on Wednesday, Saturday and Sunday also at 7 p.m.*

Inventorium: an activity centre specially for kids, to make them aware of the world around them. Divided into sections for two age groups, from 3 to 6 and from 6 to 12 (see page 176 for opening hours).

Espace-entreprise: an exhibition of French industrial production.

Maison de l'industrie: how the French economy works.

Médiathèque: a resources centre with books, magazines, videos, computer software related to techniques and industry. Includes a Braille library. *Open for adults every day except Monday, from noon to 8 p.m. (9 p.m. on Wednesday); for children, Wednesday, Saturday and Sunday from 2 to 6.30 p.m.* (See also page 177).

Salle science-actualités: a newsroom for all the latest happenings in the scientific world.

Galerie expérimentale: exhibitions of works of art by film-makers, writers, musicians and so on, linking arts, techniques and science.

Cinéma Louis Lumière: science fiction and scientific films, documentaries and cartoons. *Call 40.35.79.40 for information on the daily programme.*

In the rest of the park:

Géode: the biggest attraction of the Villette complex. The sparkling sphere is made up of 6,433 triangles of stainless steel, fitted together as closely as on a spaceship. It contains a hemispheric cinema screen, 36 metres in diameter, and reclining seats. When you watch a film you feel as if you are part of it—travelling through space or sinking to the bottom of the ocean. *Every hour from 10 a.m. to 9 p.m., Wednesday, Friday, Saturday and Sunday; from 10 a.m. to 6 p.m. Tuesday and Thursday. During the school holidays: from 10 a.m. to 9 p.m. Tuesday to Sunday. Tickets are on sale on the spot. For group bookings phone 40.05.06.07; enquiries 40.05.12.12. Seat reservations can be made at the reception desk from 11 a.m. onwards for the same day or the following 8 weeks, or by Minitel, 36 15 VILLETTE.*

Grande Halle (entrance Porte de Pantin): the old cattle market transformed into a hall for trade fairs, exhibitions, concerts etc.

Zénith: a temple dedicated to the sacred monsters of rock; with space for 6,500 spectators. *(For details on concerts call 42.40.60.00; reservations from Monday to Friday, from 11 a.m. to 6 p.m., tel. 42.40.01.01).*

The **Cité de la Musique** is still undergoing construction; it will hold a **41** concert hall for classical and contemporary music, and exhibitions of musical instruments.

The big red metallic sculptures dotted around the park are in fact Swiss architect Bernard Tschumi's Follies, sheltering refreshment stands.

Minitel

The Minitel is there to stay, having invaded most French homes and public buildings. It's used for everything from looking up phone numbers to ordering a case of Bordeaux. A little brochure–*Passeport Tourisme Minitel*–with operating instructions in English and a list of useful codes is available from tourist offices. Some of the 7,000 services are in English.

To call up the directory, switch on the Minitel, lift the telephone receiver and dial 3615. As soon as you hear a loud beep, press the "Connexion/Fin" key and put the phone receiver back. Type in the code MGS, and press the green "Envoi" key. Proceed forwards through the directory using the "Suite" key, and backwards with "Retour". For the British news, type 3615 BBC. The code 3615 LIBE will give you the news in English from USA Today, and 3615 UPI the international news from the United Press International agency. 3614 ED calls up the electronic phone directory in English.

MUSÉE DES ARTS DÉCORATIFS   23 N10   Ⓜ Palais-Royal
107–109, rue de Rivoli (1st); tel. 42.60.32.14. Wednesday to Saturday 12.30–6.00 p.m., Sunday 11.30 a.m.–5.30 p.m. Closed Monday and Tuesday.
Tapestries, porcelain, furnishings from French homes in the Middle Ages to modern times. Temporary exhibitions focus on aspects of historical or contemporary design, or the works of individual designers.

MUSÉE D'ART MODERNE   13/22 H10   Ⓜ Iéna
DE LA VILLE DE PARIS
Palais de Tokyo, 11, avenue Président-Wilson (16th); tel. 47.23.61.27. Daily except Monday, 10 a.m.–5.30 p.m., Wednesday until 8.30 p.m.
20th-century visual arts, from Matisse to Picasso. The museum boasts the biggest painting in the world—Dufy's *La Fée Électricité*, which depicts the story of electricity in 600 square metres.

42   The section called **ARC** (Animation-Recherche-Confrontation) has exhibitions of all kinds of contemporary and experimental art, including music and poetry. The **Musée des Enfants** offers instructive displays for children (see page 177).

MUSÉE CARNAVALET   25 S9   Ⓜ Saint-Paul
23, rue de Sévigné (3rd); tel. 42.72.21.13. Daily except Monday 10 a.m.–5.40 p.m.
Madame de Sévigné lived in this mansion in the heart of the Marais from 1677 until her death in 1696. It was built in the 16th century; the bas-reliefs on the façade are by Jean Goujon.

The collections trace the dramatic history of the City of Paris from the 16th century to the present day, with special emphasis on relics of the Revolution—models of the guillotine, the original Declaration of the Rights of Man and the Citizen, liberty caps and cockades. There are lots of old maps, scale models of monuments, engravings and photos, and a rich collection of paintings by François Clouet and his school.

MUSÉE CERNUSCHI   14 K13   Ⓜ Villiers/Monceau
7, avenue Velasquez (8th); tel 45.63.50.75. Daily except Monday and holidays 10 a.m.–5.40 p.m.

Since this museum was opened in 1898, Henri Cernuschi's collection of Oriental art has been considerably enriched. Treasures include neolithic terracottas and a 5th-century bodhisattva.

MUSÉE DE CLUNY   **32** P7   •   Ⓜ Cluny-La Sorbonne
6, place Paul Painlevé (5th); tel. 43.25.62.00. Daily except Tuesday 9.45 a.m.–12.30 p.m. and 2–5.15 p.m.
The abbots of Cluny lived in this 15th-century Gothic mansion, which now houses a magnificent collection of tapestries. The exquisite *Lady with the Unicorn* is the chief attraction, but there are also Byzantine fabrics, relics of the Visigoths, precious ivories and enamels.

   While you're there, go to see the (restored) ruins of the Cluny thermal baths, 24, rue du Sommerard (5th); métro Maubert-Mutualité, partly incorporated into the museum—they date from Gallo-Roman times.

MUSÉE DU   **14/22** K11   Ⓜ Champs-Elysées–Clemenceau
GRAND PALAIS
Avenue Winston-Churchill (8th); tel. 42.89.54.10 (answering machine, in French: 42.56.09.24). Daily except Tuesday 10 a.m.–8 p.m., Wednesday 10 p.m.
Important temporary exhibitions are held in this colossal iron, glass and stone construction, built for the 1900 World's Fair. It's a wonderful example of the flowery Belle Epoque style. Logically enough, the best exhibitions attract crowds of people, and the queues go all round the block.

43

MUSÉE GUIMET   **13** H10   Ⓜ Iéna
6, place d'Iéna (16th); tel. 47.23.61.65. Daily except Tuesday, from 9.45 a.m. to 5.15 p.m.
A beautifully displayed collection of Oriental Arts, in three sections: South-East Asia (Khmer, Javanese, Thai, Laotian); Tibet, China, India and Afghanistan; then Japan, Korea and Central Asia. Of special interest: examples of Greco-Buddhist art discovered in Afghanistan, including the treasure of Begram.

MUSÉE DE L'HISTOIRE DE FRANCE   **25** R9   Ⓜ Rambuteau
60, rue des Francs-Bourgeois (3rd); tel. 42.77.11.30. Daily except Tuesday and holidays 2–5 p.m.
In the Hôtel de Soubise, a beautiful 18th-century mansion: historical manuscripts and documents from all periods, including the Edict of Nantes, the Declaration of the Rights of Man, Louis XVI's testament, and so on.

MUSÉE JACQUEMART-ANDRÉ   **14** K12   Ⓜ Saint-Philippe-du-Roule

158, boulevard Haussmann (8th); tel. 42.89.04.91. Daily except Tuesday and holidays, 1–6 p.m.

Italian Renaissance art blends harmoniously with 17th- and 18th-century European works in this elegant 19th-century mansion, beautifully furnished and decorated. Paintings by great masters such as Botticelli, Canaletto, Chardin, Fragonard, Greuze, Guardi, Mantegna, Nattier, Rembrandt, as well as sculptures by Donatello and Houdon. Note on the staircase Tiepolo's fine murals, from a Venetian villa.

MUSÉE MARMOTTAN   **20** E9   Ⓜ La Muette

2, rue Louis-Boilly (16th); tel. 42.24.07.02. Daily except Monday 10 a.m.–5.30 p.m. (visits with commentary by appointment).

A fabulous collection of Monets, bequeathed by his son, as well as works by other Impressionists and First Empire and Renaissance pieces. Most of the Monets date from his last years at Giverny (see page 203), but the major work *Impression, soleil levant*, which gave the Impressionist movement its name, was stolen in 1985.

44

MUSÉE NATIONAL DES MONUMENTS FRANÇAIS   **21** G10   Ⓜ Trocadéro

Palais de Chaillot, place du Trocadéro (16th); tel. 47.27.35.74. Daily except Tuesday, 9.45 a.m.–12.30 p.m. and 2–5.15 p.m.

Full-scale reproductions of the major French monuments from the 3rd to 19th centuries, from the Roman tympanum of Vézelay to the Gothic statues of the great cathedrals. The idea of this "France in a nutshell" came from the illustrious architect Viollet-le-Duc.

MUSÉE NISSIM DE CAMONDO   **14** K13   Ⓜ Villiers/Monceau

63, rue de Monceau (8th); tel. 45.63.26.32. Daily except Monday, Tuesday and holidays, 10 a.m.–noon and 2–5 p.m.

Nissim de Camondo, the owner of this handsome turn-of-the-century mansion, furnished it in handsome style—mainly beautiful l8th-century antiques. A must for lovers of Louis XV and Louis XVI furnishings, porcelains and tapestries. Paintings by Guardi, Hubert Robert and Mme Vigée-Lebrun.

MUSÉE DE L'ORANGERIE   **23** L10   Ⓜ Concorde

Terrasse des Tuileries (1st), place de la Concorde side; tel. 42.97.48.16. Daily except Tuesday, 9.45 a.m.–5.15 p.m.

Completely renovated, and reopened in 1984, this museum contains the magnificent Walter-Guillaume collection, with works by Cézanne, Miró, Renoir and Soutine. But the main attraction is Monet's *Nymphéas* occupying oval rooms on the ground floor.

MUSÉE DU   **14/22** K11   Ⓜ Champs-Elysées–Clemenceau
PETIT PALAIS
Avenue Winston-Churchill (8th); tel. 42.65.12.73. Daily except Monday and holidays 10 a.m.–5.45 p.m.
Like the Grand Palais, it was built for the 1900 World's Fair. It contains three valuable though somewhat eclectic collections: Egyptian, Greek, Etruscan and Roman antiquities, together with objects from the Middle Ages and the Renaissance, in the Dutuit collection; the Tuck collection of 18th-century furniture and objets d'art; and late-19th-century paintings by Bonnard, Courbet, Odilon, Redon, Vuillard, and others.

MUSÉE PICASSO   **25** S9   Ⓜ Chemin-Vert
Hôtel Salé, 5, rue de Thorigny (3rd); tel. 42.71.25.21; daily except Tuesday, 9.15 a.m.–5.15 p.m., Wednesday until 10 p.m.

45

A striking 17th-century mansion, the Hôtel Salé was beautifully restored by architect Roland Simounet and furnished by designer Diego Giacometti to make way for Picasso's works, tracing the evolution of his art, and his own private collection, which includes paintings by Balthus, Cézanne, Matisse and Renoir. The museum also exhibits photographs of Picasso's family and mistresses, copies of letters and even his French Communist Party membership card.

MUSÉE DE SCULPTURE   **33** R/S 6/7   Ⓜ Gare d'Austerlitz
EN PLEIN AIR
Quai Saint-Bernard (5th). For details, ask at the Zadkine Museum (see page 53). Admission free.
An open-air sculpture garden on the banks of the Seine. Contemporary work by Arman, Brancusi, César, Gilioli, Ipousteguy, Schöffer, and so on, renewed every two years.

PALAIS DE TOKYO   **13/22** H10   Ⓜ Iéna
13, avenue du Président-Wilson (16th); tel. 47.23.36.53. Daily except Tuesday, 9.45 a.m.–5.15 p.m.
The National Centre of Photography, in the right wing of the building, has regular temporary showings of French and international photography.

MUSÉE DE L'AFFICHE ET DE LA PUBLICITÉ   **17** Q13   Ⓜ Château d'Eau or Gare de l'Est

18, rue de Paradis (10th); tel. 42.46.13.09. Daily except Tuesday noon–6 p.m.

In a fantastic Art Nouveau ceramic décor, the art of advertising, from the 18th century to the present. The 50,000 posters are shown in rotation. You can also watch videos of TV commercials, and there's a big library with appropriate reference works.

MUSÉE DE L'ARMÉE   **22** K9   Ⓜ Latour-Maubourg

Hôtel des Invalides, Esplanade des Invalides (7th); tel. 45.55.92.30. Daily 10 a.m.–5 p.m.

The military museum displays 40,000 objects and documents tracing the history of war through the ages, but largely concerned with Napoleon's armies. In the attic is a collection of relief maps showing the towns and fortresses that defended France from the 17th to 19th centuries.

46

MUSÉE ARMÉNIEN   **13** F12   Ⓜ Porte Dauphine

59, avenue Foch (16th); tel. 45.56.15.88. Thursday and Sunday 2–6 p.m. Admission free.

The centrepiece of this quaint collection is the crown of the last king of Armenia, Leon VI, who died in Paris in 1393.

MUSÉE D'ART JUIF   **8** O15   Ⓜ Lamarck-Caulaincourt

42, rue des Saules (18th); tel. 42.57.84.15. Daily except Friday, Saturday and Jewish holidays 3–6 p.m.

Jewish religious art objects, together with works signed Mané-Kaz, Lipschitz and Soutine, and a bible illustrated by Chagall.

MUSÉE DES ARTS AFRICAINS ET OCÉANIENS   Ⓜ Porte Dorée

293, ave. Daumesnil (12th); tel. 43.43.14.54. Daily except Tuesday, 10 a.m.–noon and 1.30–5.30 p.m.; Saturday and Sunday 10 a.m.–6 p.m.

In the basement of this hall, built for the Colonial Exhibition of 1931, lives a whole colony of undersea denizens—piranhas, giant turtles, crocodiles and frogs. The ground floor displays art and artefacts from the Pacific, the first floor objects from Black Africa, while the second is devoted to North Africa.

MUSÉE DES ARTS   **23/24** N10   Ⓜ Palais-Royal
ET DE LA MODE
109, rue de Rivoli (1st); tel. 42.60.32.14. Wednesday–Saturday 12.30–6.30 p.m., Sunday 11 a.m.–6 p.m., closed Monday and Tuesday.
A retrospective of the famous names of French fashion, from Chanel's little black dresses to Poiret's graceful *drapés.*

MUSÉE D'ART RUSSE   **25** Q10   Ⓜ Rambuteau
CONTEMPORAIN
49, rue Quincampoix (4th); tel. 48.04.94.16. Tuesday to Saturday 2–7 p.m. Admission free.
Four hundred works by non-conformist Soviet painters who managed to avoid the straitjacket of socialist realism.

MUSÉE DE   **25/33** Q7   Ⓜ Maubert-Mutualité
L'ASSISTANCE PUBLIQUE
47, quai de la Tournelle (5th); tel. 46.33.01.43. Daily except Monday, Tuesday and holidays 10 a.m–5 p.m.
History of Paris hospitals since the Middle Ages—pharmaceutical containers, surgical instruments and all.

47

MUSÉE DE LA CHASSE   **25** R10   Ⓜ Rambuteau
ET DE LA NATURE
60, rue des Archives (3rd); tel. 42.72.86.43. Daily except Tuesday and holidays, 10 a.m.–5.30 p.m.
Stuffed trophies, guns and art works celebrate the history of the hunt in this attractive historical house in the old Marais district. Temporary exhibitions relating to the protection of nature.

MUSÉE DU CINÉMA HENRI-LANGLOIS   **21** G10   Ⓜ Trocadéro
Palais de Chaillot, place du Trocadéro (16th); tel. 45.53.74.39 or 45.53.21.86. Guided tours daily except Tuesday, 10 and 11 a.m., 2, 3 and 4 p.m., (can be arranged in English). Closed 1–2 p.m.
Named for a celebrated French director who died in 1977, the museum illustrates the history of cinema, with exhibits of cameras, projectors, original scenarios, sets, posters, costumes worn by Greta Garbo and Catherine Deneuve, even John Wayne's hat.

MUSÉE DE LA CONTREFAÇON   **13** F11   Ⓜ Porte Dauphine
16, rue de la Faisanderie (16th); tel. 45.01.51.11. Monday and Wednesday, 2–4 p.m.; Friday 9.30 a.m.–noon. Admission free.
The fine art of forgery—even the Gaulois were experts. See how Chanel became Sanel in Turkey; try to smell the difference between "Soir de Paris" and "Soir de Toyko".

MUSÉE GRÉVIN　　**16** O12　　　　　Ⓜ Montmartre
10, boulevard Montmartre (9th); tel. 47.70.85.05. Daily including Sunday and holidays I–7 p.m.; school holidays 10 a.m.–7 p.m.
Paris's answer to Madame Tussaud's wax museum, with historical figures upstairs, people in the news today on the ground floor (see also page 177).

　The new museum, on the first level of the Forum des Halles (1st) displays a moving tableau depicting Paris in 1900 *(métro Les Halles; tel. 40.26.28.50. Daily 10.30 a.m.–7.30 p.m., Sunday and holidays 1–8 p.m.)*

MUSÉE EN HERBE　　**12** E13　　　　　Ⓜ Les Sablons
Jardin d'Acclimatation, Bois de Boulogne (16th); tel. 40.67.97.66. Daily 10 a.m.–6 p.m.; Saturday 2–6 p.m.
Workshops and leisure activities for children: outdoor games, from 4 years. Museum visit and written game (in English), from 7 years. Museum visit and show, from 7 years, 10.15 a.m. and 2.45 p.m.

48

HISTORIAL DE MONTMARTRE　　**8** O15　　　　Ⓜ Abbesses
11, rue Poulbot (18th); tel. 46.06.78.92. Daily from noon to 8 p.m.
The history of Montmartre in waxworks.

MUSÉE DE L'HOLOGRAPHIE　　**24** P10　　　　Ⓜ Les Halles
Forum des Halles (1st); Level 1, 15–21, Grand Balcon; tel. 42.96.96.83. Daily from 10.30 a.m.–7 p.m., Sunday, Monday and holidays 1–7 p.m.
How to make three-dimensional pictures, and ways to use them.

MUSÉE DE L'HOMME　　**21** G10　　　　　Ⓜ Trocadéro
Palais de Chaillot, place du Trocadéro (16th); tel. 45.53.70.60. Daily except Tuesday and holidays, 9.45 a.m.–5.15 p.m.
Well laid-out exhibits illustrate anthropology and ethnology from prehistoric times. A fascinating glimpse of ancient civilizations, with a collection of strange costumes (note the fish-skin robes from Asia), and a giant head from Easter Island. You can even contemplate the skull of Descartes, inside which the great thinker proved his existence ("I think, therefore I am").

MUSÉE DES INSTRUMENTS　　**25** Q10　　　　Ⓜ Rambuteau
DE MUSIQUE MÉCANIQUE
Impasse Berthaud (3rd); tel. 42.71.99.54. Saturday, Sunday and holidays 2–7 p.m.
Musical machines from grandma's days.

MUSÉE KWOK ON   **25** R9   Ⓜ Saint-Paul
*41, rue des Francs-Bourgeois (4th); tel. 42.72.99.42. Monday to Friday,
10 a.m.–5.30 p.m.*
The many colourful genres of Asian theatre, with musical instruments, puppets, masks and costumes.

MUSÉE DES LORGNETTES   **20** E9   Ⓜ La Muette
ET DES LUNETTES
*2, avenue Mozart (16th); tel. 45.27.21.05. Daily except Sunday,
9.30 a.m.–noon and 2–6.30 p.m.*
Monocles and pince-nez, microscopes and telescopes, binoculars
and bejewelled opera-glasses—a delightful array of aids for the
shortsighted, from the time specs were invented in the Middle Ages.
With a special collection of glasses that have sat upon famous noses.

MUSÉE DU LUXEMBOURG   **32** O7   ㋮ (line B) Luxembourg
*19, rue de Vaugirard (6th); tel. 42.34.25.95. Daily except Monday,
10 a.m.–7 p.m. Friday until 10 p.m.*
Temporary exhibitions of painting, sculpture and photography.   **49**

MUSÉE DE LA MARINE   **21** G10   Ⓜ Trocadéro
*Palais de Chaillot, place du Trocadéro (16th); tel. 45.53.31.70. Daily
except Tuesday 10 a.m.–6 p.m. (guided tours or lectures on request).*
The Naval Museum displays a vast flotilla of historical model ships,
including Louis XIV's fleet and the first-ever battleship, *La Gloire.*

MUSÉE DE LA MODE ET DU COSTUME   **13/22** H11   Ⓜ Iéna
*Palais Galliera, 10, avenue Pierre-1er-de-Serbie (16th); tel. 47.20.85.23.
Daily except Monday, 10 a.m.–5.30 p.m.*
Five thousand costumes and 30,000 articles of clothing, displayed in
rotation—a veritable panorama of men's, women's and children's
fashions from 1730 to the present.

MUSÉE DE MONTMARTRE   **8** O15   Ⓜ Lamarck-Caulaincourt
*12, rue Cortot (18th); tel. 46.06.61.11. Daily except Monday 2.30–6 p.m.,
Sunday 11 a.m.–6 p.m.*
Life at the top of the hill, illustrated by mementos of the turn of the
century—notably in the work of the artist Poulbot, who lived here and
immortalized a Montmartre street urchin, henceforth known as a
poulbot, in a drawing, *Le Gamin de Montmartre.*

MUSÉE NATIONAL DES ARTS   **12** E13   Ⓜ Les Sablons
ET TRADITIONS POPULAIRES
6, route du Mahatma-Gandhi (16th); tel. 40.67.90.00. Daily except Tuesday, 10 a.m.–5.15 p.m.
   Nostalgia for life in pre-industrial days, splendidly depicted by tableaux showing artisans' workshops and regional interiors.

MUSÉE NATIONAL   **17/25** Q11   Ⓜ Arts-et-Métiers
DES TECHNIQUES   or Réaumur-Sébastopol
270, rue Saint-Martin (3rd); tel. 42.71.24.14. Daily except Monday and holidays 1–5.30 p.m., Sunday 10 a.m.–5.15 p.m. Admission free on Sunday.
Located in the old priory of Saint-Martin-des-Champs, the museum gives an overview of the evolution of technology from the 17th century, from Pascal's calculator to the camera invented by the Lumière brothers. It includes the magnificent flying machines of Clément Ader and Louis Blériot.

MUSÉE DE LA PARFUMERIE FRAGONARD   **15** N12   Ⓜ Opéra
50 *9, rue Scribe (9th); tel. 47.42.04.56. Daily except Sunday, 9.30 a.m.–5.30 p.m.*
In the elegant setting of a small Second Empire residence, the story of perfume through the ages. You can see how to extract the essential oils from plants, objects relating to the conservation of perfumes, "artificial beauty spot" boxes, a 13th-century vanity case, and all the paraphernalia a lady required to make herself beautiful in the past centuries. The most fascinating exhibit, however, is the "perfume manufacturer's organ", which shows how different essences are mixed to create a new fragrance.

MUSÉE DE LA POSTE   **31** L5   Ⓜ Montparnasse-Bienvenüe
34, boulevard de Vaugirard (15th); tel. 43.20.15.30. Daily except Sunday and holidays 10 a.m.–5 p.m.
Keep yourself posted on everything to do with the mail, from the "clay letter" (2500 B.C.) to a fine collection of French postage stamps.

MUSÉE DE RADIO-FRANCE   **21** F8   Ⓜ Passy/Ranelagh
116, avenue du Président-Kennedy (16th); tel. 42.30.21.80. Daily except Sunday and holidays; guided visits at 10.30 and 11.30 a.m., 2.30, 3.30, 4.30 p.m.
The history of broadcasting, in the circular national TV and radio building. Visits of radio and TV studios.

MUSÉE DE LA SEITA   **22** K10   Ⓜ Invalides
12, rue Surcouf (7th); tel. 45.56.60.17. Daily except Sunday and holidays, 11 a.m.–6 p.m. Admission free.
The story of tobacco and its uses, related by the Régie des Tabacs, the state tobacco monopoly. A delightful collection of 17th- to 19th-century snuff-boxes, and pipes from the four corners of the world.

MUSÉE DE LA SERRURE   **25** R9   Ⓜ St-Sébastien-Froissart
Hôtel Libéral Bruant, 1, rue de la Perle (3rd); tel. 42.77.79.62. Daily except Sunday and Monday, 10 a.m.–noon and 2–5 p.m.
Locks of all kinds, in a Marais mansion. An old locksmith's workshop has been reconstructed in the courtyard.

MUSÉUM NATIONAL   **33** R5   Ⓜ Gare d'Austerlitz
D'HISTOIRE NATURELLE
Jardin des Plantes, 57, rue Cuvier (5th); tel. 43.36.14.41. Galleries daily except Tuesday 10.30 a.m.–5 p.m., Sunday 10 a.m.–5 p.m.; menagerie daily 9 a.m.–6 p.m.
Louis XIII created the Royal Garden of Medicinal Plants, which was nationalized during the Revolution. Of the many botanists and naturalists who have worked in the natural history museum, the best-known is perhaps Buffon, author of the 36-volume *Histoire naturelle*, and creator of many of the museum's galleries. Rock collectors will be fascinated by the **Galerie de minéralogie et de géologie,** with 500,000 specimens including an enormous quartz crystal that Napoleon brought back from Italy. The collection of meteorites is one of the finest in the world.

51

   The unique *zoothèque*, a reinforced concrete structure 13 metres underground, was designed and built in 1976 to permit conservation of very fragile specimens of animal life, most of which are about 100 years old—80,000 birds, countless invertebrates and 500,000 fish (see also page 174).

PALAIS DE LA   **14/22** K11   Ⓜ Champs-Elysées–Clemenceau
DÉCOUVERTE
Grand Palais, avenue Franklin-D.-Roosevelt (8th); tel. 43.59.16.65. Daily except Monday and holidays 10 a.m.–5.45 p.m. Planetarium: showings weekdays 3.15 and 4.30 p.m., Saturday and Sunday 11.30 a.m., 2, 3.15, 4.30 and 5 p.m.
An educational institution devoted to the vulgarization of scientific research, for children and adults alike. The Planetarium offers a 45-minute journey into space (see also page 179).

MAISON DE BALZAC   21 F8   Ⓜ Passy
*47, rue Raynouard (16th); tel. 42.24.56.38. Daily except Monday from
10 a.m.–5.40 p.m.*
An intimate look at Balzac's modest but charming Paris house.
Drawings by Gavarni, Boulanger and Daumier, as well as Balzac's
personal belongings—including his beloved coffee pot (he was a
coffee addict and died of caffeine poisoning).

MUSÉE BOURDELLE   31 L6   Ⓜ Falguière
*16, rue Antoine-Bourdelle (15th); tel. 45.48.67.27. Daily except Monday
10 a.m.–5.40 p.m.*
The home and workshop of the sculptor Antoine Bourdelle (1861–
1929), with portraits of the artist, his family and friends, and his
sculptures including his first triumph, *Héraklès archer.*

MUSÉE NATIONAL   24 N8   Ⓜ St-Germain-des-Prés
EUGÈNE DELACROIX   or Mabillon

52

*6, rue de Furstenberg (6th); tel. 43.54.04.87. Daily except Tuesday
9.45 a.m.–5.15 p.m.*
In the studio and three rooms of the apartment you'll see some of the
Romanticist's drawings and prints, reproductions and sketches, his
easel and palette, and his portrait by George Sand.

MUSÉE NATIONAL   6/14 K14   Ⓜ Malesherbes
JEAN-JACQUES HENNER
*43, avenue de Villiers (17th); tel. 47.63.42.73. Daily except Monday
10 a.m.–noon and 2 p.m.–5 p.m.*
An illustration of Belle Epoque taste in 500 paintings and 1,000
drawings by this prolific artist much inspired by sensuous nymphs
and naiads.

MAISON DE VICTOR HUGO   26 S8   Ⓜ Bastille
*6, place des Vosges, 4th; tel. 42.72.16.65. Daily except Monday
10 a.m.–5.10 p.m.*
Much of the furniture in the seven rooms Hugo lived in from 1840 to
1847 was made by the writer himself, an ardent do-it-yourself fan. He
wrote several chapters of *Les Misérables* here. See his drawings on
the first floor, and his bust by Rodin on the second.

MUSÉE GUSTAVE MOREAU   16 N13   Ⓜ Trinité
*14, rue de la Rochefoucauld (9th); tel. 48.74.38.50. Daily except Tues-
day, 10 a.m.–12.45 p.m. and 2–5.15 p.m.*

Symbolist par excellence and precursor of Abstract Expressionism, Gustave Moreau bequeathed his house and about 8,000 of his paintings to the state. Note especially *Orphée sur la tombe d'Eurydice* and *Les Licornes.*

MUSÉE RENAN-SCHEFFER   **16** N14   Ⓜ Saint-Georges
16, rue Chaptal (9th); tel. 48.74.95.38. Daily except Tuesday 10 a.m.–5.15 p.m.
The house of artist Ary Scheffer presents temporary exhibitions of 19th-century paintings, largely Romanticists; while the permanent collections are devoted to the writer George Sand, with many of her personal belongings and drawings.

MUSÉE RODIN   **22/23** K8   Ⓜ Varenne
77, rue de Varenne (7th); tel. 47.05.01.34. Daily except Tuesday, 10 a.m.–5 p.m.
Undoubtedly one of the city's most pleasant and least taxing museums to visit. Once a convent, the 18th-century Hôtel Biron was given to Rodin in 1908 to live and work in. From the lovely English-style garden (created in 1753, restored in 1927) to the airy interior, you can admire the sculptor's most famous works like *The Thinker, The Bourgeois of Calais* and *The Kiss,* along with works by Camille Claudel.

53

MUSÉE ZADKINE   **31/32** N5   Ⓜ Vavin
100 bis, rue d'Assas (6th); tel. 43.26.91.90. Tuesday–Sunday 10 a.m.–5.40 p.m., free admission on Sunday.
Works by the Russian sculptor Ossip Zadkine exhibited in the garden and studio where he worked, showing his progression from Cubism to a very personal Baroque Expressionist technique.

PARIS IN PRINT

The streets of Paris are a backdrop for countless novels. The following may add to your understanding of the city.

Victor Hugo's **Notre-Dame-de-Paris** for a wonderful picture of the medieval city, centred on the cathedral, and **Les Misérables**, which relates the turmoil of the 1848 Revolution—follow Jean Valjean through the sewers and Gavroche on the barricades.

In **A Tale of Two Cities** (Paris and London), Charles Dickens gives a vivid—though melodramatic—portrayal of the French Revolution.

Many of the novels in Emile Zola's Rougon-Macquart cycle are based in 19th-century Paris. The most enjoyable are **L'Assommoir** (translated as *Drunkard*), the decline and fall of a laundress in the Goutte-d'Or quarter; **Nana**, the life of a courtesan; **L'Argent** *(Money)*, Second-Empire Golden Boys; **Le Ventre de Paris** *(Savage Paris)*, a pork butcher's in the old Halles district; **Pot-Bouille** *(Restless House)*, bourgeois goings-on in an apartment building; and **Au Bonheur des Dames** *(Ladies' Delight)*, the birth of a department store.

For a chilling account of the state of the penniless at the end of the 1920s, read George Orwell's very entertaining **Down and Out in Paris and London.** And the American literary crowd in the Thirties with Hemingway's classic **A Moveable Feast**, or Waverley Root's stint as a journalist on the Chicago Tribune in **The Paris Edition.**

Jean Rhys's **Good Morning, Midnight**, largely situated in the Latin Quarter, evokes a haunting Paris of despair.

Léon-Paul Fargue is himself the pedestrian in his **Le Piéton de Paris** (you'll have to read this and the following titles in French), a very poetic evocation of all he saw on his leisurely walks through pre-war Paris.

54

A former surrealist, Léo Malet wrote a series of detective stories *(Nouveaux Mystères de Paris)*, each one set in a different arrondissement. **Brouillard au Pont de Tolbiac** is one of the most exciting, following a case of ace detective Nestor Burma through the 13th arrondissement—before the little Passage des Hautes-Formes became a fully fledged street in the area's recent urban development (see page 57). The same story has been published by Casterman as a comic strip, illustrated by Tardi. Other good novels in this series are **121, rue de la Gare** and **Les Rats de Montsouris**.

Another detective, imperturbable Inspecteur Maigret, carries out most of his investigations in seedy parts of Paris; his creator, Georges Simenon, has written his own guide, **Le Paris de Simenon.**

In **Rue des Boutiques Obscures**, by Patrick Modiano, the protagonist is searching for himself, but through people he meets, rather than places. A victim of amnesia, he looks for his past through the western areas of Paris, in places off the beaten track depicted with the accuracy of a map.

Patrick Grainville's **Les Forteresses noires** portrays the chilly skyscraper area of La Défense both realistically and poetically.

And Georges Perec's **La vie mode d'emploi**, a weighty volume describing a Parisian *immeuble* in the most minute and fascinating detail, where all the characters fit into their surroundings like pieces in a jigsaw puzzle, but go about their business, ignoring for the most part each other's existence.

PARIS AND ITS FACELIFTS

Paris is a museum in itself, tracing the history of architecture from medieval times to the present...and the future.

Like the elegant Parisian girls, the capital never lets itself go. Besides regular facials to smooth away the ravages of time, it has always kept up with the latest in avant-garde fashions. The Eighties transformed it radically—as much as Baron Haussman's upheavals last century.

The occasional visitor to Paris sees only the most spectacular results of this stealthy transformation—and in most cases, he isn't missing much. The Sixties and Seventies were largely marked by anarchic attempts to make Paris another version of Manhattan or Chicago, with controversial projects such as the Pompidou Centre, the Forum des Halles, and the glass and steel towers of the Défense office district which exiles 10,000 commuters to the outskirts every day.

But in the Eighties the trends changed. The last generations of Presidents have all wanted to leave their own mark on Paris. Their "great projects" are now almost all completed. And while they were under way, more modest, but no less interesting, constructions were going up all over the city. As a result, the centre of gravity has moved towards the east (Bercy, Bastille, La Villette, etc.), and under the influence of Rossi, Ricardo Bofill and Richard Rogers, a new school of architecture has flourished. The big names today are Castro, Gaudin, Grumbach, Nouvel, de Portzamparc. They cut their teeth in the new towns, like Cergy-Pontoise and Marne-la-Vallée. But Paris soon invited them in, mainly to undertake the renovation of insalubrious parts of the 13th and 20th arrondissements. The "great projects", listed below, are well worth a visit.

55

If you are interested in modern town planning, go to visit the information centres that organize exhibitions of architecture.

Pavillon de l'Arsenal: 21, boulevard Morland (4th); map **33** S7, métro Sully-Morland.

Institut français d'architecture: 6, rue de Tournon (6th); map **32** O7, métro Odéon.

GRANDE ARCHE DE LA DÉFENSE · La Défense
1, parvis de la Défense, Puteaux. Architect von Spreckelsen. This monumental marble arch honeycombed with offices completes the perspective of the Champs-Elysées at the Défense. A company belonging to Robert Maxwell occupies the base, while Edgar Faure's Foundation of the Rights of Man is under the roof.

GRAND LOUVRE · 24 O9/10 · Ⓜ Palais-Royal
Right Bank (1st). Architect Ieoh Ming Pei. Complete restructuration of the museum, involving the removal of the Ministry of Finance to Bercy. The only visible part is the famous glass pyramid.

MINISTÈRE DE L'ÉCONOMIE · 34 U5 · Ⓜ Bercy
ET DES FINANCES
1, boulevard de Bercy (12th). Architects Chemetov and Huidobro. Three buildings perpendicular to the Seine, forming a huge inhabited bridge with one end in the river, behind the Gare de Lyon.

PALAIS OMNISPORTS PARIS-BERCY · 34 U5 · Ⓜ Bercy
8, boulevard de Bercy (12th). Architects Andrault and Parat. An immense grass-covered tumulus in the style of a Mayan pyramid, used for cultural or sporting events.

56

INSTITUT DU · 33 Q7 · Ⓜ Cardinal Lemoine
MONDE ARABE · or Jussieu
23, quai Saint-Bernard, main entrance 1, rue des Fossés-Saint-Bernard (5th). Architects Nouvel, Soria, Lezenes and Architecture Studio. A resolutely contemporary edifice of glass and aluminium, which pays homage to traditional Islam architecture by incorporating the delicate tracery of moucharaby work in the décor.

OPÉRA DE PARIS-BASTILLE · 26 T8 · Ⓜ Bastille
2–6 place de la Bastille (12th). Architect Ott. The new opera house contains a theatre seating 2,700, an amphitheatre with 500 seats, and the Studio de la Tour d'Argent, a book-, record- and video library, workshops for costumes and décors, restaurants, bookshops and exhibition space.

PARC DE LA · 10/11 U/W15/16 · Ⓜ Porte de Pantin
VILLETTE · or Porte de la Villette
211, avenue Jean-Jaurès/30, avenue Corentin-Cariou (19th). Architects Fainsilber, de Portzamparc, Tschumi. The museums of science and music, the Géode, the Zénith rock concert hall and an exhibition hall, in Paris's biggest park.

MÉDIATHÈQUE JEAN-PIERRE MELVILLE   39 S3   Ⓜ Nationale

99, rue Nationale (13th); tel. 45.70.80.50. In the heart of the Tolbiac district stands the City of Paris's first *médiathèque*, or resources centre. Its aluminium and glass architecture, in "ocean liner" style, was specially designed to admit as much light as possible into the offices and working areas, while one side of the building is darkened by a huge semi-transparent canvas in an aluminium frame, to diminish reflection on the computer screens.

The centre comprises a reference library of more than 10,000 compact discs and audio-cassettes, and a video-cassette lending library. And in the Marguerite-Durand computerized library, you can find out all you ever wanted to know about bits and bytes and microchips.

If they understand French, your children might like "Story Time", Wednesdays and Saturdays on the mezzanine.

57

WHAT THE FUTURE HAS IN STORE...

The building boom is not restricted to grandiose monuments—it has also had some influence on the little world of boutiques and cafés. The cafés Costes and Beaubourg have become hallowed sanctuaries of the Eighties' style, and the boutiques around Les Halles and Rue Etienne-Marcel rivalize in audacity. If you venture into the residential districts of Paris, look up one or two of the following addresses to get an idea of France's futuristic housing programme.

13th arrondissement:
Two hundred council flats designed by de Portzamparc: *Rue des Hautes-Formes. Map 39 S3; métro Tolbiac.*
Blocks of flats: *152, avenue d'Italie. Map 39 R2; métro Maison-Blanche.*
A home for the elderly: *120, rue du Château-des-Rentiers. Map 39 S3; métro Nationale.*

Artists' workshops in a converted warehouse: *26, rue Edmond-Flamand. Map 34 T4; métro Quai de la Gare.*

14th arrondissement:
Ricardo Bofill's ''Baroque Columns''—council flats inspired by classical architecture: *78, rue du Château. Map 37 L4; métro Pernety.*

20th arrondissement:
Block of flats, an anthology of Paris's renovation policy: *Rue Bisson. Map 18 U12; métro Couronnes.*
Studios and flats for musicians: *116, rue des Pyrénées. Métro Maraîchers.*
High school: *39, rue Vitruve. Métro Porte de Bagnolet.*
Industrial workshop building: *64, boulevard Davout. Métro Porte de Montreuil.*
Academy of music: *54, rue des Cendriers. Map 19 V11; métro Ménilmontant.*
A whole district undergoing renovation: *rues de la Mare and des Cascades. Map 19 V12; métro Pyrénées.*

...AND A TOUCH OF NOSTALGIA

Two great architectural styles have left their mark on the capital, Art Nouveau (buildings by Hector Guimard, Georges Chédanne, Ernest Herscher and Jules Lavirotte) and Art Deco (Le Corbusier, Mallet-Stevens, Carlu, Boileau and Azéma).

Guimard
Hôtel Jassédé: *41, rue Chardon-Lagache (16th); métro Chardon-Lagache.*
Jassédé flats: *142, avenue de Versailles/1, rue Lancret (16th). Map 28 E6; métro Chardon-Lagache.*
Hôtel Mezzara: *60, rue La Fontaine (16th). Map 20 E7; métro Jasmin.* In the same street: Castel Béranger at no. 14; flats nos. 17–21. In the neighbourhood: flats at 43, rue Gros and 8–10, rue Agar. Stop for a coffee at Café Antoine, 17, rue de la Fontaine, a tiny café-bar with Art Nouveau front and sign.
Hôtel Guimard: *122, avenue Mozart (16th). Map 20 E8; métro Jasmin.* Métro entrance at Porte Dauphine: exit corner of Boulevard de l'Amiral-Bruix and Avenue Foch. *Map 13 F12.*

Chédanne
Block of flats: 9, *rue de Presbourg (16th. Map 13/14 H12; métro Kléber.*

Herscher
Block of flats: 39, *rue Scheffer (16th). Map 21 F10; métro Rue de la Pompe.*

Lavirotte
Block of flats: 29, *avenue Rapp (7th). Map 22 J10; RER (line C) Pont de l'Alma.*

Le Corbusier
Jeanneret and La Roche villas (Le Corbusier Foundation): *8 and 10, square du Dr-Blanche (16th). Map 20 D8; métro Jasmin.*

Mallet-Stevens
Group of houses: *Rue Mallet-Stevens (16th). Map 20 E8; métro Ranelagh.*

Carlu, Boileau, Azéma
Palais de Chaillot: *Place du Trocadéro (16th). Map 21 G10; métro Trocadéro.*

59

The art world was once divided into two camps on either side of the Seine. The fat-cat Right Bank area around the Faubourg Saint-Honoré was the pristine realm of old masters and establishment contemporaries, while the Left Bank galleries revelled in the exciting, unorthodox shocks of the avant-garde. Today the distinction is less clear-cut, as Left-Bank galleries have aged into conservatives, sticking mainly to established post-war artists.

For many years, art lovers and collectors believed that the creative instinct had deserted Paris. Now, however, the capital has recaptured its key position in the art world and can be considered on an equal footing with New York. The new wave of avant-gardists has been drawn towards the magnetic Pompidou Centre, with galleries throughout the Marais right up to the Bastille area, where more than 100 artists live and work.

As a rule, art galleries are open Tuesday to Saturday between 2 and 7.30 p.m.

ANTOINETTE   **24** N8   Ⓜ Saint-Germain-des-Prés
7, rue Jacob (6th); tel. 43.26.84.85. For admirers of naive art.

ARTCURIAL   **14** K11   Ⓜ Franklin-D.-Roosevelt
9, avenue Matignon (8th); tel. 42.99.16.16. A slick and spacious gallery showing works by well-known contemporary artists. If you can't afford a painting, try an art book, or a sculpture, print, scarf, rug, **61** pottery or jewellery from the boutique (see also pages 87 and 106).

BEAUBOURG   **25** Q9   Ⓜ Hôtel-de-Ville
23, rue du Renard (4th); tel. 42.71.20.50, and 3, rue Pierre-au-Lard (4th); tel. 48.04.34.40. Displays the most popular neo-Realists and other works from its vast collection.

BERGGRUEN   **23** M9   Ⓜ Solférino
70, rue de l'Université (7th); tel. 42.22.02.12. A cosseted, elegant retreat near the Musée d'Orsay, with a splendid showing of first-rate works by Dubuffet, Klee, Léger, Miró (as well as some newer artists).

MARCEL BERNHEIM   **14** K12   Ⓜ Franklin-D.-Roosevelt
18, avenue Matignon (8th); tel. 42.65.22.23. Big names of the 20th century: Impressionists and post-Impressionists, but also Picasso, Poliakoff and Dalí.

Every little gallery has its own special atmosphere and charm.

FABIEN BOULAKIA   **23/24** N8   Ⓜ Saint-Germain-des-Prés
20, rue Bonaparte (6th); tel. 43.26.56.79. Masters of the Fifties (Fautrier, Tapiès), and colourful, semi-abstract works of the Cobra group.

JEANNE BUCHER   **24** N8   Ⓜ Mabillon
53, rue de Seine (6th); tel. 43.26.22.32. A discerning gallery, more tasteful than trendy, showing works as diverse as those of Nicolas de Staël and way-out Fred Deux.

CLAIRE BURRUS   **26** T8   Ⓜ Bastille
30–32, rue de Lappe (11th); tel. 43.55.36.90. In a little courtyard near the Bastille, Claire Burrus directs her gallery with the same professional, personal touch instituted in *Le Dessin* gallery of Saint-Germain-des-Prés.

FARIDEH CADOT   **25** R10   Ⓜ Arts-et-Métiers
77, rue des Archives (3rd); tel. 42.78.08.36. With a gallery in New York as well, Farideh Cadot is at the peak of the international scene.

ANTOINE CANDAU   **26** U8   Ⓜ Ledru-Rollin
17, rue Keller (11th); tel. 43.38.75.51. This young man offers abstract works by equally young painters at reasonable prices.

PHILIPPE CASINI   **25** R10   Ⓜ Arts-et-Métiers
13, rue Chapon (3rd); tel. 48.04.00.34. In a gallery located at the far end of a magnificent 18th-century courtyard in Paris's Chinatown, Philippe Casini has a sharp eye for discovering avant-garde French and German artists.

CREDAC   Ⓜ Mairie d'Ivry
93, avenue Georges Gosnat, Ivry-sur-Seine; tel. 46.70.15.71. Five rooms of the research, exchange and distribution centre for modern art are used for various exhibitions ranging from painting and sculpture to photography and video.
  The centre welcomes artists, who can stay here and exhibit their works on the premises.

CROUSEL-ROBELIN   **25** Q10   Ⓜ Rambuteau
40, rue Quincampoix (4th); tel. 42.77.38.87. Contemporary works of a very high standard by well-established artists.

MICHEL DELORME   **33** Q6   Ⓜ Jussieu
9, rue Linné (5th); tel. 43.31.23.84. Magnificent canvases in the Expressionist manner by Appel and Jorn of the Cobra group.

DONGUY   **26** T8   Ⓜ Bastille
57, rue de la Roquette (11th); tel. 47.00.10.94. The experimental section

of this gallery is devoted to video and sound, while the more conventional part is given over to photography (Fluxus visual poetry and the South-American Constructivist movement, Madi).

LILIANE ET MICHEL DURAND-DESSERT 25 R10 ⓜ Rambuteau
3, rue des Haudriettes (3rd); tel. 42.77.63.60. An old warehouse-turned-gallery, displaying paintings and sculpture by internationally renowned artists, particularly members of the Italian Arte Povera group such as Mario Merz, Luciano Fabro and Kounellis.

JEAN FOURNIER 25 Q10 ⓜ Rambuteau
44, rue Quincampoix (4th); tel. 42.77.32.31. Once the red-light district, the area has turned respectable, with several art galleries. The Fournier gallery is outstanding, both for the way its space is exploited and for the quality of the artists represented—both American and French, mainly abstract.

GALERIE DE FRANCE 25 Q9 ⓜ Hôtel-de-Ville
50–52, rue de la Verrerie (4th); tel. 42.74.38.00. A little bit of everything: the well-known (Brancusi, Soulages), the avant-garde, and Soviet contemporaries.

GALERIE DE PARIS 24 O8 ⓜ Odéon
6, rue du Pont-de-Lodi (6th); tel. 43.25.42.63. Among the trendiest of the capital.

LA HUNE 24 N8 ⓜ Saint-Germain-des-Prés
14, rue de l'Abbaye (6th); tel. 43.25.54.06. In the shade of the church of Saint-Germain-des-Prés, opposite the little Square Laurent-Prache where you can see a Picasso sculpture dedicated to Guillaume Apollinaire. Reminiscent of the Fifties, the gallery specializes in post-war engravings and prints by Dubuffet, Picasso, Vieira da Silva and others. It also has a very good book department featuring works on art and architecture.

KRIEF 24 O8 ⓜ Odéon
50, rue Mazarine (6th); tel. 43.29.32.37. A dynamic owner, who has followed all the European trends from the Fifties on.

LAAGE-SALOMON 25 Q9 ⓜ Rambuteau
57, rue du Temple (4th); tel. 42.78.11.71. A collection based on artists from the U.S. and Germany, with a special affection for Baselitz.

LAHUMIÈRE 14 J13 ⓜ Courcelles
88, boulevard de Courcelles (17th); tel. 47.63.03.96. An enlightened choice of turn-of-the-century paintings, pastels, water-colours, drawings and collages, and a wide range of original prints.

YVON LAMBERT   **25** S10   Ⓜ Saint-Sébastien-Froissart
108, rue Vieille-du-Temple (4th); tel. 42.71.09.33. A gathering of Minimalists and Conceptualists, as well as painters like Combas or Schnabel, beneath the beautiful glass skylight of an old warehouse. Another gallery at 5, rue du Grenier-Saint-Lazare (3rd); tel. 42.71.04.25 (map **25** Q10; métro Rambuteau).

LARA VINCY   **24** N8   Ⓜ Mabillon
47, rue de Seine (6th); tel. 43.26.72.51. A multi-media gallery displaying neo-Realist, ultra-modern paintings, sculpture and videos.

BAUDOUIN LEBON   **25** R9   Ⓜ Hôtel-de-Ville
34, rue des Archives (4th); tel. 42.72.09.10. In a historical old street, the gallery is a beacon for the avant-garde, widening its scope to include photographs, as well as mainstream painters such as Dubuffet, now considered a classic.

LELONG   **14** K13   Ⓜ Miromesnil
13, rue de Téhéran (8th); tel. 45.63.13.19. Pursuing a similar course to Aimé Maeght, his predecessor on the premises, Lelong has extended his choice to include a few up-and-coming talents.

64 **ADRIEN MAEGHT**   **23** M9   Ⓜ Rue du Bac
42–46, rue du Bac (7th); tel. 45.48.45.15. The son of Aimé Maeght deals in top celebrities such as Braque and Calder, as well as lesser-known artists.

NIKKI DIANA MARQUARDT   **26** S8   Ⓜ Saint-Paul/Bastille
9, place des Vosges (4th); tel. 42.78.21.00. In an impressive renovated 19th-century workshop, American dealer Nikki Diana Marquardt shows the brightest new stars of visionary art.

MATIGNON   **14** K12   Ⓜ Franklin-D.-Roosevelt
18, avenue Matignon (8th); tel. 42.66.60.32. Early 20th-century French masters, great and small.

GHISLAIN MOLLET-VIEVILLE   **25** Q10   Ⓜ Rambuteau
26, rue Beaubourg (3rd); tel. 42.78.72.31. Conceptual and Minimal art in superb premises; by appointment only.

MONTENAY   **24** 08   Ⓜ Odéon
31, rue Mazarine (6th); tel. 43.54.85.30. One of the few galleries in the heart of Saint-Germain-des-Prés to show the best of the latest international contemporary art.

PAVILLON DES ARTS   **24/25** P10   Ⓜ Les Halles
101, rue Rambuteau (1st); tel. 42.33.82.50. An attractive gallery showing contemporary artists only.

DENISE RENÉ   **23** M8   Ⓜ Rue du Bac
196, boulevard Saint-Germain (7th); tel. 42.22.77.57. Geometric abstraction of all tendencies from Constructivism to kinetic art, by Vasarely and his followers.

DANIEL TEMPLON   **25** Q10   Ⓜ Rambuteau
30, rue Beaubourg (3rd); tel. 42.72.14.10. High-class, top-quality works with an international flavour. Has links with New York's Castelli Gallery.

DINA VIERNY   **23/24** N8   Ⓜ Saint-Germain-des-Prés
36, rue Jacob (6th); tel. 42.60.23.18. The owner, an eclectic and enthusiastic collector, modelled for Maillol; the display of his works is incomparable—not to be missed.

Optical Illusions

65

The fading, flaking, old-fashioned advertisements painted on the blank end walls of Paris's apartment buildings are slowly disappearing, making way for bright contemporary murals, many in the trompe-l'œil style made popular by Richard Haas in Chicago and New York.

Worthy of interest: **Fabio Rieti's** "Imaginary windows", 27, rue Quincampoix (4th), map **25** Q10, métro Rambuteau; and his "Staircase" on the corner of rues Turbigo and Pierre-Lescot, map **24** P10, métro Etienne-Marcel.

Bertin and **Sanabria's** vision of an "Imaginary town"—a factory landscape set in a valley—disguises a blind façade on rue Dussoubs, between rues Greneta and Marie-Stuart (2nd), map **16/24** P11, métro Réaumur-Sébastopol. While a double marine vista, signed by **Irena Dedicova**, unfurls on the Ménilmontant sportsground, 47–49, boulevard de Ménilmontant (11th), map **19/27** V10, métro Père-Lachaise.

You may be bewildered by **Yvaral's** gigantic kinetic artwork on 105, rue du Faubourg Saint-Denis (19th), map **17** R13, métro Gare de l'Est. From close up, the juxtaposition of narrow strips makes no sense. You'll have to cross to the other side of the road to see the face of Saint Vincent de Paul come into focus.

Parisians feel that their city is the centre of the world, and they aren't far wrong when it comes to a shopping spree. Witty, chic, inventive or daring, the seductive displays are an irresistible appeal to make you get out your purse—from the piles of fruit on the smallest street stall to a single jewel artistically placed next to a draped silk scarf.

There's so much to buy that for some visitors the entire stay is one long trek from boutique to tempting boutique—interrupted only by time off for a meal—in a quest for the latest fashions, an enamel snuffbox or a gadget for the kitchen. But for those who want to save all their energy for sightseeing, shopping can be less harassing in the big department stores, which also have restaurants on the spot (*Le Grill* in Printemps is the best; in the Samaritaine the food is overshadowed by the lovely view of the Seine). Galeries Lafayette and Printemps both provide hostesses to help confused shoppers negotiate the labyrinth.

Value-added tax (TVA) is imposed on almost all goods and services in France. Visitors from non-EEC countries can obtain a refund of up to 22% on large purchases—ask the sales assistant for a *détaxe* form. You must present this form to the French Customs, where it will be officially stamped. You keep one copy and send the other back to the store; the refund will be sent to you within three months, or paid into your credit card account. The large department stores will deduct it directly from your bill—take all your purchases to the *détaxe* **67** desk, along with your passport and plane ticket.

As most shops close on Sunday, we have only mentioned the other closing days, whenever applicable. Many shops open later on Monday and close for lunch on Saturday. Annual holidays change from one year to the next but always include weeks in July or August. If you hate crowds and congestion, you'll love the city in August—but if you intend visiting a specific shop, you'd better phone first to make sure it's open—and check the opening hours, too, as they may change in summer.

"Let's treat Fido to that nice gold collar!"

Late-night Shopping

If you run out of aspirin in the middle of the night—no problem, the **Pharmacie Dehry** never closes (84, avenue des Champs-Elysées, tel. 45.62.02.41; map **14** H12; métro George V).

There's also an all-night post office: **Bureau de Poste Paris-Louvre** (52, rue du Louvre (1st); tel. 40.28.20.00; map **24** O10; métro Louvre). It functions day and night, and every day of the year. While the **Bureau de Poste des Champs-Elysées** is open daily 8 a.m.–10 p.m.; Sunday 8 a.m.–8 p.m. (71, avenue des Champs-Elysées (8th); tel. 43.59.55.18; map **14** J12; métro George V).

Plenty of shops open late; for convenience we have listed them below, with a reference to the relevant page in this chapter.

Food Shops
Au Régal: daily until 10.30 p.m. (page 92)
Boulangerie de l'Ancienne Comédie: open non-stop, except Sunday 6 a.m.–9 p.m. (page 92)
La Boutique Layrac: daily 9 a.m.–3 a.m. (page 92)
Le Cochon Rose: Friday to Wednesday 6 p.m.–5.30 a.m. (page 93)
Dalloyau: daily until 9 p.m. (page 94)
Fauchon: weekdays until 10 p.m. (page 94)
Flo Prestige: daily 8 a.m.–midnight (page 94)
Jo Goldenberg: daily until midnight (page 95)
Hédiard: weekdays until 11 p.m. (page 95)
Lenôtre: daily until 9 p.m. (page 96)
Nicolas Madeleine: weekdays until 8 p.m. (page 97)

General
B.H.V.: late closing Wednesday 10 p.m. (page 69)
Drugstore Publicis: 9 a.m.–2 a.m. (page 89)
Prisunic Champs-Elysées: Monday to Saturday 9.45 a.m.–midnight (page 90)
La Samaritaine: late closing Tuesday and Friday 8.30 p.m. (page 70)
Soho: weekdays until 11 p.m. (page 90)

Books
Flammarion 4: daily except Tuesday until 10 p.m. (page 107)
La Hune: weekdays until midnight (page 108)
Marais Plus: daily except Sunday until midnight (page 108)

Records
Clémentine Disques: open until 9 p.m., 11.p.m. or 1 a.m. (page 105)
Lido Musique: 10 a.m.–1.30 a.m.; Sunday 1.30–8 p.m. (page 106)
Virgin Megastore: daily until midnight (page 106)

DEPARTMENT STORES

AU BON MARCHÉ   31 M7   Ⓜ Sèvres-Babylone
38, rue de Sèvres (7th); tel. 45.49.21.22. 9.30 a.m.–6.30 p.m.; food department 9.30 a.m.–7.30 p.m.
A general department store, but the vast food department offers a big choice in luxury items like smoked salmon, foie gras and exotic fruit. **Les Trois Hiboux** (The Three Owls) is a library-bookshop for children with games and workshop facilities for weaving, clay modelling, playing music.

AU PRINTEMPS   15 M12   Ⓜ Havre-Caumartin
64, boulevard Haussmann (9th); tel. 42.82.50.00. 10 a.m.–7 p.m.
Top billing: womenswear department in the **Nouveau Magasin,** menswear in the **Magasin Brummell.** Also popular: perfume and cosmetics, wedding gifts, personalized gifts, toys, book department, music and computers, household goods, travel agent, restaurants. High-quality all-round shopping. Stop for a cuppa under the turquoise dome of the 6th-floor cafeteria.

B.H.V. (BAZAR DE   25 Q9   Ⓜ Hôtel-de-Ville
L'HÔTEL DE VILLE)
52–64, rue de Rivoli (4th); tel. 42.74.90.00. 9 a.m.–6.30 p.m.; Wednesday late closing 10 p.m.; Saturday 9 a.m.–7 p.m.
The place to go if you're moving or redecorating. The hardware **69** department is a favourite of do-it-yourselfers. But the store has everything for the home, including kitchen appliances, electric fittings, bathroom accessories, carpets and paint, a sporting goods department, a book and music department (stereo equipment, radios, cassettes, CDs, and so on).

GALERIES LAFAYETTE   15/16 N12   Ⓜ Chaussée d'Antin
40, boulevard Haussmann (9th); tel. 42.82.34.56. 9.30 a.m.–6.30 p.m.
A grand old institution, in a vast building with a superb stained-glass dome in the centre. It may be traditional, but behind times it's not; the latest clothes for men, women and children are a speciality, in all categories—sportswear to big-name labels. Also a marvellous array of crystal, china and silverware, home furnishings and appliances, music and books, cosmetics and sundries, plus various services including hairdresser, money exchange and restaurant. If you'd like a ticket for a Wednesday morning fashion show, ask the hostess at the Opéra entrance.

MARKS & SPENCER   **15/16** N12   Ⓜ Chausse d'Antin
35, boulevard Haussmann (9th); tel. 47.42.42.91. 9.30 a.m.–6.30 p.m.;
Tuesday 10 a.m.–6.30 p.m.
The Paris branch of the English bargain hunter's favourite attracts
the natives for its layette-infants and childrens' department, sweaters
and lingerie. The food department offers everything from good Scot-
tish salmon and shortbread to excellent fresh sandwiches.

LA SAMARITAINE   **24** O9   Ⓜ Pont-Neuf
19, rue de la Monnaie (1st); tel. 40.41.20.20. 9.30 a.m.–7 p.m.; Tuesday
and Friday 9.30 a.m.–8.30 p.m.
You can find just about everything in this enormous store—women's
clothing, home furnishings and bathroom equipment, even a pets'
department.

As you go along, you'll notice that some neighbourhoods seem to
specialize in certain categories of shops. The 8th arrondissement is
definitely high in high fashion. The 5th and 6th abound in books,
antiques, art, younger fashions. The 7th and 9th are also good for
antiques and art, shoes and clothes. The 1st and 2nd have all kinds of
avant-garde gear, several duty-free perfume shops and much more.
As for prices, Paris has never been the bargain basement of the
world. And it just isn't done to bargain. But there are many discount
houses as well as good sales in late December–January, late June–
July and August. French stores may exchange faulty or damaged
merchandise or give you credit, but they never, never give your money
back.

   You'll probably want to concentrate on the things the French are
best at, namely food, fashions and luxury items such as glass,
porcelain and perfume. Here are ideas for various categories of
shopping.

FASHION

AGNÈS B.   **32** N5   ⓇⒺⓇ Port-Royal/Ⓜ Vavin
81, rue d'Assas (6th); tel. 46.33.70.20. 10.30 a.m.–7 p.m.
Popular sportswear (mother and daughter), but no longer the high
quality it once was.

AGNES B. LOLITA   **24** P10   Ⓜ Les Halles
1, rue du Jour (1st); tel. 45.08.49.89. 10.30 a.m.–7 p.m.
For teenage girls (12–18).

AZZEDINE ALAÏA   **25/26** S9   Ⓜ Chemin Vert
17, rue du Parc-Royal (3rd); tel. 42.72.19.19. 10 a.m.–7 p.m.
It's a stark white place with no show window, but Azzedine from Tunisia has won fame for his slinky creations.

ANOUSCHKA   **14** J11   Ⓜ Franklin-D.-Roosevelt
33, rue Marbeuf (8th) (2nd floor); tel. 45.61.00.58. 1–8 p.m.
Clothes from the Thirties to the Seventies—designers, fashion models and actors come for inspiration.

APOSTROPHE   **14** K12   Ⓜ Saint-Philippe-du-Roule
93, rue du Faubourg Saint-Honoré (8th); tel. 42.65.34.35. 10 a.m.–7 p.m. Other branches in the 1st, 6th, 8th and 16th arrondissements.
Well-made outfits and separates in the latest colours and cut. Prices fairly high, but not catastrophic.

FRANÇOIS BAUDIN   **23** L9   Ⓜ Rue du Bac
84 bis, rue de Grenelle (7th); tel. 45.49.20.11. 10.30 a.m.–2 p.m. and 3–6.30 p.m.; Monday 2–6.30 p.m.
Adorable shoes, handbags and women's clothes decorated with metal and stones. Out of the ordinary.

MARINA DE BOURBON   **14** J13   Ⓜ Courcelles
112, boulevard de Courcelles (17th); tel. 47.63.42.01. 10.30 a.m.–8 p.m.
Superbly designed ladies' clothes, sweaters, travel bags. A wide price range.

71

BROWNS   **23** N8   Ⓜ Saint-Germain-des-Prés
182, boulevard Saint-Germain (6th); tel. 45.44.49.76. 10.30 a.m.–7 p.m.; Monday noon–7 p.m.
British clothes for men—comfortable, smart, sometimes original. Off-the-peg casuals by young designers.

BURBERRY   **15** M12   Ⓜ Madeleine
8, boulevard Malesherbes (8th); tel. 42.66.13.01. 9.45 a.m.–6.45 p.m. Other branches in the 6th and 16th arrondissements.
World-famous trench coat—the best for Paris drizzle.

CADOLLE   **15** M11   Ⓜ Concorde
14, rue Cambon (1st); tel. 42.60.94.94. 9.30 a.m.–1 p.m. and 2–6.30 p.m.
The bra was invented here by the present owner's great-great-grandmother, Hermine Cadolle. The tradition of quality lingerie is carried on, and you can choose from pretty ready-to-wear or have your undies custom-made (Saturday, by appointment).

PIERRE CARDIN ESPACE BOUTIQUE   **15** L11   Ⓜ Madeleine
29 (women) and 59 (men), rue du Faubourg Saint-Honoré (8th);
tel. 42.65.36.91. 10 a.m.–6.30 p.m.
Between ready-to-wear and haute couture—from fairly conservative
chic to wilder numbers expressing the designer's ingenuity.

CAREL   **14** J12   Ⓜ Franklin-D.-Roosevelt
22, avenue des Champs-Elysées (8th); tel. 45.62.30.62. 10 a.m.–7 p.m.;
Monday 11 a.m.–7 p.m. Other branches in the 6th, 8th and 16th
arrondissements and the department stores.
A shoe shop offering a good choice of current seasonal colours and
styles, at reasonable prices considering the quality.

CÉLINE   **14** J11   Ⓜ Franklin-D.-Roosevelt
24, rue François-1er (8th); tel. 47.20.22.83. 10 a.m.–7 p.m.. Other
branches in the 6th and 16th arrondissements.
High-quality shoes and accessories for the French preppy crowd, as
well as attractive conservative fashions.

CERRUTI 1881   **15** M11   Ⓜ Madeleine
For women: 15, place de la Madeleine (8th); tel. 47.42.10.78;
10.15 a.m.–7 p.m.
For men: 27, rue Royale (8th); tel. 42.65.68.72. 10 a.m.–7 p.m.; Monday
2–7 p.m.
Impeccably cut suits by Nino Cerruti in fine Italian fabrics. Four
boutiques in Paris; these are the main ones.

72 **CHANEL**   **15** M11   Ⓜ Concorde
31, rue Cambon (1st); tel. 42.61.54.55. 9.30 a.m.–6.30 p.m.; Saturday
10 a.m.–1 p.m. and 2–6.30 p.m.
Also 42, avenue Montaigne (8th); tel. 47.23.74.12; map 14 J11.
Perhaps the most-copied big name in the world. But The Real Thing,
even in Karl Lagerfeld's pricey ready-to-wear and accessories, is
much better than the counterfeits.

CHARVET   **15** M11   Ⓜ Opéra
28, place Vendôme (1st); tel. 42.60.30.70. 9.45 a.m.–6.30 p.m.
Custom-made shirts for men and women, from a fabulous array of
fabrics. Off-the-peg shirts and ties.

CHEVIGNON   **16** O11   Ⓜ Bourse
5, place des Victoires (2nd); tel. 42.36.10.16. 10.15 a.m.–7 p.m. Other
branches in the 1st and 6th arrondissements.
The sporty look for men (women like it, too) in leather, denim, linen,
covered with badges, labels and insignia. Famous for the blouson.

COMME DES GARÇONS   **16/24** P10   Ⓜ Etienne-Marcel
40 (men) and 42 (women), rue Etienne-Marcel (1st); tel. 42.33.05.21. 11 a.m.–7 p.m.
A very personal asymmetrical style by Japanese designer Rei Kawakubo—for men and women.

COW-BOY DREAM   **25** Q10   Ⓜ Etienne-Marcel
110, rue Saint-Denis (1st); tel. 42.36.38.15. 9.30 a.m.–7.30 p.m. Open Sunday.
The biggest selection of cowboy boots this side of Texas.
Also 16 and 21, rue de Turbigo (1st); tel. 42.36.30.05; map 24 P10. 9.30 a.m.–7.30 p.m.
Modern clothes and Western-style accessories—saddles, cowboy hats, gloves, belts, Indian headdresses, moccasins, Navajo jewellery.

LE DEVERNOIS   **22** J9   Ⓜ Latour-Maubourg
70, rue Saint-Dominique (7th); tel. 47.05.69.28. 10 a.m.–7 p.m.; Monday 11 a.m.–7 p.m.
A conservative line of high-quality separates in attractive colours for reasonable prices. The Devernois label is sold all over town.

CHRISTIAN DIOR   **14/22** J11   Ⓜ Franklin-D.-Roosevelt
30, avenue Montaigne (8th); tel. 40.73.54.44. 9.30 a.m.–6.30 p.m.; Monday 10 a.m.–6.30 p.m.; Saturday 10 a.m.–1 p.m. and 2.30–6.30 p.m.
A great place to browse in style, with everything from clothing (men, women, children) to linen, lingerie and gifts. High prices drop drastically at sales times–June and January.

73

ÉRÈS   **15** M12   Ⓜ Madeleine
2, rue Tronchet (8th); tel. 47.42.24.55. 9.30 a.m.–7 p.m.
Beautiful beachwear—bikinis, dresses, shirts—at spectacular, if not exorbitant—prices.

FIL À FIL   **15** M12   Ⓜ Madeleine
8, rue Tronchet (9th); tel. 47.42.55.24. 10 a.m.–7 p.m. Other branches in the 1st and 16th arrondissements.
An attractive selection of shirts, ties, scarves and belts for men and women.

LOUIS FÉRAUD   **15** L12   Ⓜ Saint-Philippe-du-Roule
88, rue du Faubourg Saint-Honoré (8th); tel. 42.65.32.84; 10 a.m.–7 p.m. Other branches in the 1st, 6th and 17th arrondissements.
Superb and colourful clothes for the woman-around-town by artistic Féraud. His wife or daughter may be around to help you choose what looks best on you.

GABRIEL **15** M11 ⓜ Madeleine
9, rue Richepance (8th); tel. 42.60.12.78. 9.30 a.m.–7 p.m.
A rainbow selection of 100% cashmere sweaters by Charles of Scotland. And shoes and bags to match.

JEAN-PAUL GAULTIER **16** O11 ⓜ Bourse
6, rue Vivienne (2nd); tel. 42.86.05.05. 10 a.m.–7 p.m.; Saturday 11 a.m.–7 p.m.
Also Junior Gaultier, 7, rue du Jour (1st); tel. 40.28.01.91; map 24 P10, métro Les Halles.
The enfant terrible of the fashion world who pioneered breastplates and padded hips also sells good old striped blazers in a kitschy décor.

FORUM DES HALLES **24** P10 ⓜ Les Halles
The unsightly hole left when the old central market buildings were torn down in 1969 lingered so long that a film was shot there. No one could agree on what to do with it, and while the city planners bickered among themselves, the *"trou des Halles"* became a legend. Finally taken up by Jacques Chirac, the Forum was completed in 1979.

It's a huge, glittering shopping mall on four subterranean levels cascading to a square down below. There are dozens of boutiques of every description, as well as three big stores—La Fnac, Go Sport and Habitat—several cinemas, restaurants, cafés and two museums.

The gardens, at ground level, are surrounded by delicate glass and steel buildings occupied by cultural exhibition halls (an arts pavilion, a library, Commandant Cousteau's Oceanic Centre, and so on). Underneath the gardens, the Nouveau Forum, completed in 1985, houses shops and boutiques, a discotheque, and sports facilities. There's also a videotheque where for 18 F you can select a videocassette and watch it on an individual TV screen.
Vidéothèque: Nouveau Forum des Halles, Saint-Eustache entrance, 2, Grande Galerie (1st); tel. 40.26.30.60. Open Tuesday to Sunday 12.30–7.30 p.m.; Wednesday 12.30–10.30 p.m. Time limit two hours.

The whole complex is such a maze of tunnels that a computer system has been installed with monitors at strategic points to help you find your way. Touch the screen to choose the place you are looking for, then the "Return" key for the address and a map with your route traced out with arrows.

GIVENCHY NOUVELLE BOUTIQUE   14/22 J11   Ⓜ Alma-Marceau
3 and 8, avenue George-V (8th); tel. 47.23.81.36. 10 a.m.–7 p.m.
*Also 8, avenue Montaigne (8th); tel. 47.23.44.40; map **14** J11.*
Superb evening-wear. Off-the-peg and haute couture at number 3;
new label "Givenchy Life"—sports and knitwear at number 8.

HERMÈS   15 L11   Ⓜ Madeleine
24, rue du Faubourg Saint-Honoré (8th); tel. 42.65.21.60. 10 a.m.–
6.30 p.m.; Monday and Saturday 10 a.m.–1 p.m. and 2.15–6.30 p.m.
The grand old family business is legendary for its leather goods and
silks; also specializes in watches, jewellery, china, sportswear.

CHARLES JOURDAN   15 M11   Ⓜ Madeleine
86, avenue des Champs-Elysées (8th); tel. 45.62.29.28. 9.45 a.m.–
7 p.m. Other branches in the 1st, 6th and 16th arrondissements.
Well-made and fashionable shoes and accessories in a wide range of
sizes and colours.

STÉPHANE KÉLIAN   23 M8   Ⓜ Sèvres-Babylone
13 bis, rue de Grenelle (7th); tel. 42.22.93.03. 10.30 a.m.–7 p.m. Other
branches in the 2nd, 3rd, 8th, 9th and 16th arrondissements.
Beautiful shoes and boots of all colours and design, way-out and
conservative. Comfortable woven leather; boots with zip-off tops....

KENZO   16/24 O11   Ⓜ Bourse
3, place des Victoires (1st); tel. 42.36.81.41. 10 a.m.–7 p.m.; Monday
11 a.m.–7 p.m.
*Also 16, boulevard Raspail (7th); tel. 42.22.09.38, map **23** M8.*
Colourful, modern, ample clothes by the first Japanese to hit the big
time in Paris over 20 years ago. His newer, attractive branch on
Boulevard Raspail also sells sportswear and home accessories.

75

Shopping Arcades
Charming reminders of the 18th or 19th centuries, these hideaway
galeries are lined with picturesque little boutiques.
Galerie Véro-Dodat (1st); map 24 O10; métro Louvre–Rue de Rivoli
Galerie Vivienne (2nd); map 16 O11; métro Bourse
Passage du Caire (2nd); map 17 Q11; métro Réaumur-Sébastopol
Passage de Choiseul (2nd); map 16 N11; métro Quatre-Septembre
Passage Jouffroy (9th); map 16 O12; métro Richelieu-Drouot
Passage des Pavillons, 6, rue de Beaujolais (1st); map 16/24 O11;
métro Pyramides
Passage des Princes (2nd); map 16 O12; métro Richelieu-Drouot
Passage Verdeau (9th); map 16 O12; métro Richelieu-Drouot

TOKIO KUMAGAÏ   **23** M8   Ⓜ Saint-Sulpice
32, rue de Grenelle (7th); tel. 45.44.23.11. 10 a.m.–7 p.m.; Saturday
11 a.m.–7 p.m.
*Also 52, rue Croix-des-Petits-Champs (1st); tel. 42.36.08.01, map **24***
C10.
High-class ready-to-wear clothes for women by a Japanese designer.
Unusual shoes (with a few models for men).

CHRISTIAN LACROIX   **14** K12   Ⓜ Franklin-D.-Roosevelt
73, rue du Faubourg Saint-Honoré (8th); tel. 42.65.79.08. 10 a.m.–
7 p.m.
Glamorous party and daytime clothes by the exuberant designer from
Arles, the man who re-invented the bustle and put fun back into
fashion. Expensive.

KARL LAGERFELD   **15** L11   Ⓜ Madeleine
17, rue du Faubourg Saint-Honoré (8th); tel. 42.66.60.60. 10 a.m.–
7 p.m.
His intriguing clothes in the Révillon boutique make him one of the
kings of feminine fashion.

LANCEL   **15/16** N12   Ⓜ Opéra
1–8, place de l'Opéra (9th); tel. 47.42.37.29. 9.30 a.m.–7 p.m. Other
branches in the 6th, 8th and 17th arrondissements.
Hold-alls of all shapes and sizes, from wallets to suitcases. Wide
range of appealing colours.

76

LANVIN   **15** L11   Ⓜ Madeleine
15 (men) and 22 (women), rue du Faubourg Saint-Honoré (8th); tel.
42.65.14.40. 9.30 a.m.–6.30 p.m.; Monday and Saturday 10 a.m.–1 p.m.
and 2–6.30 p.m. Other branches in the 1st and 8th arrondissements.
Strikingly fresh clothes by Maryll Lanvin, who knows that women like
to look feminine. For men: snappy tailored suits, beautiful shirts and
ties.

GUY LAROCHE   **14/22** J11   Ⓜ Alma-Marceau
For women: 29, avenue Montaigne (8th); tel. 47.23.78.72. 9.30 a.m.–
6.30 p.m.
For men and women: 30, rue du Faubourg Saint-Honoré (8th); tel.
42.65.62.74; 10 a.m.–6.30 p.m.
The classic, beautifully made ready-to-wear won't rock any boats but
strikes a sure note of elegance and is known to be least expensive of
big-name couture houses. Six boutiques in Paris; these are the main
ones.

LECOANET-HEMANT   **15** L12   Ⓜ Champs-Elysées–Clemenceau
*84, rue du Faubourg Saint-Honoré (8th); tel. 42.65.43.37. 10.30 a.m.–
7 p.m.*
An Indian and a Frenchman from Brittany joined their talents to
create a dressy couture line. This is their ready-to-wear shop, with
some chic wool suits, silk blouses and scarves.

LOLITA LEMPICKA   **25** R9   Ⓜ Saint-Paul
*3 bis, rue des Rosiers (4th); tel. 42.74.42.94. Tuesday to Saturday
10.30 a.m.–7 p.m.*
Without being too classic, Lolita Lempicka respects traditional
shapes; her creations are superb but prices reach astronomical
heights.

LESAGE   **15** M11   Ⓜ Opéra
*21, place Vendôme (1st); tel. 40.20.95.79. Tuesday to Friday
10.30 a.m.–7 p.m.; Saturday 10.30 a.m.–1 p.m. and 2.30–7 p.m.*
The master of haute couture embroidery has a select address near
the Ritz. Expensive creations, but oh so enticing and unexpected.

DIDIER LUDOT   **16/24** O11   Ⓜ Palais-Royal
*23–24, galerie Montpensier, Jardin du Palais-Royal (1st); tel.
42.96.06.56. Monday to Friday 11 a.m.–2 p.m. and 3–7 p.m.; Saturday
11 a.m.–1 p.m. and 2 p.m.–7 p.m.*
Period pieces from the Thirties to Sixties: beautiful second-hand
clothes at reasonable prices. Accessories too, such as crocodile-skin **77**
handbags.

MANUFACTURE DE BEAUX VÊTEMENTS   **24** P9   Ⓜ Les Halles
21, rue des Halles (1st); tel. 42.33.07.70. 10.30 a.m.–7 p.m.
Reproductions of clothes from the great Hollywood era (Forties to
Sixties)—mainly for men. Including accessories like shoes, specs,
watches...

MISSONI   **23** M9   Ⓜ Rue du Bac
43, rue du Bac (7th), tel. 45.48.38.02. 10 a.m.–7 p.m.
Wonderful knitwear: sweaters, twin-sets, dresses....

ISSEY MIYAKE   **23** M9   Ⓜ Rue du Bac
*201, boulevard Saint-Germain (7th); tel. 45.44.60.88. 10 a.m.–12.30 p.m.
and 1.30–7 p.m.*
Fabric is the medium for this artist-designer whose stunning, original
garments are priced in the art-work category.

PHILIPPE MODEL   **15/23** N11   Ⓜ Pyramides
33, place du Marché-Saint-Honoré (1st); tel. 42.96.89.02. 10 a.m.–
7.30 p.m.; Monday 1–7.30 p.m.
Eccentric but opulent-looking shoes and matching hats, gloves,
glasses and earrings.

MONTANA   **23** M8   Ⓜ Rue du Bac
31, rue de Grenelle (7th); tel. 42.22.69.56. 10.15 a.m.–7 p.m. Other
branches in the 1st and 8th arrondissements.
Super-chic clothes by a great creator. Almost in the haute couture
category and price range, they're not for everyone, nor do they look
like everyday wear.

POPY MORENI   **26** S8   Ⓜ Chemin Vert
13, place des Vosges (4th) tel. 42.77.09.96. Tuesday to Saturday
10 a.m.–7 p.m.; Monday 3–7 p.m.
Italian chic for young women and children. Expensive but absolutely
irresistible.

THIERRY MUGLER   **16** O11   Ⓜ Bourse
10, place des Victoires (2nd); tel. 42.60.06.37. Tuesday to Saturday
10 a.m.–7 p.m.; Monday 11 a.m.–1 p.m. and 2–7 p.m.
Science fiction with a touch of whimsy in the creations of this
designer with a flair for the dramatic.

FRANK NAMANI   **14** J11   Ⓜ Alma-Marceau
6, rue Marbeuf (8th); tel. 47.20.47.28. 9.30 a.m.–7 p.m.
78 Luxurious ready-to-wear in noble materials, for men and women.

LES NUITS D'ÉLODIE   **13/14** H12   Ⓜ Charles-de-Gaulle–Etoile
1 bis, avenue Mac-Mahon (8th); tel. 42.67.68.95. 10.20 a.m.–7 p.m.;
Monday 11 a.m.–7 p.m.
Luscious lingerie, négligées and women's clothes. Expensive haute
couture.

OLD ENGLAND   **15** M/N11   Ⓜ Opéra
12, boulevard des Capucines (9th); tel. 47.42.81.99. 9.30 a.m.–
6.30 p.m.; Monday 9.30 a.m.–12.30 p.m. and 2–6.30 p.m.
Very British. Smart, hard-wearing clothes for the whole family, but
prices are high.

PER SPOOK   **14/22** J11   Ⓜ Alma-Marceau
18, avenue George-V (8th); tel. 47.23.00.19. Monday to Friday 10 a.m.–
1 p.m.; and 2–6.30 p.m.
Spacious coordinated clothes in harmonious colours by the most
Parisian of Norwegian designers.

POLO RALPH LAUREN　　**15** M11　　Ⓜ Madeleine
2, place de la Madeleine (8th); tel. 42.86.90.83. 10 a.m.–7 p.m.
Smart leisure wear and a classic line in the American designer's
superb boutique, where everyone gets a friendly reception. Men's
clothes downstairs, women's on the first floor.

GEORGES RECH　　**23/24** N8　　Ⓜ Saint-Germain-des-Prés
*54, rue Bonaparte (6th); tel. 43.26.84.11. 10 a.m.–7 p.m.; Monday
11 a.m.–7 p.m. Other branches in the 1st and 16th arrondissements.*
Reasonably priced classics, never outmoded.

SONIA RYKIEL　　**23** M8　　Ⓜ Sèvres-Babylone
4–8, rue de Grenelle (6th); tel. 42.22.43.22. 10 a.m.–7 p.m.
*Also 70, rue du Faubourg Saint-Honoré (8th); tel. 42.65.20.81; map
15 L11.*
Her fans can't get enough of her sophisticated sweater outfits and
sexy knits–both day and evening wear (expensive). At number 4,
leisure wear, at number 6, classics, and 8, children's clothes.

SAINT-LAURENT RIVE GAUCHE　　**31/32** N7　　Ⓜ Saint-Sulpice
*6 (women) and 12 (men), place Saint-Sulpice (6th); tel. 43.26.84.40;
10 a.m.–7 p.m. Other branches in the 8th and 16th arrondissements.*
Periodically hailed as the reigning king of Paris fashion, Saint Laurent consistently turns out chic clothes with timeless elegance—good
investments in spite of their high price. His clothes for men are
exceptionally well made and in fabulous fabrics and colours, without
being way-out or precious.

79

JEAN-LOUIS SCHERRER　　**14** J11　　Ⓜ Franklin-D.-Roosevelt
*51, avenue Montaigne (8th); tel. 43.59.55.39. 9.30 a.m.–6.30 p.m.;
Saturday 10 a.m.–6.30 p.m. Other branches in the 6th, 8th and 16th
arrondissements.*
Opulent clothes approaching haute couture in quality.

ÉLISABETH DE SENNEVILLE　　**24** P10　　Ⓜ Etienne Marcel
3, rue de Turbigo (1st); tel. 42.33.90.83. 10.45 a.m.–7.15 p.m.
Also 55. rue Bonaparte (6th); tel. 46.33.57.90; map 23/24 N8.
Always up-to-date, ever innovating, Elisabeth de Senneville has
gained renown over the last ten years for her prints and unusual
fabrics. Big shop with several departments for women and children.

SMUGGLER　　**13** F10　　Ⓜ Pompe/Trocadéro
*93, rue de Longchamp (16th); tel. 47.04.23.27. 10.30 a.m.–8 p.m.;
Monday 2–8 p.m.*
Good quality classic clothes, at reasonable prices, for preppy men
from 25 to 35.

TANT QU'IL Y AURA   **31** M7   Ⓜ Saint-Sulpice
DES HOMMES   or Sèvres-Babylone
23, rue du Cherche-Midi (6th); tel. 45.48.48.17. 10.30 a.m.–7 p.m.;
Monday noon–7 p.m.
Men only: shirts, sweaters, boxer shorts and kinky gadgets.

TAXI-BROUSSE ALMEN GIBIRILA   **7** M15   Ⓜ La Fourche
1, rue Dautancourt (17th); tel. 42.63.20.73. 1–9 p.m., or by appointment
(it's better to phone before you go).
A souk-like boutique, where Benin/Congolese owner Almen Gibirila
creates long flowing garments inspired by the desert robes of the
Tuaregs, Basari and Masai.

CHANTAL THOMASS   **14** K11   Ⓜ Franklin-D.-Roosevelt
12, rond-point des Champs-Elysées (8th); tel. 43.59.87.34. 10 a.m.–
7 p.m.; Monday 11 a.m.–7 p.m.
Also 11, rue Madame (6th); tel. 45.44.60.11; map **31** *N7.*
She designs regular clothes for women, but lively lingerie of lace and
silk is her speciality.

EMMANUEL UNGARO   **14/22** J11   Ⓜ Alma-Marceau
2, avenue Montaigne (8th); tel. 47.23.61.94. 9.30 a.m.–7 p.m.
Also 58, rue du Faubourg Saint-Honoré (8th); tel. 47.42.16.06; map **15**
L11.
Inimitable design, sometimes quite sexy.

80
UPLA   **24** P9   Ⓜ Châtelet
17, rue des Halles (1st); tel. 40.26.49.96. 10.30 a.m.–7 p.m. Other
branches in the 6th and 16th arrondissements.
Bags, scarves and chic leisure wear for a trendy bourgeoise clientele.

VALENTINO   **14/22** J11   Ⓜ Alma-Marceau
17, avenue Montaigne (8th); tel. 47.23.64.61. 10 a.m.–7 p.m.
The Italian look for men—classic suits, and a big selection of luxury
sportswear for tennis or yachting. And smooth sophistication in black
and white for women.

MARIA-PIA VARNIER   **24** P10   Ⓜ Les Halles
22, rue Mondétour (1st); tel. 40.26.43.04. 11 a.m.–7 p.m.
Fine leather goods, classic in form, up-to-date in colour and craft.
Expensive.

GIANNI VERSACE   **23** N9   Ⓜ Saint-Germain-des-Prés
67, rue des Saints-Pères (6th); tel. 45.44.09.52. 10.15 a.m.–7 p.m.;
Monday 11.15 a.m.–7 p.m.
Sophisticated, prestigious, avant-garde fashion for men.

VICTOIRE **16/24** O11 Ⓜ Bourse
12, place des Victoires (2nd); tel. 45.08.53.29. 9.30 a.m.–7 p.m.
A fine selection of big-name designers of ready-to-wear. And at
no. 10 (tel. 42.60.96.21), less pricey models for younger people by
up-and-coming Parisian designers.

WESTON **14** J12 Ⓜ George-V
114, avenue des Champs-Elysées (8th); tel. 45.62.26.47. 9 a.m.–7 p.m.;
Monday 10 a.m.–7 p.m. Other branches in the 6th, 8th, 9th and 16th
arrondissements.
Gained a reputation for hard-wearing mocassins. Good-looking
shoes for men, but quality said to be on the decline.

YOHJI YAMAMOTO **24** O10 Ⓜ Louvre–Rue de Rivoli
or Etienne-Marcel
25, rue du Louvre (women) and 47, rue Etienne-Marcel (men) (1st);
tel. 45.08.82.45. 10.30 am–7 p.m.; Monday 11.30 a.m.–7 p.m.
Stark décor for clothes by the master of strict styling and sober
colours, mainly black, for the avant-garde.

ERMENEGILDO ZEGNA **15** N11 Ⓜ Opéra
10, rue de la Paix (2nd); tel. 42.61.67.61. 10 a.m.–7 p.m.
Elegance à l'italienne for men, by the genial inventor of crease-proof
high-performance woollen fabrics.

DISCOUNTS AND DÉGRIFFE

For high fashion at a fraction of the price, don't miss these discount
and stock shops, where the designer labels have usually been re-
moved.

ACCESSOIRES À SOIE **13** H13 Ⓜ Argentine
21, rue des Acacias (17th); tel. 42.27.78.77. 10.30 a.m.–2 p.m. and
3–7.30 p.m.; Monday 12.30–7.30 p.m.
Lots of elegant accessories—ties, shawls, squares—all made from
pure silk; even silk-covered handbags. And 50% cheaper than anywhere else.

L'APRÈS-MIDI **13** G13 Ⓜ Argentine
23, rue Brunel (17th); tel. 45.74.00.25. Monday to Friday 1.30–7.30 p.m.
Discounts on big names like Saint Laurent, Chanel, Alaïa, Montana,
Karl Lagerfeld...depending on arrivals.

CACHAREL STOCK   **37** M3   Ⓜ Alésia
114, rue Alésia; tel. 45.42.53.04. 10 a.m.–6.45 p.m.
Up to 50% reduction on last year's models for men, women and
children.

CHERCHEMINIPPES   **31** L6   Ⓜ Falguière
109, rue du Cherche-Midi (6th); tel. 42.22.45.23; 10.30 a.m.–7 p.m.
Also 111, rue du Cherche-Midi; tel. 42.22.53.76; same hours.
Resale shops with a few first-hand unlabelled designer clothes.
At number 109, very up-to-date women's models. At number 111,
menswear. All in perfect condition. There's a children's boutique
between the two (see page 186).

CLUB DES DIX   **15** L11   Ⓜ Concorde
58, rue du Faubourg Saint-Honoré (8th); tel. 42.66.43.61. 10 a.m.–
6 p.m.; open seven days a week.
At least 30% off well-known labels for women and men.

DOROTHÉE BIS STOCK   **37** M3   Ⓜ Alésia
74, rue d'Alésia (14th); tel. 45.42.49.99. 10.15 a.m.–7 p.m.; Monday 2–
7 p.m.
The biggest markdowns are on models from two seasons back. At the
same address, **Tennis Stock** sells sportswear at half price.

LE MOUTON À CINQ PATTES   **31** M7   Ⓜ Sevres-Babylone
Women and children: 8–10 and 18, rue Saint-Placide (6th); tel.
82 *45.48.86.26. 10 a.m.–7 p.m.; Monday 2–7 p.m.*
Women and men: 19, rue Grégoire-de-Tours (6th); tel. 43.29.73.56;
map 24 O8.
Men only: L'Annexe, 48, rue Saint-Placide; tel. 45.48.82.85.
Clothes by the avant-garde or more classic names (Krizia, Montana,
Saint Laurent).

BOUTIQUE NINA RICCI   **14** J11   Ⓜ Franklin-D.-Roosevelt
39, avenue Montaigne (8th); tel. 47.23.78.88. 10 a.m.–6.30 p.m.; Sat-
urday 2.15–6 p.m. (basement closed).
Forty per cent reductions on models from recent collections, in the
basement of the elegant couture house.

RÉCIPROQUE   **13/21** F10   Ⓜ Rue de la Pompe
95, rue de la Pompe (16th); tel. 47.04.30.28. Tuesday to Saturday
10 a.m.–6.45 p.m.
An exchange shop with as-new second-hand clothes for men and
women. A good place for a bargain.

Boubou Boutiques
Rue Doudeauville is almost entirely devoted to African fabrics—tie-dyes, batiks—in riotous colours. Just what you need to run up an exclusive little number to put a bit of sun into a rainy summer's day.
Rue Doudeauville (18th); map 9 Q/R15; métro Château Rouge.

TATI   **8** P14   ⓂBarbès-Rochechouart
4, boulevard Rochechouart (18th); tel. 42.55.13.09. Monday to Friday 10 a.m.–7 p.m.; Saturday 10 a.m.–7.30 p.m. Other branches in the 3rd and 6th arrondissements.
An infernal mêlée where you rub shoulders and everything else with all and sundry to get your bargain. Watch your wallet in the scrummage, and steer clear of the place on Saturdays. The other branches are very slightly tamer.

TOTO SOLDES   **9** Q15   ⓂChâteau-Rouge
49, boulevard Barbès (18th); tel. 42.52.90.53. 10 a.m.–7 p.m. Other branches in the 2nd, 8th, 13th, 17th, 18th, 19th and 20th arrondissements.
Heaps of superb African fabrics sold cheaper than in Africa. Also house linen, carpets, soft furnishings....

TOUTES GRIFFES DEHORS   **22** J9   ⓂLatour-Maubourg
76, rue Saint-Dominique (7th); tel. 45.51.68.14. 10 a.m.–7 p.m.
If you're lucky, you may find the Balmain, Guy Laroche or Gaston Jaunet of your dreams.

83

JEWELLERY

If you want to see all the latest trends in jewellery in record time, window-shop your way along Rue de la Paix and round Place Vendôme, where all the great designer names hold sway.

L'ATELIER   **8** P15   ⓂJules Joffrin
52, rue Custine (18th); tel. 42.54.07.04. 9.30 a.m.–12.30 p.m. and 3–7.30 p.m.; Monday 3–7.30 p.m.
The window is full of beautiful rare timepieces from the Thirties to Sixties, including a few fob watches. Reasonable prices.

BOUCHERON   **15** M11   ⓂOpéra
26, place Vendôme (1st); tel. 42.61.58.16. Monday to Friday 9.30 a.m.–1 p.m. and 2.30 p.m.–6.30 p.m.
Renowned jewellers in a venerable historic building.

BURMA **15** M11 Ⓜ Madeleine
15, boulevard de la Madeleine (9th); tel. 42.61.11.63. 9.30 a.m.–6.30 p.m.
Costume jewellery in gold, silver or vermeil—big-name look-alikes.

CARTIER **15** N11 Ⓜ Opéra
13, rue de la Paix (2nd); tel. 42.61.58.56. 10 a.m.–6.30 p.m.; Monday 10.30 a.m.–6.30 p.m. Other branches in the 1st, 2nd, 8th, 10th and 12th arrondissements.
No need to introduce Cartier. A "must", as the slogan for their gift department proclaims.

DARY'S **15/23** M11 Ⓜ Concorde
362, rue Saint-Honoré (8th); tel. 42.60.95.23. 10 a.m.–6 p.m.
Take your time to rummage in this tiny shop crammed with old-fashioned and modern jewellery, watches and antiques.

DÉMONS ET MERVEILLES **23/24** N8 Ⓜ Saint-Germain-des-Prés
45, rue Jacob (6th); tel. 43.24.59.97. 10 a.m.–8 p.m.
Bewitching oriental jewellery, plus painted boxes, embroidered clothes and flowery fabrics.

LA DROGUERIE **24** P10 Ⓜ Les Halles
9, rue du Jour (1st); tel. 45.08.93.27. 10.30 a.m.–6.45 p.m.; Monday 2–6.45 p.m.
An Ali Baba's cave of baubles, bangles and especially beads—with ribbons, strings and clasps to do-it-yourself.

84

FABRICE **23** N8 Ⓜ Saint-Germain-des-Prés
33/33 bis, rue Bonaparte (6th); tel. 43.26.57.95. 11.30 a.m.–7 p.m.
Spectacular or discreet, every kind of costume jewellery, in wood, metal, leather, ivory, silk.... Prices for all pockets.

MAUBOUSSIN **15** M11 Ⓜ Opéra
20, place Vendôme (1st); tel. 42.60.32.54. 9.30 a.m.–1 p.m. and 2.30–6.30 p.m.
Wonderful work in semi-precious stones as well as dazzling gems.

PREMIER ÉTAGE **15/24** P10 Ⓜ Etienne-Marcel
32, rue Etienne-Marcel (2nd); tel. 42.33.20.30. 11 a.m.–7 p.m.
To make you stand out in a crowd, flashy but attractive jewellery: red copper spangled with multicoloured stones, hammered metal chains.... The interior design by Denis Colomb is also worth seeing.

REMINISCENCE **24** N8 Ⓜ Mabillon
22, rue du Four (6th); tel. 46.33.32.61. 10 a.m.–7 p.m.
The dazzling glitter of strass and rhinestones...and a few oriental jewels.

SACRILÈGE **25** Q10 Ⓜ Les Halles
6, rue du Cygne (1st); tel. 42.33.51.29. 10.30 a.m.–7.30 p.m.; Monday 1.30–7.30 p.m.
Top-fashion costume jewellery to please all tastes.

SCOOTER **24** P10 Ⓜ Les Halles
10, rue de Turbigo (2nd); tel. 45.08.89.31. 10 a.m.–7 p.m.; Monday 2–7 p.m.
Lovely contemporary pieces inspired by North African and Indian traditional styles.

SOUCHE LAPARRA **17/25** R11 Ⓜ Temple
157, rue du Temple (3rd); tel. 42.72.16.20. Monday to Friday 9 a.m.– noon and 2–5 p.m.
Gold chains cut to measure—by the metre or centimetre.

SWAROVSKI **15** M11 Ⓜ Tuileries
249, rue Saint-Honoré (1st); tel. 42.60.06.27. 10 a.m.–7 p.m. Also 50, rue du Four (6th), tel. 45.48.73.58; map 23/24 N8.
Purveyor of gems to the great Parisian jewellers for more than a century, Swarovski sells its own line and creations by Dior, Yves Saint Laurent, Céline, Valentino as well as new designers like Pierre Bex and Robi Roja.

UTILITY BIBI **24** N8 Ⓜ Mabillon
27, rue du Four (6th); tel. 43.25.53.77. 10 a.m.–7 p.m.
American Billy Boy's hilarious baroque creations, among those of two dozen other contemporary designers.

85

PERFUME AND COSMETICS

Everyone knows that France is the world's leader in the art of fragrance—so go on, spoil yourself. Perfume, eau de cologne and eau de toilette are good buys, not just because they're so very French but because they are sold duty-free all over the city (at the airport the counters are usually mobbed). Balmain, Carven, Givenchy, Nina Ricci, Ungaro and so on all are all entrenched on the Right Bank, but their perfumes can be found in the department stores and every neighbourhood *parfumerie*. Some others, including duty-free stores, are listed below.

CARON **14** J11 Ⓜ Franklin-D.-Roosevelt
34, avenue Montaigne (8th); tel. 47.23.40.82. 10 a.m.–6.30 p.m.
Excellent traditional scents going back some years, or appealing up-to-date fragrances.

CATHERINE   **15/23** M11   Ⓜ Tuileries
6, rue de Castiglione (1st); tel. 42.60.81.49. 9.30 a.m.–6.30 p.m.
A duty-free perfume shop (30% off) selling all major brands, plus cosmetics and gifts.

CENTRE FRANCO-AMÉRICAIN   **16** P11   Ⓜ Sentier
49, rue d'Aboukir (2nd); tel. 42.36.77.46. 9 a.m.–6.30 p.m.; Saturday 10 a.m.–5.30 p.m.
Most of the well-known brands, 25% cheaper. The same goes for the ties and scarves signed Cardin, Yves Saint Laurent and so on.

COMPTOIR SUD-PACIFIC   **15** N8   Ⓜ Opéra
17, rue de la Paix (2nd); tel. 42.61.74.44. 9.30 a.m.–7 p.m.
Stars of show-biz and the cinema love Josée Fournier's fruity eaux de toilette—*Vanille, Pamplemousse, Cerise.* Luxury luggage as well.

FREDDY   **15** N12   Ⓜ Opéra/Ⓡ (line A) Auber
10, rue Auber (9th); tel. 47.42.63.41. Monday to Friday 9 a.m.–6.30 p.m.
25% reduction on cosmetics and perfumes, leatherware and accessories of all the big brands; also on Yves Saint Laurent pens and watches.

ANNICK GOUTAL   **15/23** M11   Ⓜ Tuileries
14, rue de Castiglione (1st); tel. 42.60.52.82. 10 a.m.–7.30 p.m. Other branches in the 7th, 8th and 17th arrondissements.
One of France's top "noses", Mme Goutal has opened four shops selling her popular perfumes (some named after her children), which won her the European Prize for Excellence. Collectors take note—her bottles are beautiful. Soap and beauty products available as well.

GUERLAIN   **14** J12   Ⓜ Franklin-D.-Roosevelt
68, avenue des Champs-Elysées (8th); tel. 45.62.52.57. 9.30 a.m.–6.45 p.m.; Saturday 9.30 a.m.–7 p.m. Other branches in the 7th, 8th and 16th arrondissements.
Founded in Paris in 1828, this venerable, family-owned perfume house is an institution, still offering the scents devised for Empress Eugénie *(Eau de Cologne impériale)* alongside the latest heady successes, *Chamade* and *Parure*. Guerlain's first perfume, *Gicki*, was created in 1879.

GRAIN DE BEAUTÉ   **31** M7   Ⓜ Saint-Sulpice
9, rue du Cherche-Midi (6th); tel. 45.48.07.55. 10.30 a.m.–7 p.m.; Monday 2.30–7 p.m.
A chintzy "beauty spot" with the best of British fragrances, pot-pourris, old-fashioned soaps.

GIFTS

À PROPOS   **31** L6   Ⓜ Duroc
86, rue de Sèvres (7th); tel. 43.06.61.16. 10 a.m.–7 p.m.
Original, tasteful gifts: household objects, stationery, handsome pens
and cigarette lighters.

ARTCURIAL   **14** K11   Ⓜ Franklin-D.-Roosevelt
*9, avenue Matignon (8th); tel. 42.99.16.16. Tuesday to Saturday
10.30 a.m.–7.15 p.m.*
This display centre offers limited editions by contemporary artists—
sculpture, jewellery, scarves, porcelain, carpets, furniture, as well as
paintings, etchings, posters and modern art books.

AUGUSTINE, LA MAISON   **24** O8   Ⓜ Saint-Michel
DES BOÎTES   or Odéon
*18, rue des Grands-Augustins (6th); tel. 43.25.11.66. Tuesday to Satur-
day 11 a.m.–6 p.m.*
There's nothing square about these decorative or amusing trick
boxes that come in all shapes and sizes, from all over the world, in
every kind of material—ceramic, rosewood, coral, glass, silver....

AU VIEUX DOCUMENT   **16** O13   Ⓜ Notre-Dame-de-Lorette
*6 bis, rue de Châteaudun (9th); tel. 48.78.77.84. Monday to Friday
11 a.m.–6 p.m. (or by appointment).*
17th-, 18th- and 19th-century engravings (with an official stamp of
guarantee), old topographical maps, 19th-century lithographs, old
posters and rare books for bibliomaniacs.

87

BOUCHARA   **15** M12   Ⓜ Havre-Caumartin
*54, boulevard Haussmann (9th); tel. 42.80.66.95. 9.15 a.m.–6.30 p.m.
Other branches in the 16th and 17th arrondissements.*
A vast store, well-stocked with high-quality fabrics of all kinds and
colours, French or foreign-made.

BOUTIQUE CHIC ET CHOC   **24** P10   ⓔ Châtelet–Les Halles
*Connections Hall, RER Châtelet–Les Halles (1st); tel. 40.02.38.40.
9.30 a.m.–7 p.m.; Monday and Saturday 11 a.m.–7 p.m.*
Part of a PR campaign by the public transport authority, the shop
sells a multitude of gimmicks with the métro motif—T-shirts, sneakers,
kimonos and mugs.

BOUTIQUE DU MUSÉE DES ARTS DÉCORATIFS **23/24** N10 Ⓜ Louvre– Rue de Rivoli

107, rue de Rivoli (1st); tel. 42.60.32.14. Daily (including Sunday) 12.30–6 p.m.
Reproductions of works exhibited in the museum, such as Sèvres porcelain and 18th-century furnishing fabrics. There's also a section for contemporary pieces based on temporary exhibitions.

CÉRAMIQUE INTERNATIONAL **15** M11 Ⓜ Madeleine

9, place de la Madeleine (8th); tel. 42.65.75.70. 10 a.m.–7 p.m.
If you want to eat off a Dali or a Cocteau, don't miss this boutique offering china tableware printed with paintings or drawings by famous artists—machine resistant.

C.F.O.C. **23** M8 Ⓜ Saint-Germain-des-Prés

163/167 boulevard Saint-Germain (6th); tel. 45.48.00.18. 10 a.m.–7 p.m. Other branches in the 1st and 16th arrondissements.
Exotic boutiques devoted to the Far East. Clothes are sold at number 163, crafts at 167.

LE CHAT HUANT **24** P7 Ⓜ Saint-Michel/Maubert-Mutualité

50, rue Galande (5th); tel. 46.33.67.56. Daily (including Sunday) 11 a.m.–7 p.m.
Mainly Far Eastern imports, an inexpensive choice of knickknacks and gifts (lacquered boxes, silk scarves, ashtrays, and so on).

COCODY **25** R9 Ⓜ Saint-Paul

1 bis, rue Ferdinand-Duval (4th); tel. 42.77.28.82. 11 a.m.–7 p.m.; Sunday noon–7 p.m.
Also 14, rue Descartes (5th); tel. 43.26.05.49; map 32 P6.
Gaily coloured fabrics from Mali, the Ivory Coast and Ghana, and African handicrafts—jewellery, pottery, naïve paintings.

Crystal Paradise

Rue de Paradis positively sparkles. Here you'll find, grouped together and keenly competing, most of France's renowned porcelain and crystal manufacturers—Baccarat, Bernadaud, Daum, Haviland, Limoges-Unic, Madronet, Villeroy & Boch. Part of Baccarat is devoted to a fascinating museum displaying all its historic pieces. You'll also find Lalique crystal (though the selection is more comprehensive in the shop on Rue Royale), Meissen porcelain and Christofle silverware.
Rue du Paradis (10th); map 17 Q13; métro Château d'Eau/Poissonnière

DEHILLERIN   **24** O/P10   Ⓜ Les Halles
18, rue Coquillière (1st); tel. 42.36.53.13. 8 a.m.–12.30 p.m. and 2–6 p.m.
Everything in professional kitchenware to help you master the art of French cooking...from all sizes of tartlet tins and cast-iron saucepans to *chinois* sieves. Come at opening time and you may avoid the crush; it's very popular.

DESCAMPS   **24** P9   Ⓜ Châtelet
88, rue de Rivoli (4th); tel. 42.78.20.88. 10 a.m.–7 p.m. Other branches in the 1st, 6th, 7th, 8th, 9th, 11th, 13th, 14th, 15th, 16th and 17th arrondissements.
Beautiful bathroom and bedroom linens.

DRUGSTORE PUBLICIS   **14** H12   Ⓜ Charles-de-Gaulle–Etoile
133, avenue des Champs-Elysées (8th); tel. 47.23.54.34. 9 a.m.–2 a.m.; Sunday 10 a.m.–2 a.m. Other branches in the 6th and 8th arrondissements.
Open until 2 a.m., so handy if you're out of cigarettes or need a book to send you to sleep.... Sells just about everything, from ice cream to hi-fis.

ALFRED DUNHILL   **15** N11   Ⓜ Opéra
15, rue de la Paix (2nd); tel. 42.61.57.58. 9.30 a.m.–6.30 p.m.; Monday 10.30 a.m.–6.30 p.m.
As tobacco is a state monopoly, you won't find any here. But there are lots of fine quality smoking accessories—pipes, humidors, cigarette lighters—and other gifts for men, such as fountain pens, tie pins, and an exclusive line of eaux de toilette and skin care products.

89

L'ESPRIT ET LE VIN   **15** L12   Ⓜ Madeleine
65, boulevard Malesherbes (8th); tel. 45.22.60.40. Tuesday to Saturday 10 a.m.–7 p.m.
Nothing is missing from this shop dedicated to wine-tasting. From the latest in streamlined corkscrews to carafes and expert oenological tomes.

JANSEN   **15** L11   Ⓜ Concorde
9, rue Royale (8th); tel. 42.66.51.52. 10 a.m.–7 p.m.
The fabulous gift shop specializing in tableware is only part of this elegant store specializing in antiques and modern furnishings in all styles, arranged as if in a private home.

KANGOUROU   **15** M13   Ⓜ Saint-Augustin
10, rue de la Pépinière (8th); tel. 42.94.05.59. 10 a.m.–7 p.m. Other branches in the 4th, 9th, 14th and 15th arrondissements.
Amusing gifts and gadgets at unbeatable prices.

RITA KIM   **17** S12   Ⓜ Jacques-Bonsergent
79, quai de Valmy (10th); tel. 46.07.50.88. Tuesday to Saturday 12.30–7 p.m.
Chock-a-block with plastic American kitsch the French find irresistible—inflatable hats, parrot lamps, Marilyn Monroe watches, T-shirts, toys and tableware.

KIMOMOYA   **25** R8   Ⓜ Pont-Marie/Saint-Paul
11, rue du Pont-Louis-Philippe (4th); tel. 48.87.30.24. 11 a.m.–7 p.m.; Monday 1.30–7 p.m.
From paintbrushes to kimonos, every object is a Japanese work of art.

PILONES ET PARMENTIER   **8** O14   Ⓜ Abbesses
7, rue Tardieu (18th); tel. 46.06.37.00. Tuesday to Sunday 11 a.m.–12.30 p.m. and 3–7 p.m.
Greetings cards of all shapes—bananas, hearts, etc. And postcards to cut out and make into rings or earrings.

PRISUNIC CHAMPS-ÉLYSÉES   **14** J12   Ⓜ Franklin-D.-Roosevelt
109, rue La Boétie (8th); tel. 42.25.27.46. Monday to Saturday 9.45 a.m.–midnight.
Lots of attractive articles at bargain prices: clothing, food, cosmetics, household goods, school stationery, and so on.

PUIFORCAT   **14** J11   Ⓜ Franklin-D.-Roosevelt
22, rue François 1er (8th); tel. 47.20.74.27. Tuesday to Saturday 10 a.m.–7 p.m.
Renowned for beautiful designs in silverware and porcelain by famous designers (Andrée Putman, Manuel Canovas); Lalique crystal; good gift department.

SOHO   **14** K11   Ⓜ Franklin-D.-Roosevelt
26, avenue des Champs-Elysées (8th); tel. 45.62.09.16. Daily, including Sunday, 10.30 a.m.–11 p.m.
Gadgets, gimmicks and gifts at all prices.

FRANÇOISE THIBAULT   **24** N8   Ⓜ Saint Germain-des-Prés
1, rue Bourbon-le-Château (6th); tel. 43.26.40.23. Tuesday to Saturday 10.30 a.m.–7.15 p.m.
Amusing, tasteful, decorative objects such as cushion-cats, music boxes, painted bibelots, mirrors and artisan-made furniture.

TORVINOKA   **24** N8   Ⓜ Saint-Germain-des-Prés
4, rue Cardinale (6th); tel. 43.25.09.13. Tuesday to Saturday 10 a.m.–7 p.m.

The best in Finnish design: furniture by Alvar Aalto, stoneware and faïence by Arabia. Also kitchen- and tableware by French, Italian, English, Spanish and Portuguese designers.

LOUIS VUITTON   **14** J11   Ⓜ Franklin-D.-Roosevelt
57, avenue Montaigne (8th); tel. 45.62.47.00. 9.30 a.m.–6.30 p.m. Also 78 bis, avenue Marceau (8th); tel. 47.20.47.00; map 13/14 H12.
If you still haven't a Louis Vuitton bag, satchel, suitcase or trunk and want the real McCoy (with its familiar LV logo) here's your chance. They aren't giving anything away, but it's less expensive than abroad.

FLORISTS

The French are great at the art of bouquets, which make a wonderful "thank-you" gift if you're invited to a French home.

CHARLANE   **6** J14   Ⓜ Wagram
95, avenue de Villiers (17th); tel. 42.27.17.04. 10 a.m.–7.30 p.m. Also 29, rue du Roi-de-Sicile (4th); tel. 42.72.63.73; map 25 R8/9.
Specializes in beautiful bonsaï.

MAXIM'S FLEURS   **15** L11   Ⓜ Concorde
5, rue Royale (8th); tel. 47.42.88.46. 10 a.m.–7 p.m.
Belle-Epoque bouquets in the Maxim's style. Reproductions of period vases and *barbotines*, faïence pots decorated with figures in relief.

MONCEAU FLEURS   **14** K13   Ⓜ Villiers **91**
92, boulevard Malesherbes (17th); tel. 45.63.88.23. 9 a.m.–8 p.m.; Sunday 9 a.m.–5 p.m.
A profusion of plants and flowers, not too costly.

GOURMET PARIS

The food shops will drive you wild. You'll find authentic regional produce from every corner of the country, in addition to specialities from the world over. Some of the addresses we have selected have acquired an international reputation; others are secrets you'll be delighted to discover.

À LA MOTTE AU BEURRE   **22** J8   Ⓜ Ecole Militaire
23 bis, avenue de La Motte-Picquet (7th); tel. 45.51.99.49. Thursday to Tuesday 7 a.m.–8 p.m.
A large choice of **sandwiches**, generously filled and not too expensive. And a delicious farmhouse baguette.

ANDROUET   **15** M13   Ⓜ Liège
41, rue d'Amsterdam (8th); tel. 48.74.26.90. Tuesday to Saturday 10 a.m.–7 p.m. Restaurant tel. 48.74.26.93. Noon–2 p.m. and 7–10.30 p.m.
A master **cheese** maker. Top quality in more than 200 cheeses, aged on the premises. The comfortable upstairs restaurant offers a regular menu or a cheese-tasting—sample as many as you can.

APOLLON   **37** L4   Ⓜ Pernety
66, rue Raymond-Losserand (14th); tel. 45.45.77.59. 10 a.m.–1 p.m. and 2–9 p.m.; closed Monday morning.
Wonderful **Greek** produce—moussaka, tarama, stuffed vine leaves, olives, wines and spirits—all of excellent quality.

AU RÉGAL   **21** F9   Ⓜ La Muette
4, rue Nicolo (16th); tel. 42.88.49.15. Daily including Sunday 9.30 a.m.–10.30 p.m.
High-class **Russian** specialities—blinis, salmon, caviar, vodka.... The restaurant next door is open daily from noon to 11 p.m. (closed Sundays from 3 to 8 p.m.).

AUX CINQ CONTINENTS   **26** U9   Ⓜ Voltaire
75, rue de la Roquette (11th); tel. 43.79.75.51. Monday to Friday 9.30 a.m.–1 p.m. and 3.30–8 p.m.; Sunday 9.30 a.m.–1 p.m.
A cosmopolitan array of **spices** and savours to bring the whole world to your dinner table.

AUX DUCS DE PRASLIN   **14** J11   Ⓜ Franklin-D.-Roosevelt
44, avenue Montaigne (8th); tel. 47.20.99.63. 10 a.m.–7 p.m.
The great **praline** specialist. Sweets from every French province.

BERTHILLON   **25/33** R7   Ⓜ Pont Marie
31, rue Saint-Louis-en-l'Ile (4th); tel. 43.54.31.61. Wednesday to Sunday 10 a.m.–8 p.m.
A renowned **ice-cream** parlour, as French as can be. Dozens of traditional and innovative flavours.

BOULANGERIE DE L'ANCIENNE-COMÉDIE   **24** O8   Ⓜ Odéon
10, rue de l'Ancienne-Comédie (6th); tel. 43.26.89.72. Closed Sunday 6 a.m.–9 p.m.
An all-night **bakery**—bread, sandwiches, croissants, cakes. Prices go up after 11 p.m.

LA BOUTIQUE LAYRAC   **24** O8   Ⓜ Mabillon
29, rue de Buci (6th); tel. 43.25.17.72. Daily including Sunday 9 a.m.–3 a.m.
Cooked dishes to take away; also foie gras, caviar and shellfish.

ANNE-MARIE CANTIN **22** J8/9 Ⓜ Ecole Militaire
12, rue du Champ-de-Mars (7th); tel. 45.50.43.94. 8.30 a.m.–1 p.m. and 4–7.30 p.m.
A fine selection of **cheeses**, both fresh from the farm and aged, by a young woman who learned it all from her father. You can visit of the cellars and participate in a cheese-tasting—five cheeses, bread and a glass of good wine, 50 F.

CAVES DE LA MADELEINE **15** L/M11 Ⓜ Madeleine
Cité Berryer, 25, rue Royale (8th); tel. 42.65.92.40. 9 a.m.–7 p.m.
An extraordinary **cellar** with all the best French vintages: 150 Bordeaux, 170 Burgundies, 50 Côtes-du-Rhône, wines of the Loire, Provence, Jura....

CAVES TAILLEVENT **14** J12 Ⓜ Saint-Philippe-du-Roule
199, rue du Faubourg Saint-Honoré (8th); tel. 45.61.14.09. Tuesday to Friday 10 a.m.–7.30 p.m.; Monday 2–7.30 p.m.; Saturday 10 a.m.– 7 p.m.
An eclectic **cellar** with wines from France, Italy, Spain, Australia, California...and a few specialities like Churchill's Graham port and pure malt whiskies.

LE CHOCOLAT PAR MICHEL CHAUDUN **22** K10 Ⓜ Invalides
149, rue de l'Université (7th); tel. 47.53.74.40. 9.30 a.m.–7.30 p.m.
For inveterate chocoholics. The tiny shop even looks like a chocolate box. Chaudun won awards from the chocolate-tasters' club for two of his five chocolate gâteaux—bitter truffle *Esmeralda*, and caramel praline *Veragua*.

93

LE COCHON ROSE **8** O14 Ⓜ Pigalle
44, boulevard de Clichy (18th); tel. 46.06.86.25. Friday to Wednesday 6 p.m.–5.30 a.m.
Famous **caterer**, 200 yards from the Moulin Rouge. Cold meats, fruit, wine and spirits, bread, sandwiches and cooked dishes.

COMPAGNIE ANGLAISE DES THÉS **24** P10 Ⓜ Les Halles
Forum des Halles, 3, rue Basse (1st); tel. 42.97.45.43. 10.30 a.m.– 7.30 p.m. Other branches in the 8th and 15th arrondissements.
More kinds of **tea** than you can imagine, stored in superb red canisters and sold loose. Traditional blends directly imported from India, China and Sri Lanka; perfumed teas like raspberry or whisky; special house-blends such as Scheherazade and Hawaii. Also English cakes and biscuits, teapots and other small tea-brewing gifts.

CHRISTIAN CONSTANT   **23** M9   Ⓜ Rue du Bac
26, rue du Bac (7th); tel. 47.03.30.00. Daily including Sunday 8 a.m.–
8 p.m. Also 37, rue d'Assas (6th); tel. 45.48.45.51.
Ice creams and sorbets made from natural products, but relatively
expensive. **Chocolates** are also a specialty, and delectable pastries—
try the *Caracas*, a bitter-chocolate cake. Tea-room for on-the-spot
sampling.

DALLOYAU   **14** K12   Ⓜ Saint-Philippe-du-Roule
99, rue du Faubourg Saint-Honoré (8th); tel. 43.59.18.10. Daily in-
cluding Sunday 9 a.m.–9 p.m. Other branches in the 2nd, 6th, 7th and
15th arrondissements.
Fabulous **macaroons** in three flavours boosted this caterer to fame.
Fine pastries, chocolates, ice cream, and prepared dishes such as
duck in aspic for take-away. Tea and light lunch served as well.

DEBAUVE ET GALLAIS   **23** N8   Ⓜ Saint-Germain-des-Prés
30, rue des Saints-Pères (7th); tel. 45.48.54.67. Tuesday to Friday
10 a.m.–1 p.m. and 2–7 p.m.; Saturday early closing 6 p.m.
Excellent **chocolate**, caramels, fruit drops, and so on, in a beautiful
Empire-style setting. Don't be put off by the old-fashioned sign
outside proclaiming "Chocolats hygiéniques". It's a relic of the 1800s,
when a neighbouring pharmacist persuaded the confectioner to sell
his curative potions and powders disguised with a chocolate coating.
Today's soft-centres are a bit easier to swallow.

94
FAUCHON   **15** M11   Ⓜ Madeleine
26, place de la Madeleine (8th); tel. 47.42.60.11. 9.40 a.m.–7 p.m. Open
until 10 p.m. for "gastronomie" products.
The high temple of **fancy groceries**—a fabulous selection of food-
stuffs from all over the world, many attractively wrapped for your
gourmet gifts. Fresh foods to take out; personal delivery service.

LA FERME DU HAMEAU   **29** G4   Ⓜ Porte de Versailles
223, rue de la Croix-Nivert (15th); tel. 45.32.88.70. Tuesday to Saturday
8.30 a.m.–1 p.m. and 3.30–5.30 p.m.
A shop that looks like a Norman cottage, where you'll find authentic
country produce such as camembert, black pudding *(boudin)* and
andouillettes from Normandy, quenelles and rosette sausage from
Lyon. Excellent wine cellar.

FLO PRESTIGE   **15/16** N11   Ⓜ Pyramides
42, place du Marché Saint-Honoré (1st); tel. 42.61.45.46. Daily in-
cluding Sunday 8 a.m.–midnight. Other branches in the 12th, 15th and
16th arrondissements.

Reputed **caterer,** selling everything from sandwiches to cooked meals to their prestigious chocolate cake. Wines and champagne, too.

JO GOLDENBERG   25 R9   Ⓜ Saint-Paul
7, rue des Rosiers (4th); tel. 48.87.20.16. Daily including Sunday 8.30 a.m.–midnight.
The famed **delicatessen** with excellent chopped liver and onions, gefilte fish and eggplant caviar is a restaurant as well, with high-spirited musical ambience at dinner.

GRAND'MÈRE L'OYE   8/16 P14   Ⓜ Anvers
57, rue de Dunkerque (9th); tel. 42.81.33.55. (answering machine 42.80.11.30). Tuesday to Saturday 10 a.m.–noon and 4–7.30 p.m.
Grandmother Goose, alias André-François Biancarelli, offers not only **foie gras,** but potted meats, duck *magret*, goose *confit*, and a nice range of hearty dishes from south-west France, including *cassoulet*. Mr. Biancarelli is backstage in his *laboratoire*, demonstrating the delicate art of cooking goose liver. Also Norwegian smoked salmon (whole or hand-sliced) and caviar from Iran (to order). Everything free from preservatives and artificial colourings.

HÉDIARD   15 M11   Ⓜ Madeleine
21, place de la Madeleine (8th); tel. 42.66.44.36. 9 a.m.–11 p.m. Other branches in the 1st, 7th, 15th, 16th and 17th arrondissements.
Very **fancy groceries.** If you're looking for vintage sardines, rose-petal jam, 25-year-old vinegar, try Hédiard, just slightly more esoteric than Fauchon across the square. The epicure's dream.

95

HÉRATCHIAN   16 P13   Ⓜ Cadet
6, rue Lamartine (9th); tel. 48.78.43.19. 8.30 a.m.–7.30 p.m.; Monday 2–7.30 p.m.
A **Middle Eastern bazaar** where exotic spices, dried fruit and vegetables, nuts and olives are sold by the ladle from sacks or jars. Also ready-prepared dishes to take away. In business since 1935, Hératchian has become an institution.

IZRAËL (LE MONDE DES ÉPICES)   25 R8   Ⓜ Saint-Paul
30, rue François-Miron (4th); tel. 42.72.66.23. Tuesday to Friday 9.30 a.m.–1 p.m. and 2.30–7 p.m.; Saturday 9 a.m.–7 p.m.
A bonanza of **exotic ingredients** for every kind of ethnic cuisine. Dried fruit, Turkish Delight, cakes from Chile and Argentina, beans and lentils, six kinds of rice sold loose from huge sacks, olives marinating in barrels, jams and marmelades, rum, vodka...and a tantalizing mingling of spicy fragrances to make your mouth water.

LUCIEN LEGRAND FILLES & FILS   **16** O11   Ⓜ Bourse
1, rue de la Banque (2nd); tel. 42.60.07.12. Tuesday to Friday 8.30 a.m.–7.30 p.m.; Monday 10 a.m.–7.30 p.m.; Saturday 8.30 a.m.– 1 p.m. and 3–7 p.m.
From interesting little local **wines** to great vintages, recommended by the owner, who travels to vineyards all over France to find the best. Wine-tastings on Saturdays.

LENÔTRE   **20/28** E7   Ⓜ Michel-Ange-Auteuil
44, rue d'Auteuil (16th); tel. 45.24.52.52. Daily including Sunday 9 a.m.–9 p.m. Other branches in the 7th, 8th, 15th, 16th and 17th arrondissements.
Caterer and **pastry-maker** par excellence, Gaston Lenôtre reigns in the world of *haute gastronomie* along with the likes of Paul Bocuse. From his *fantasme* (layers of bittersweet chocolate cake and chocolate mousse) to cherry tartlets, everything is a masterpiece.

LA MAISON DU CHOCOLAT   **14** J11   Ⓜ Franklin-D.-Roosevelt
52, rue François 1er (8th); tel. 47.23.38.25. 9.30 a.m.–7 p.m. Also 225, rue du Faubourg Saint-Honoré (8th); tel. 42.27.39.44; map 14 J13.
Irresistible **chocolates**, including big macaroons and cakes, by Robert Linxe, the chocolate wizard of Paris. People passing by are so bowled over by the tempting aroma that they rush inside to buy.

LA MAISON DU MIEL   **15** M12   Ⓜ Madeleine
24, rue Vignon (9th); tel. 47.42.26.70. Tuesday to Saturday 9.30 a.m.– 7 p.m.; Monday 11 a.m.–6 p.m.
A sweet-smelling shop for **honey** connoisseurs—at least 30 varieties from the French provinces and the rest of the world, from thick, white, clover honey to dark, runny pine. And other products of the hive like pollen and royal jelly.

MARIAGE   **25** R9   Ⓜ Hôtel-de-Ville
30, rue de Bourg-Tibourg (4th); tel. 42.72.28.11. Tuesday to Sunday 11 a.m.–7.30 p.m.
A **tea** den that may be your "cuppa", whose walls are lined with pretty metal canisters storing teas from all over the world. And perhaps the world's only tea-flavoured chocolates. Also a tea-room for light lunches and afternoon teas. Brunch noon–4 p.m., 115 F.

LE MOULIN DE LA VIERGE   **31** L4   Ⓜ Pernety
105, rue Vercingétorix (14th); tel. 45.43.09.84. Tuesday to Saturday 8 a.m.–8 p.m. Other branches in the 14th and 15th arrondissements.
Wholemeal farmhouse **bread**—a welcome breath of tradition in this bakery surrounded by urban-renewal modernity.

NICOLAS MADELEINE   **15** M11   Ⓜ Madeleine
31, place de la Madeleine (8th); tel. 42.68.00.16. 9 a.m.–8 p.m.
A comprehensive **wine** centre, with a wide range of prices and vintages. Wine-tasting corner, and specialized books.

LE PALAIS DE LA VIANDE   **22** J8/9   Ⓜ Ecole Militaire
15, rue du Champ-de-Mars (7th); tel. 47.05.07.02. Tuesday to Saturday 6 a.m.–1 p.m. and 3.30–8 p.m.; Sunday 6 a.m.–noon.
A deliriously surreal setting for a wide range of **cooked dishes** to take away.

PETROSSIAN   **22** K10   Ⓜ Invalides
18, boulevard de Latour-Maubourg (7th); tel. 45.51.70.64. Tuesday to Saturday 9 a.m.–1 p.m. and 2.30–7 p.m.
The king of **caviar,** also known for high-quality smoked salmon, vodka and foie gras.

POILÂNE   **31** M7   Ⓜ Sèvres-Babylone
8, rue du Cherche-Midi (6th); tel. 45.48.42.59. 7.15 a.m.–8.15 p.m. Other branches in the 14th and 15th arrondissements.
People from all over the world queue up to catch Poilâne's **bread** fresh from the charcoal oven. Legendary for the big rounds of bread made with unrefined flour, Poilâne also offers delicious nut breads, home-made cookies and country-style tarts.

SAIBRON   **31** L4   Ⓜ Gaîté
4, place Brancusi, (14th); tel. 43.21.76.18. Tuesday to Saturday 7.30 a.m.–8 p.m.; Sunday 7.30 a.m.–1.30 p.m.
Delicious crusty **baguettes,** and inventive pâtisseries—to take away or devour on the spot.

97

SANDAGA   **9** R15   Ⓜ Marx-Dormoy
24, rue Doudeauville (18th); tel. 42.64.07.35. Tuesday to Sunday 9 a.m.– 8 p.m.
Tropical fruit and vegetables, smoked and dried fish, *gari,* mil, cassava and other **exotic produce** from Africa and the Antilles. And calabashes, mortars and cooking pots to do it the right way.

LA TABLE D'ITALIE   **24** N8   Ⓜ Mabillon
69, rue de Seine (6th); tel. 43.54.34.69. Tuesday to Saturday 9 a.m.–7.30 p.m.
More than a thousand **Italian specialities** in this shop with visible beams and mosaics outside. Excellent fresh pasta, and the owner will throw in for free his advice on how to cook it. If you want to taste right away, a *tavola calda* lunch is available after 11 a.m.

THAN BINH **32** P7 Ⓜ Maubert-Mutualité
29, place Maubert (5th); tel. 43.25.81.65. Tuesday to Sunday 9 a.m.–7 p.m. Also 18, rue Lagrange (5th); tel. 43.54.66.11.
Oriental gourmet grocery—spring rolls, swallows' nests, soybean curds, and so on.

VERLET **24** N10 Ⓜ Palais-Royal
256, rue Saint-Honoré (1st); tel 42.60.67.39. Monday to Friday 9 a.m.–7 p.m.
The smell of roasting **coffee** beans will lure you into this coffee-taster's mecca. From noon, you can sit down and sample some of the 20 blends before you make up your mind which one to buy. And 50 kinds of tea.

DESIGN

ÉDIFICE **23** M8 Ⓜ Rue du Bac
27 bis, boulevard Raspail (7th); tel. 45.48.53.60. 10 a.m.–7 p.m.
Fashionable designer Philippe Starck's whole line shown exclusively here; the trendy wares might include frosted glass tables, a folding desk, chairs and bookshelves to lower or raise at will.

98 **ESPACE TEMPS** **24** P10 Ⓜ Etienne Marcel
3, rue de Turbigo (1st); tel. 42.33.37.12. 10.30 a.m.–1 p.m. and 2–7 p.m.
Futuristic furniture and objects look right at home in the pared-down, spaced-out setting.

GALERIE PRIMITIF **24** N/O8 Ⓜ Mabillon
5, rue Jacques-Callot (6th); tel. 43.25.21.64. 10 a.m.–12.30 p.m. and 2–7 p.m.
Lots of rare finds in this little gallery. Owner Franck Robichez sells his own creations—small pieces of furniture in stainless steel—as well as primitive and contemporary jewellery, and examples of African primitive art.

HABITAT **24** P10 Ⓜ Les Halles
Forum des Halles, Rambuteau entrance, Level 2 (1st); tel. 42.97.51.06. 10 a.m.–7 p.m.; Monday noon–7 p.m. Other branches in the 8th and 15th arrondissements.
Young, modern, practical furniture at moderate prices to fill your house from top to bottom.

HOMICIDE   **24** P10   Ⓜ Les Halles
Forum des Halles, Saint-Eustache entrance, 5, Grande Galerie (1st);
tel. 40.26.40.15. 10.30 a.m.–7 p.m.
The latest designs in household objects, from kettles to pens.

MODERNISMES   **21** G9   Ⓜ Passy
16, rue Franklin (16th); tel. 46.47.90.10. 9 a.m.–6 p.m.; Saturday
10 a.m.–7 p.m.
Copies of classic works by big names such as Le Corbusier and
Mallet-Stevens alongside recent Italian and other European creations, attractively displayed.

NÉOTU   **25** Q9   Ⓜ Hôtel-de-Ville
25, rue du Renard (4th); tel. 42.78.91.83. 9 a.m.–1 p.m. and 2–7 p.m.
The furniture and lamps combined with the display space form a
work of art. Creations by Garouste and Bonetti and Martin Szekely.

PERKAL   **25** R10   Ⓜ Rambuteau
8, rue des Quatre-Fils (3rd); tel. 42.77.46.80. 11 a.m.–7 p.m.; Monday
2–7 p.m.
Nestor Perkal, a Spanish designer, offers colourful imports from
Totem Memphis and the Spanish company Ediciones, as well
as an international selection. Perkal gives casual advice but may
also be hired to decorate a whole apartment.

RÉGALI   **24** P10   Ⓜ Les Halles **99**
15, rue Pierre-Lescot (1st); tel. 42.33.32.33. 10 a.m.–7 p.m. Other
branches all over the city.
Gifts, glass- and silverware, and halogen lamps at unbeatable prices.

TAÏR ET MERCIER   **33** Q7   Ⓜ Maubert-Mutualité
7, boulevard Saint-Germain (5th); tel. 43.54.19.97. Monday to Friday
10 a.m.–7 p.m.
Plastic never looked so good.... Taïr and Mercier's line of tableware in
polypropylene is practically indestructible.

VIA   **24** P9   Ⓜ Châtelet
10, place Sainte-Opportune (1st); tel. 42.33.14.33. 10.30 a.m.–7 p.m.;
Saturday 11 a.m.–7 p.m.
The name is the acronym for Valorisation de l'Innovation dans
l'Ameublement, in other words, "Let's give those young designers a
chance." Exclusives from young French designers on their way up, in
a showroom designed by Philippe Starck.

ANTIQUES AND COLLECTORS' ITEMS

À LA PLACE CLICHY   **7/15** M14   Ⓜ Place de Clichy
93, rue d'Amsterdam (8th); tel. 45.26.15.16. 9.45 a.m.–6.30 p.m.; Saturday 9.45 a.m.–7 p.m.
Besides modern rugs and floor coverings, this shop has an extremely good department devoted to antique carpets from Asia, North Africa and Portugal.

L'ARLEQUIN   **25** R9   Ⓜ Saint-Paul
13, rue des Francs-Bourgeois (4th); tel. 42.78.77.00. Tuesday to Saturday noon–7 p.m.
19th-century glassware and crystal—you might find the odd piece to match up your liqueur set or complete your collection of perfume bottles.

ARMÉE DU SALUT   Ⓡ (line C) Boulevard Masséna
12, rue Cantagrel (13th); tel. 45.83.54.40. Tuesday to Saturday 9 a.m.–noon and 2–6 p.m.
Hunt for bargains in the Salvation Army's huge warehouse next to its shelter, designed by Le Corbusier in 1933.

AU VIEUX PARIS   **15** N11   Ⓜ Opéra
4, rue de la Paix (2nd); tel. 42.61.00.89. Tuesday to Saturday 10 a.m.–12.30 p.m. and 2.30–6 p.m.; Monday 2.30–6 p.m.
The oldest shop of its kind in Paris, with a good reputation for antique silverware.

MICHEL CACHOUX   **24** O8   Ⓜ Odéon
16, rue Guénégaud (6th); tel. 43.54.52.15. Tuesday to Saturday 11 a.m.–12.30 p.m. and 2.30–7.30 p.m.
With his geologist's eye, Cachoux has sought out the most fabulous minerals and semi-precious stones from around the world. The displays are often renewed: minerals, polished and mounted stones, fossils, petrified wood, geodes, sculpted stone, rock crystal boxes.

ROBERT CAPIA   **24** O10   Ⓜ Louvre
26, galerie Véro-Dodat (1st); tel. 42.36.25.94. 10 a.m.–7 p.m.
In one of the city's most attractive, old-fashioned shopping galeries, an array of antique dolls—some of them pricey, signed originals, chosen by the top specialist. Also antique games and old phonographs for listening to warbly old records by Caruso or Sarah Bernhardt.

LA COUR AUX ANTIQUAIRES   **15** L11   Ⓜ Madeleine
*54, rue du Faubourg Saint-Honoré (8th); tel. 42.66.38.60. 10.30 a.m.–
6 p.m.; Monday 2.30–6 p.m.*
Eighteen shops in a charming cobbled courtyard each with a speciality: paintings, ceramics, furniture, Art Nouveau, Indian and African
art, gilded bronze.... High prices in this high-rent district.

DÉPÔT-VENTE DE PARIS   **27** X7   Ⓜ Porte de Vincennes
81, rue de Lagny (20th); tel. 43.72.13.91. 9.30 a.m.–7.30 p.m.
The biggest used-furniture sale warehouse in Paris. Breton ward-
robes, period pieces, Twenties' dining-room suites side-by-side with
second-hand electrical appliances going for a song.

GALERIE DENISE ORSONI   **24** O10/11   Ⓜ Palais-Royal
*170, galerie de Valois (parallel with rue de Valois) (1st); tel. 42.96.32.30.
Tuesday to Saturday 1–7 p.m.*
Art Nouveau chairs, turn-of-the-century lamps and Viennese furnishings, 1920–1940 ceramics.

RAOUL GUIRAUD   **23** M8   Ⓜ Rue du Bac
*90, rue de Grenelle (7th); tel. 42.22.61.04. 10.30 a.m.–12.30 p.m. and
2.30–7 p.m.*
Antiques and curios of the 18th and 19th centuries. Scientific objects,
furniture, engravings, marine paintings.... If you want to sell something, have no qualms—speed and honesty are guaranteed.

HÔTEL DROUOT   **16** O12   Ⓜ Richelieu-Drouot
*9, rue Drouot (9th); tel. 48.00.20.20. 11 a.m.–6 p.m. Also Drouot-
Montaigne, 15, avenue Montaigne (8th); tel. 48.00.20.80; map
14/22 J11.*
Rebuilt in unattractive-modern (and not very practical) style in 1980,
the centenarian Drouot has remained, nevertheless, Paris's most
important auction hall. Sixteen auction rooms run by 100 official
commissaires-priseurs, who are responsible for authenticity for
30 years under French law. The objects on sale are on show from
11 a.m.–6 p.m. and auctioned the next day from 2 or 2.30 p.m. Details
of future auctions are given in the *Gazette de l'Hôtel Drouot.*
   Prestige sales by the top Drouot auctioneers are held in special
rooms at the Théâtre des Champs-Elysées.

LE LOUVRE DES ANTIQUAIRES   **24** N/O10   Ⓜ Palais-Royal
*2, place du Palais-Royal (1st); tel. 42.97.27.00. Tuesday to Sunday
11 a.m.–7 p.m.*
A fabulous selection of all kinds of antiques to satisfy even the most
discriminating collector. Two hundred and fifty dealers share three

101

floors with a restaurant and offices for expertise, currency exchange and delivery service (closed Sunday).

MEUBLES PEINTS   **25** S9   Ⓜ Saint Paul
32, rue de Sévigné (4th); tel. 42.77.54.60. Tuesday to Sunday noon– 7 p.m.
The owner, Jean-Pierre Besenval, restores old rural furniture of the 18th and 19th centuries and paints them beautifully, copying old designs or inventing his own.

VILLAGE SAINT-PAUL   **25/26** S8   Ⓜ Saint-Paul
Area between Quai des Célestins, rues Saint-Paul and Saint-Antoine (4th). Open Thursday to Monday.
When this district was renovated in 1979, around 80 boutiques were set up in the courtyards and along the river banks, specializing in wickerwork, paintings, furniture, Art Deco, and so on.

VILLAGE SUISSE   **22/30** H7   Ⓜ La Motte-Piquet
78, avenue de Suffren (15th); 10.30 a.m.–7 p.m. Open Thursday to Monday.
On the site of the Swiss Pavilion for the 1889 World's Fair, 100 dealers show a wide variety of antique furniture and objects, tastefully displayed. A pleasant place to browse or shop seriously.

MARKETS

Every district of Paris has its own little street market, where housewives buy their fresh fruit, vegetables, meat and fish. They are held from 7.30 a.m.–1.30 p.m., two or three days a week, sometimes on Sundays. From the noise and bustle, you'll soon get to know the whereabouts of your own local market; here are just a few.

Carmes: Place Maubert (5th); map **32** P7. Tuesday, Thursday, Saturday.

Buci: Rue de Buci (6th); map **24** N/O8. Daily until 7 p.m.

Popincourt: Boulevard Richard-Lenoir (11th); map **18** T10. Tuesday, Friday.

Rue de Levis (17th); map **6/7** K/L 14. Daily except Monday until 7 p.m.

Ordener: between rues Montcalm et Championnet (18th); map **8** N/O16. Wednesday, Saturday.

Clignancourt: Boulevard Ornano (18th); map **8** P16. Tuesday, Friday, Sunday.

Place des Fêtes: rues Pré-Saint-Gervais and Petitot (19th), map **19** W13. Tuesday, Friday, Sunday.

In addition to street stalls, there are several covered markets, which open every day except Sunday afternoon and Monday, from 8 a.m. to 1 p.m. and 4 to 7 p.m., and markets on specific themes, like flowers, postcards, stamps or birds—not to mention the wonderful jumble of the flea markets.

MARCHÉ AUX CARTES POSTALES   Ⓜ Corentin Celton
Issy-les-Moulineaux, corner Boulevard Gambetta and Rue Vaudetard. Tuesday and Thursday 9.30 a.m.–7 p.m.
For collectors of postcards, stamps, coins and old documents.

MARCHÉ AUX CARTES   **24** N7/8   Ⓜ Mabillon
POSTALES ANCIENNES
Marché Saint-Germain, 3, rue Mabillon (6th); Wednesday 11 a.m.–6 p.m.
You could come across a magnificent find among the thousands of faded old postcards.

MARCHÉ AUX FLEURS DE L'ÎLE DE LA CITÉ   **24** P8   Ⓜ Cité
Place Louis Lépine (4th). Daily 8 a.m.–7 p.m.
Beautiful flower market, taken over by exotic birds on Sunday.

MARCHÉ DE LA PLACE DE JOINVILLE   **10** U15   Ⓜ Crimée
Place de Joinville (19th). Thursday and Sunday 7 a.m.–1.30 p.m.
An open-air market on the Quai de l'Oise, along the Ourcq Canal. It's not exactly central but picturesque—swarming with people shopping for food or old clothes.

103

MARCHÉ DE   **37** M/N4   Ⓜ Denfert-Rochereau
LA RUE DAGUERRE
19, rue Daguerre (14th).
A covered market, devoted to food. You may like to rest your weary feet at the Café au Marché in the marketplace, or try a glass of wine at the excellent wine bar just beside the market at 6, rue Daguerre, the **Rallye**.

MARCHÉ SAINT-PIERRE (DREYFUS)   **8** P14/15   Ⓜ Anvers
2, rue Charles-Nodier (18th); tel. 46.06.92.25. Monday to Saturday 9.30 a.m.–6.30 p.m. (closed Monday morning).
Fabrics are the speciality, and five floors display everything from fine brocades to fake furs. Prices are bargains for Paris. Neighbouring shops also overflow with fabrics.

MARCHÉ AUX TIMBRES **14** K11 Ⓜ Champs-Elysées–Clemenceau

Cours Marigny (8th); Thursday, Saturday, Sunday and holidays, 10 a.m.–6 p.m.
Seventy stands where avid stamp collectors buy, sell and swop their treasures.

FLEA MARKETS

MARCHÉ D'ALIGRE **26** U7 Ⓜ Ledru-Rollin

Place d'Aligre (12th); daily until 1 p.m.
The smallest and most picturesque of the city's flea markets, with lively bargaining in every language imaginable.

MARCHÉ AUX PUCES PORTE DE MONTREUIL Ⓜ Porte de Montreuil

Porte de Montreuil (20th); Saturday, Sunday and Monday 6.30 a.m.– 1 p.m.
As authentic as they come, with lots of tatty clothes—though if you rummage well enough you might find just what you've always been looking for.

MARCHÉ AUX PUCES PORTE DE SAINT-OUEN **7/8** N/P17 Ⓜ Porte de Clignancourt or Porte de Saint-Ouen

Between portes de Saint-Ouen and de Clignancourt (18th); Saturday, Sunday and Monday 7.30 a.m.–7 p.m.
This is really six different flea markets, on the northern edge of Paris in the commune of Saint-Ouen, grouping more than 3,000 dealers. It's *the* place for choice antiques—though nothing is cheap anymore. You need a good eye, all your wits about you, and the nerve to bargain.

Paul Bert: more provincial in style than the others. Old trunks, doors, spiral staircases.

Biron: authenticated antiques. Furniture, bronze statuettes, lace, old clothes and Art Deco posters.

Malik: a treasurehouse of vintage clothes, some of them very glamorous, and all kinds of accessories.

Serpette: the most recent, and the trendiest. Furniture, posters, lamps and bric-à-brac from the good old days.

Jules-Vallès: the cheapest and the greatest fun. Among the heaps of jumble and junk, look out for the specialists in clocks, dolls, cameras, military medals and postcards.

Vernaison: where it all started in 1920. A veritable maze of alleyways full of furniture of all styles—genuine or not. Toys and trinkets, silver cutlery—you name it, they've got it.

MARCHÉ AUX PUCES **36** K2 Ⓜ Porte de Vanves
PORTE DE VANVES
Avenues Marc Sangnier and Georges Lafenestre (14th). Saturday and Sunday, from dawn to 7 p.m.
A small market, worth a visit for the china, paintings, books, clothes and antique furnishings.

MUSIC AND PHOTOGRAPHY

CLÉMENTINE **31** M5 Ⓜ Montparnasse-Bienvenüe
89, boulevard du Montparnasse (6th); tel. 45.48.18.35. Monday to Thursday 10 a.m.–11.30 p.m.; Friday and Saturday 10 a.m.–1 a.m.; Sunday 2–9 p.m.
Convenient late-night opening hours to pick up records, tapes, CDs—the latest French hits, and sales on US imports. Also sells tickets for rock and pop concerts.

FNAC **24** P10 Ⓜ Les Halles
Forum des Halles, Pierre-Lescot entrance, 2nd level (1st); tel. 40.26.81.18. 10 a.m.–7.30 p.m.; Monday 1–7.30 p.m.
Also 136, rue de Rennes (6th); tel. 49.54.30.00; map 31 M6, 10 a.m.– 7 p.m.; Monday 1–7 p.m.
And 26, avenue de Wagram (8th); tel. 47.66.52.50; map 13/14 H13; 10 a.m.–7 p.m.; Monday 1–7 p.m.

105

The music department of the famed discount store is taken by storm at weekends and during the two months of extra discounts on new releases. Prices for hi-fi/video sets are reasonable, quality is good, and the sales assistants are always ready to give sound advice. Also computer and photo departments, and concert or theatre tickets.
    In addition to the addresses given above, there's another large FNAC in the CNIT building at the Défense (see page 193).

L'HEUR MAXIME **26** T7 Ⓜ Ledru-Rollin
Cour Bel Air, 56, rue du Faubourg Saint-Antoine (12th); tel. 43.41.33.55. Wednesday to Saturday 11 a.m.–7 p.m.; Sunday 2–7 p.m.
A cosmopolitan selection of recordings, including such oddities as a single of Pope Jean-Paul II singing Gounod's Ave Maria and the Lord's Prayer in Polish, French pop singers warbling in Japanese. There's an art gallery separated from the shop by a 17th-century

cobbled courtyard, where Cardinal Richelieu's musketeers used to meet. The big paving stone in the middle served as a table for their card and dice games.

LIDO MUSIQUE **14** J12 Ⓜ Franklin-D.-Roosevelt
68, avenue des Champs-Elysées (8th); tel. 45.62.30.86. 10 a.m.–1.30 a.m.; Sunday 1.30–8 p.m.
Classical music and jazz get the lion's share in the record department, but there's a good selective choice of pop, folk and film music, too. And five thousand video cassettes (VHS system) on sale.

LA MAISON DU LEICA **26** S9 Ⓜ Chemin Vert
52, boulevard Beaumarchais (11th); tel. 48.05.77.67. Tuesday to Saturday 9.30 a.m.–1 p.m. and 2–7 p.m.
Leica cameras and accessories—new and second-hand at unbeatable prices, and repairs.

NEW ROSE **24/32** O7 Ⓜ Odéon
7, rue Pierre-Sarrazin (6th); tel. 43.54.28.90. 11 a.m.–7 p.m.
Rock'n'roll, punk rock, heavy metal—records, CDs, cassettes, and all the English specialized magazines. Tickets on sale for most of the rock concerts (no booking by phone).

VIRGIN MEGASTORE **14** J12 Ⓜ Franklin-D.-Roosevelt
52–60 avenue des Champs-Elysées (8th); tel. 40.74.06.48. 10 a.m.–midnight; Sunday noon–midnight.
The spectacular Paris version of the British Virgin record shop, selling the latest in everything, including film music well before the film is out. Records, cassettes, CDs in all genres from jazz to Latin, with classical music in a big room off to the side, away from the madding crowd. Prices are expensive as all recordings are in France, but there are always specials. They also sell ghettoblasters and compact disc sets, and there's a bookshop, a cafeteria, a conference room, and facilities for previews of video clips. You can get tickets for most concerts and shows here.

BOOKS

ARTCURIAL **14** K11 Ⓜ Franklin-D.-Roosevelt
9, avenue Matignon (8th); tel. 42.99.16.19. Tuesday to Saturday 10.30 a.m.–7.15 p.m.
Thousands of French and foreign books and magazines on art, architecture and modern design.

ATTICA   **32** P7   Ⓜ Maubert-Mutualité
34, rue des Ecoles (5th); tel. 43.26.09.53. 10 a.m.–1 p.m. and 2–7 p.m.; Monday 2–7 p.m.
Straight from the USA, the latest American literature. English books sold for the same price as in Britain. Also novels and plays on cassette.

ATTICA 2   **32** O5   Ⓜ Saint-Michel
84, boulevard Saint-Michel (5th); tel. 46.34.16.30. 10 a.m.–1 p.m. and 2–7 p.m.; Monday 2–7 p.m.
Computer software and videos, and language tapes, videos and dictionaries.

ATTICA JUNIOR   **32** P7   Ⓜ Maubert-Mutualité
23, rue Jean-de-Beauvais (5th); tel. 46.34.62.03. 10 a.m.–1 p.m. and 2–7 p.m.; Monday 2–7 p.m.
Children's books in English, and teaching programmes.

BOULINIER   **24/32** O7   Ⓜ Odéon
20, boulevard Saint-Michel (6th); tel. 43.26.90.57. 10 a.m.–7.30 p.m.
New and second-hand comic books (*bandes dessinés*, or BDs) for classics like Astérix and Tintin, including first editions and other collectors' items. Also school text books, French literature in second-hand editions, and stationery.

CHAMBRE CLAIRE   **24** O7   Ⓜ Odéon
14, rue Saint-Sulpice (6th); tel. 46.34.04.31. Tuesday to Saturday 11 a.m.–7 p.m.
Works on photography, in French and other languages.

107

CINÉ DOC   **16** O12   Ⓜ Richelieu-Drouot
45, passage Jouffroy (9th); tel. 48.24.71.36. 10 a.m.–7 pm.; Saturday 10 a.m.–1 p.m. and 2–7 p.m.
Books, magazines, posters and photographs on everything to do with the cinema.

BRENTANO'S   **15** N11   Ⓜ Opéra
37, avenue de l'Opéra (2nd); tel. 42.61.52.50. 10 a.m.–7 p.m.
Paris's largest English-language bookshop has recently been renovated for greater ease of choice in paperbacks, best-sellers, specialized and reference books, with a music and stationery department.

FLAMMARION 4   **25** Q10   Ⓜ Rambuteau
19, rue Beaubourg (4th); tel. 42.77.12.33. Wednesday to Monday noon–10 p.m.; Saturday, Sunday and holidays 10 a.m.–10 p.m.
The Centre Pompidou's bookshop—everything concerned with contemporary design.

FNAC   **24** P10   Ⓜ Les Halles
Forum des Halles, Pierre-Lescot entrance, level 2 (1st); tel. 40.26.81.18;
10 a.m.–7.30 p.m.; Monday 1–7.30 p.m. See page 105 for the other
branches.
The book supermarket. Somewhat of a rarity in France, a place where
you can browse at your leisure, even sit down and read a comic book.

GALIGNANI   **23** M10   Ⓜ Tuileries
224, rue de Rivoli (1st); tel. 42.60.76.07. 9 a.m.–7 p.m.
Run by the same family since the beginning of the 19th century. An
excellent department of English and American books. Also guides
and art books in several languages, and rare editions.

JOSEPH GIBERT   **24/32** O7   Ⓜ Odeon
26, boulevard Saint-Michel (5th); tel. 46.34.21.41. 10 a.m.–7 p.m.
The student bookshop of the Latin Quarter, most titles in French. New
and second-hand books on every subject. Reduced-price recent
books sold in bins outside.

LA HUNE   **23/24** N8   Ⓜ Saint-Germain-des-Prés
170, boulevard Saint-Germain (6th); tel. 45.48.35.85. 10 a.m.–midnight;
Monday 2 p.m.–midnight; Saturday 10 a.m.–7.30 p.m.
The intellectuals' bookshop, conveniently open late for the local
literary crowd. Mostly French titles.

LIBRAIRIE GOURMANDE   **24/32** P7   Ⓜ Saint-Michel
4, rue Dante (5th); tel. 43.54.37.27. 10 a.m.–7 p.m.; Sunday 2.30–7 p.m.
Books for gourmets. Also deals in antiquarian editions.

108

MARAIS PLUS   **25** S9   Ⓜ Saint-Paul
20, rue des Francs-Bourgeois (3rd); tel. 48.87.01.40. 9 a.m.–midnight;
Sunday 9 a.m.–7 p.m.
The setting is charming—this was once the Marais Cultural Centre,
just a stone's throw from the Picasso and Carnavalet museums.
Besides selling books and a few select second-hand items, Charlotte
Guillaud has set up a homely tearoom—and it doesn't matter if you
read at the table. Enjoy a savoury tart, a mixed salad or a delicious
home-made cake while you browse through the guides on Paris and
France.

MOTS ET MERVEILLES   **33** Q4   Ⓜ Gobelins
7, boulevard de Port-Royal (13th); tel. 47.07.25.21. Tuesday to Sat-
urday 10 a.m.–1 p.m. and 2–7 p.m.
Not for the printed word, but for the spoken. Taped versions of two
thousand French titles, including plays, short stories and bestsellers.

Children's cassettes are sold with the book. Also audio language teaching.

Another novelty here is the "*carte postale sonore*"—cassette tapes with typical Parisian noises on side A (market bustle, restaurant babble, and the like) and a blank side B for you to record your own message. The cassette can then be addressed, stamped and posted to whoever you wish were here.

NQL INTERNATIONAL   32 Q6   Ⓜ (line B) Port-Royal
78, boulevard Saint-Michel (6th); tel. 43.26.42.70. 10 a.m.–7 p.m.
Foreign literature is a speciality. There's a very good choice of English paperbacks, foreign art books and dictionaries.

SHAKESPEARE & CO   25 P8   Ⓜ Maubert-Mutualité
37, rue de la Bucherie (5th). Noon–midnight.
Crammed top to bottom with new or second-hand books on all topics, George Whitman's bookshop is more than just a place to browse. It's a landmark among intellectuals, some of whom are honoured by an invitation to Sunday afternoon tea. The upstairs reading room is equipped with sofas and desks. Poetry readings are sometimes organized.

W.H. SMITH   15 M11   Ⓜ Concorde
248, rue de Rivoli (1st); tel. 42.60.37.97. 9.30 a.m.–6.30 p.m.
Specializes in British publications, but also stocks some American editions. Renovated in 1989.

109

LE TOUR DU MONDE   21 F9   Ⓜ La Muette
9, rue de la Pompe (16th); tel. 42.88.58.06. Research service 45.20.87.12. Tuesday to Saturday 10 a.m.–1 p.m. and 2–7 p.m.
This bookshop has a free research service to help you find books out of print.

LE VERRE ET L'ASSIETTE   32 Q5   Ⓜ (line B) Port-Royal
1, rue du Val-de-Grâce (5th); tel. 46.33.45.96. 10 a.m.–12.30 p.m. and 2–7 p.m.; Monday 2–7 p.m.
Three thousand titles on gastronomy and wines, with a big section devoted to dietetics. Includes cookbooks, textbooks for professionals and children's books.

LES YEUX FERTILES   24 O8   Ⓜ Saint-Michel/Odéon
2, rue Danton (6th); tel. 43.26.91.51. 10.30 a.m.–8 p.m.
A tiny little shop devoted to current and future trends in novels and the art world.

Every region of France has its own particular cuisine, and Paris is no exception. Creations of the great Parisian chefs figure on menus all over the world. Lobster thermidor, even lobster à l'américaine, were invented in the capital. Classic dishes like vol-au-vent, *bœuf miroton,* and *veau Marengo* are typical of Parisian *cuisine bourgeoise,* as are many world-famous desserts—millefeuille and apple charlotte, for example.

But the Parisians are said to be provincials at heart, and you can sample food from all the regions in the capital's restaurants—from Brittany's pancakes and cider to Provençal bouillabaisse. That's where the chefs excel, demonstrating with panache the culinary treasures of the whole country.

Understandably, the French are chauvinistic as regards their cuisine. But their tastes are developing, and they now enjoy the more exotic flavours introduced by the influx of immigrants from Vietnam, North Africa and elsewhere.

Most French still like a good meal at lunchtime, so snackbars and bistrots all offer a set menu with a "day's special". Many museums have a café or restaurant on the premises, some of which have gained quite a good reputation—for instance the restaurants of the Pompidou Centre and the Grand Palais, the Modern Art Museum's café, and the Picasso Museum's tearoom. There are, of course, plenty of self-service restaurants such as the Hippopotamus and Flunch chains, which serve a wide range of acceptable dishes at reasonable prices. Not to mention the army of "snacks", sandwich bars, croissanteries, pizzerias, crêperies and "buffeterias" that cater to smaller appetites (and wallets).

111

The number and variety of good restaurants is bewildering. We have tried to provide a fair selection of addresses to suit every taste, from prestigious temples of gastronomy to modest bistrots and wine bars. The approximate cost of a full meal is given, so you can estimate how much you're likely to need; and under each entry you'll find a typical example of à la carte items. Some restaurants are so reputed they are booked up months ahead; we have indicated when advance reservations are absolutely necessary, but you'd be well advised to book a table in most cases, and more so in the evening.

Come to Paris—and cast your diet to the winds.

These are twelve of the best restaurants in Paris—inevitably a subjective choice. May those we overlooked forgive us.

L'AMBROISIE   26 S8   Ⓜ Chemin Vert
9, place des Vosges (4th); tel. 42.78.51.45. Service 12.15–2 p.m. and 8.15–10 p.m. (700 F)
In the heart of the Marais, Bernard Pacaud's restaurant is attractively decorated with wood panelling, tapestries and his wife's fabulous bouquets. His cuisine is up-to-date and excellent, rivalling that of the greatest chefs of his generation.
    A la carte: *blanc de turbot à l'huile parfumée à la purée de fenouil* (turbot fillet with fennel-flavoured oil). Business lunch: 255 F.

DUQUESNOY   22 J10   ⓇⒺⓇ (line C) Pont de l'Alma
6, avenue Bosquet (7th); tel. 47.05.96.78. Service noon–2 p.m. and 8–10.15 p.m.; closed Saturday lunch, Sunday and all August. (500 F)
Chef Jean-Paul Duquesnoy has spruced up the old restaurant *La Bourgogne*, creating an elegant setting to match his equally elegant cuisine.
    A la carte: *Saint-Jacques fumé à la minute; salade de pommes de terre au caviar* (smoked scallops; potato salad with caviar).

FAUGERON   13 G10   Ⓜ léna
52, rue de Longchamp (16th); tel. 47.04.24.53. Service 12.30–3 p.m. and 7.30–10 p.m.; closed Saturday, Sunday, all August and from Christmas to New Year's Day. Reserve in advance. (600–700 F)
In a setting of yellow and blue, the customer is treated like a king. The award-winning sommelier, Jean-Claude Jambon, will be happy to help you choose your wine.
    A la carte: *œufs à la coque Faugeron à la purée de truffes; turbot au vin rouge* (soft-boiled eggs with truffle purée; turbot in red wine).

LASSERRE   14 K11   Ⓜ Franklin-D.-Roosevelt
17, avenue Franklin-D.-Roosevelt (8th); tel. 43.59.53.43. Service 12.30–2.15 p.m. and 7.30–10.30 p.m.; closed Sunday, Monday lunch and all August. Reserve 2 weeks in advance. (750–800 F)
Perfect on a summer's night with the roof rolled back to reveal the stars. Well-stocked wine cellar; attentive service.
    A la carte: *truffes en feuilletage* (truffle in puff pastry).

LAURENT **14** K11 Ⓜ Champs-Elysées–Clemenceau
*41, avenue Gabriel (8th); tel. 47.23.79.18. Service 12.30–2.30 p.m. and
7.30–11 p.m.; closed Saturday lunch and Sunday. Reserve 2 to 3 days
in advance. (750–800 F)*
The food is exquisite, the service remarkable, and the wine list as
exclusive as the bill. In summer, the terrace overlooking the Champs-
Elysées gardens is a wonderful asset.
    A la carte: *salade de homard* (lobster salad, prepared at your
table). Set lunch menu: 350 F, wine extra. Special dinner menu "*plai-
sir*": 720 F, wine extra.

LEDOYEN **14/22** K11 Ⓜ Champs-Elysées–Clemenceau
*Carré des Champs-Elysées (near the Petit Palais) (8th); tel.
47.42.23.23. Open daily.*
A renowned establishment in the heart of Paris, recently renovated by
the French singer Régine in Louis XV and Belle Epoque styles. There
are two restaurants.
    The heavy décor of the gastronomic **Guépard** is reminiscent
of Visconti's film (The Leopard). *Service 12.30–2.30 p.m. and 8.30–
10.30 p.m. (800–1,200 F).*
    The **Carré-des-Champs-Elysées** is less formal. Jacques Maximin,
who rose to fame at the Négresco in Nice, is in charge of the kitchen
brigade. *Service 12.30–2.30 p.m. and 8.30 p.m.–1 a.m. (250–350 F). Tea
is served from 4 to 6 p.m.*
    Businessmen can make use of convenient offices, drawing rooms,
a club and the luxurious, comfortable **Piano-Bar** (open 11 a.m.–
2 a.m.). And there's music and dancing on Friday and Saturday
evenings.

LUCAS-CARTON **15** M11 Ⓜ Madeleine **113**
*9, place de la Madeleine (8th); tel. 42.65.22.90. Service noon–2.30 p.m.
and 8–10.30 p.m.; closed Saturday, Sunday and all August. (800 F)*
Contrasting with the elegant 1900s' décor, Chef Alain Senderens'
cuisine has a touch of the whimsical. He is daring and inventive,
gathering and adapting ideas from other countries and ancient
culinary tomes, with spectacular results.
    A la carte: *canard Apicius rôti au miel et aux épices* (duck roast
with honey and spices). Set menus: business lunch 380 F, dinner from
605 F. Wines from 100 F for a Reuilly to 19,000 F for a 1945 Château
Petrus.

JOËL ROBUCHON (JAMIN) **13** G10 Ⓜ Iéna
*32, rue de Longchamp (16th); tel. 47.27.12.27. Service noon–2 p.m.
and 8–10 p.m.; closed Saturday, Sunday and all July. Reserve 2–
3 months in advance. (800 F, plus wine).*

Robuchon must have lost count of all the stars, toques and other honours he's been awarded, but he could never be accused of resting on his laurels. The man who gave new meaning to mashed potatoes has more than one trick up his sleeve; for example *ravioli de langoustines au jus de truffes et foie gras* (prawn raviolis with truffle juice and foie gras). Fixed sampling menu (5 courses) 790 F, seasonal menu (3 courses) 890 F, wine extra.

MICHEL ROSTANG   **14** J13   Ⓜ Ternes
20, rue Rennequin (17th); tel. 47.63.40.77. Service 12.30–2 p.m. and 7.30–10.30 p.m.; closed Saturday lunch and Sunday, and from 1–16 August. Reserve 2–3 days in advance. (600–700 F)
Originality, carefree ambience, and irreproachably fresh produce. One of the greatest restaurants in Paris.
   A la carte: *canette de Bresse au sang* (Bresse duckling cooked in its blood). Set menu 420 F; sampling menu 480 F, wine extra).

GUY SAVOY   **13/14** H12/13   Ⓜ Charles-de-Gaulle–Etoile
18, rue Troyon (17th); tel. 43.80.40.61. Service 12.15–1.30 p.m. and 7.30–10.30 p.m.; closed Saturday (except evenings October to March), Sunday, the last two weeks of July and the first week of August. (600–700 F)
Tasteful décor in tones of beige, pink and white. The food is excellent—astonishingly original.
   A la carte: *escargots et ravioli dans un coulis aux herbes* (snails and ravioli with herb sauce); *pigeon breton poché, grillé et servi avec son gâteau d'abats* (poached Breton squab, grilled and served with a little giblet flan); *canette à l'ancienne rôtie et navets confits aux épices* (roast duckling with spiced turnips). Fixed sampling menu 540 F. Special prestige menu 550 F, wine extra.
   On the other side of the street, the **Bistrot de l'Etoile** is a pleasant annexe of the Savoy, where you can lunch or dine extremely well for 130 F.

TAILLEVENT   **14** J12   Ⓜ George-V
15, rue Lamennais (8th); tel. 45.63.39.94. Service noon–1.30 p.m. and 7.30–9.30 p.m.; closed Saturday, Sunday, holidays, one week in February and and from mid-July to mid-August (700 F).
Everything is "just so" from flowers to service to wine. The effect is one of elegance and ceremony. Reserve your table a month in advance for lunch, two months for dinner.
   A la carte: *suprême de bar au gros sel* (sea bass supreme in coarse salt).

LA TOUR D'ARGENT   **33** Q7   Ⓜ Maubert-Mutualité
15–17, quai de la Tournelle (5th); tel. 43.54.23.31. Service: orders taken noon–1 p.m. and 8–9 p.m.; closed Monday. Reservation essential—one week in advance for lunch, two to three for dinner. (700–900 F, wine included)
The festive atmosphere and the glorious view of Notre-Dame enhance every meal, presided over by the legendary Claude Terrail.

A la carte: *salade de rouget de rocher; caneton Tour d'Argent* (red mullet salad; Tour d'Argent duckling). Set menu (except Sunday evening and holidays) 330 F, wine extra.

EXCELLENT ADDRESSES

Good food at reasonable prices—choose from our selection and you won't be disappointed.

AMBASSADE D'AUVERGNE   **25** Q10   Ⓜ Rambuteau
22, rue du Grenier-Saint-Lazare (3rd); tel. 42.72.31.22. Service noon–2.30 p.m. and 7.30–11.30 p.m. (220 F)
Just a few blocks from the Centre Pompidou, the "Auvergne Embassy" run by the Petrucci family serves hearty country fare: stuffed cabbage, lentil cassoulet, sausages, black pudding and *aligot*—a garlicky blend of mashed potatoes and Cantal cheese.

A la carte: *potée auvergnate* (a farmhouse casserole of fresh and salt pork, sausages, cabbage, carrots and turnips).

115

BENOÎT   **25** Q9/10   Ⓜ Hôtel-de-Ville
20, rue Saint-Martin (4th); tel. 42.72.25.76. Service noon–2 p.m. and 7.45–10 p.m.; closed Saturday, Sunday, Easter week and three weeks in August. Reserve the day before. (350–450 F)
Traditional *cuisine bourgeoise* in a real bistrot—dark panelling, mirrors, lace curtains and all. Michel Petit, the owner and chef, is the grandson of the founder.

A la carte: *daube de joue de bœuf* (braised ox cheek).

GÉRARD BESSON   **24** O10   Ⓜ Les Halles
5, rue Coq-Héron (1st); tel. 42.33.14.74. Service noon–2.30 p.m. and 7.30–10.30 p.m.; closed Saturday, Sunday, three weeks in July and 22 December–3 January. (350–450 F)
A chef held in high esteem for his delicious poultry and fish dishes.

BISTROT DE PARIS   **23** M9   Ⓜ Rue du Bac
*33, rue de Lille (7th); tel. 42.61.16.83. Service 12.30–2.30 p.m. and
7.30–10.45 p.m.; closed Saturday lunch and Sunday. (300 F)*
A typically Parisian décor, where owner Michel Oliver (a TV chef) lives
up to his excellent reputation.
   A la carte: *estouffade de bœuf* (braised beef).

LE BOURDONNAIS   **22** J8   Ⓜ Ecole Militaire
*113, avenue de la Bourdonnais (7th); tel. 47.05.47.96. Service
noon–2.30 p.m. and 8–10.30 p.m. Reserve the day before. (300 F)*
A friendly atmosphere in this little restaurant serving both traditional
and sophisticated food.
   A la carte: *noisette de canard feuilleté aux épinards* (noisette of
duck in puff pastry with spinach). Set menus: lunch 200 F, dinner
250 F, wine included. Fixed sampling menu, lunch and dinner, 380 F,
wine extra.

CARRÉ DES FEUILLANTS   **15/23** M11   Ⓜ Concorde
*14, rue de Castiglione (1st); tel. 42.86.82.82. Service noon–2.15 p.m.
and 7.30–10.30 p.m.; closed Saturday lunch and Sunday. Reserve 1–2
days ahead. (450 F)*
A touch of the Gascon in Alain Dutournier's armagnacs and excellent
cuisine, served in a luxurious yet low-key setting of blond panelled
walls and contemporary still-lifes.
   A la carte: *cul de lapereau retour des Indes* (spicy rump of rabbit).
Business lunch: 230 F.

LA FERMETTE MARBEUF 1900   **14** J11   Ⓜ Alma-Marceau
*5, rue Marbeuf (8th); tel. 47.20.63.83. Service noon–2.30 p.m. and
7.30–11.30 p.m. (150–300 F)*
116 Worth a visit for the authentic Art Nouveau setting in the back room,
with ceramics and cast-iron columns—as well as for the food.
   A la carte: *filets de sole aux pâtes fraîches* (sole fillets with fresh
pasta); *gâteau de foies de volaille et de ris de veau* (warm flan of
chicken liver and veal sweetbread); *canette de Challans rôtie* (roast
duckling). Set menu: dinner and lunch Sunday 150 F.

CHEZ FRANÇOISE   **22** K10   Ⓜ Invalides
*Aérogare des Invalides (7th); tel. 47.05.49.03. Service noon–2.30 p.m.
and 7 p.m.–midnight; closed Sunday evening and 1–15 August.
(250 F)*
A favourite rendez-vous for French parliamentarians, specializing in
smoked meat and fish.
   A la carte: *saumon fumé maison* (home-smoked salmon). Set
menu 130 F, wine extra.

GUYVONNE　　**6/14** K14　　　　　　　Ⓜ Monceau
*14, rue de Thann (17th); tel. 42.27.25.43. Service 12.15–2 p.m. and
7.45–10 p.m.; closed Saturday, Sunday, the three last weeks of July
and two weeks at Christmas. (300–350 F).*
Guy Cros likes to cook fish, and you can choose from six or seven
different kinds on the menu, depending on arrivals. But he also
specializes in offal. Set menu 186 F, wine extra.

LE MANOIR DE PARIS　　**13** H13　　　　　Ⓜ Ternes
*6, rue Pierre-Demours (17th); tel. 45.72.25.25. Service noon–2 p.m. and
7.30–10 p.m.; closed Saturday and Sunday. (400–500 F)*
You may recognize the hostess—bubbly TV presenter Denise Fabre.
Her husband, chef Francis Vandenhende, delights his fans with the
Belle Epoque setting and his contemporary cuisine—in fact carried
out by a team of talented assistants.
　A la carte: *ravioli de lapin aux cèpes en civet* (ravioli of jugged
rabbit with boletus mushrooms). Set lunch menus: 245 F, wine extra;
sampling menu 395 F.
　Upstairs, **La Niçoise** serves delicious Provençal dishes in a much
lower price range (count 200–250 F). Service noon–2 p.m. and 7.30–
11 p.m. Closed Saturday lunch and Sunday.

LA MARLOTTE　　**31** M7　　　　　　Ⓜ Saint-Placide
*55, rue du Cherche-Midi (6th); tel. 45.48.86.79. Service noon–2 p.m.
and 8–10.30 p.m.; closed Saturday, Sunday and all August. (230 F)*
Good food and a nice atmosphere.
　A la carte: *canard au vin rouge* (duck in red wine). Every day, five
specialities 80–97 F.

MINIM'S　　**15** L12　　　Ⓜ Champs-Elysées–Clemenceau **117**
*76, rue du Faubourg Saint-Honoré (8th); tel. 42.66.10.09. Service
noon–3 p.m. only; closed Sunday. Reserve in advance. (120 F)*
An old art gallery, taken over by Cardin to counterbalance the great
Maxim's. Low-priced grills and salads.

MIRAVILE　　**33** Q7　　　　　　Ⓜ Maubert-Mutualité
*25, quai de la Tournelle (5th); tel. 46.34.07.78. Service 12.30–2 p.m. and
8.30–10.30 p.m.; closed Saturday lunch, Sunday and the first two
weeks of January and August. (350 F)*
Nautical paintings on the walls recall Gilles Epié's Breton origins. His
high-quality, inventive desserts and petits-fours are irresistible.
　A la carte: *pigeon aux choux, à la moelle et aux truffes* (pigeon with
truffles, bone marrow and cabbage). Set lunch menu 150 F, wine
extra; dinner sampling menu 350 F, wine extra.

MOROT-GAUDRY   **30** H7   Ⓜ La Motte-Picquet
6, rue de la Cavalerie (15th); tel. 45.67.06.85. Service noon–3 p.m. and 7.30–10.30 p.m.; closed Saturday and Sunday. Reserve one day ahead. (350–450 F)
Roof-top dining on the 8th floor. The cooking is also on a high level, classic but full of imagination.

A la carte: *noix de Saint-Jacques poêlées à la fondue d'endives* (scallops with chicory). Business lunch 200 F, fixed sampling menus, lunch and dinner 300 F.

PILE OU FACE   **16** O11   Ⓜ Bourse
52 bis, rue Notre-Dame-des-Victoires (2nd); tel. 42.33.64.33. Service noon–2 p.m. and 8–10 p.m.; closed Saturday, Sunday, last week in July, all August, Christmas and New Year's Day. (350 F)
Popular at lunchtime with the financial wizards of the Stock Exchange.

A la carte: *confit de lapin à la purée d'ail* (rabbit preserves with garlic purée) served with potato crisps.

LE SYBARITE   **23** N8   Ⓜ Saint-Sulpice
6, rue du Sabot (6th); tel. 42.22.21.56. Service noon–2.30 p.m. and 7.30–10.30 p.m.; closed Saturday lunch and Sunday. Reserve the day before. (150–250 F)
Lively·atmosphere and food from the south-west. Jazz sessions Friday and Saturday nights.

A la carte: *foie gras de canard* (duck foie gras). Set lunch menu 70 F.

LA TABLE D'ANVERS   **8** P14   Ⓜ Anvers
2, place d'Anvers (9th); tel. 48.78.35.21. Service noon–2.30 p.m. and 8–10.30 p.m.; closed Sunday and 10 days around August 15. Reserve the day before. (250–300 F)
Creative cooking by the Conticini brothers, who inherited their talent from their father. A tempting array of desserts. Set menus, based on themes (lobster 300 F, rustic 150 F, sweet-sour 90 F, etc. Lunch menu 170 F.

LE VIVAROIS   **13** F10   Ⓜ Rue de la Pompe
192, avenue Victor Hugo (16th); tel. 45.04.04.31. Service noon–2 p.m. and 8–9.30 p.m.; closed Saturday, Sunday and all August. (450 F)
Whatever you order, you'll always be served something extra. Claude Peyrot's cuisine is excellent, inventive—and the pasta is fabulous.

A la carte: *huîtres chaudes au curry* (hot curried oysters). Business lunch 296 F.

ECONOMICAL

LE BAPTISTE **33** Q6 Ⓜ Jussieu
11, rue des Boulangers (5th); tel. 43.25.57.24. Service noon–3 p.m. and 7–10.30 p.m. (Friday and Saturday 11 p.m.); closed Saturday lunch and Sunday. (80 F)
Chicken liver pâtés, steak, fish, chocolate mousse—just a few examples of the unpretentious food served here. Inexpensive wines and a pleasant atmosphere to round off a good meal. Set menu 52 F.

CHARTIER **16** O/P12 Ⓜ Rue Montmartre
7, rue du Faubourg Montmartre (9th); tel. 47.70.86.29. Service 11 a.m.–3 p.m. and 7–9.30 p.m. (85 F)
This is one of the least expensive meals in town, attracting hordes for its low prices and charming old-fashioned décor. But go early, and for bonhomie rather than gastronomy; it's like a crowded cafeteria at peak hours.
   A la carte: *raie au beurre noisette* (skate with browned butter).

CHEZ GERMAINE **31** L7 Ⓜ Vaneau
30, rue Pierre-Leroux (7th); tel. 42.73.28.34. Service 11.30 a.m.– 2.30 p.m. and 6.30–9 p.m.; closed Saturday evening, Sunday and all August. (55 F)
It's hard to find a table here—the place is full of Frenchmen nostalgic for mother's home cooking: salt pork with lentils, cherry *clafoutis*. Why not join the queue?

HATELET **17** Q13 Ⓜ Poissonnière
89, rue d'Hauteville (10th); tel. 47.70.35.19. Service 11.30 a.m.–3 p.m.; closed Sunday. (50 F)
This "conventional" restaurant and a string of snack bars (in the 9th, 10th and 11th arrondissements) where you eat standing up all serve fish or meat kebabs, salads, vegetables, wine, fruit juice—simple, healthy food.

119

L'INCROYABLE **16** N/O11 Ⓜ Palais-Royal
26, Rue de Richelieu (1st); tel. 42.96.24.64. Service 11.45 a.m.–2.15 p.m. and 6.30–8.30 p.m.; closed Saturday evening, all Sunday, and Monday evening. (50 F)
As incredible as its name suggests—an appetizer, a meat dish, cheese or dessert at a really low price, and you're all set for a busy afternoon. You can eat outside in the summer. An address worth noting.

PERRAUDIN   **32** O6   Ⓟ (line B) Luxembourg
157, rue Saint-Jacques (5th); tel. 46.33.15.75. Service noon–2.30 p.m. (except Saturday lunch and Sunday evening) and 7.30–10.15 p.m. (100 F)
Bourgeois cuisine in the Latin Quarter: *andouillette* (chitterling sausage), beef bourguignon, *tarte Tatin* (upside-down apple tart)—served with a smile. Sunday, 11 a.m.–3 p.m., three different brunches, around 70 F for adults and 55 F for children.

LE PETIT SAINT-BENOÎT   **23/24** N8   Ⓜ Saint-Germain-des-Prés
4, rue Saint-Benoît (6th); tel. 42.60.27.92. Service noon–2.30 p.m. and 7–10 p.m.; closed Saturday and Sunday. (70 F)
An hors d'œuvre, main course, dessert and wine for 70 F: a good bargain.

LE PETIT VATEL   **24** N7   Ⓜ Odéon
5, rue Lobineau (6th); tel. 43.54.28.49. Service noon–3 p.m. and 7 p.m.–midnight; closed Sunday lunch. (60 F)
Very informal—you eat in the kitchen, and the dishes come straight from a wonderful oven that survived two world wars.

SHAKE   **26** T8   Ⓜ Bastille
16, rue Daval (11th); tel. 43.57.89.59. Service 12.30–2.30 p.m. and 8 p.m.–midnight; closed Saturday lunch and Sunday. Reserve 48 hours in advance. (80–180 F)
A tiny, colourful bistrot near the Bastille. Dishes from the Périgord, a variety of salads, savoury quiches and delicious desserts.

120 TY BREIZ   **31** L5   Ⓜ Montparnasse-Bienvenüe
52, boulevard de Vaugirard (15th); tel. 43.20.83.72. Service 11.45 a.m. (Saturday 12.15 p.m.)–1.45 p.m. and 7–9 p.m.; closed Sunday, Monday evening in winter, and all August. (50–60 F)
An excellent *crêperie* where you can gorge on savoury pancakes, sweet pancakes, flambéed pancakes to the fizz of Breton cider.

CHEZ VINCENT   **19** V10   Ⓜ Père-Lachaise
60, boulevard de Ménilmontant (20th); tel. 46.36.07.67. Service noon–2 p.m. and Friday and Saturday only 7–9.45 p.m.; closed Sunday and all August. (100 F)
Unless you choose à la carte, the wine is always included (and in unlimited quantities, on Friday and Saturday night!). At lunchtime, choose from three menus (58 F, 78 F and 115 F), and take your time to appreciate the heart-warming cuisine.

EXTRA SPECIAL

There's something "different" about the restaurants listed in this section—not the cuisine, particularly, though you can count on it being of excellent quality, but rather the intrinsic atmosphere that makes them stand out as monuments to the Parisian way of life.

BOFINGER **26** S8 Ⓜ Bastille
3, rue de la Bastille (4th); tel. 42.72.87.82. Service noon–3 p.m. and 7.30 p.m.–1 a.m. (180–200 F)
The oldest brasserie of Paris, with a superb, stylish Belle Epoque décor and traditional cuisine.

BRASSERIE FLO **17** Q12 Ⓜ Château d'Eau
7, rue des Petites-Ecuries (10th); tel. 47.70.13.59. Service noon–3 p.m. and 7 p.m.–2.30 a.m. (250 F)
Sauerkraut, shellfish, foie gras in a splendid setting.

CHARDENOUX **27** V8 Ⓜ Charonne
1, rue Jules-Vallès/23, rue Chanzy (11th); tel. 43.71.49.52. Service noon–2 p.m. and 8–11 p.m.; closed Saturday lunch, Sunday and all August. (150–200 F)
A friendly bistrot on the corner of two old, cobbled streets. Good food at reasonable prices.

CIEL DE PARIS **31** L5 Ⓜ Montparnasse-Bienvenüe
Tour Montparnasse, 33, avenuu du Maine (15th); tel. 45.38.52.35. Service noon–2.30 p.m. (Sunday 3 p.m.) and 7–11.30/midnight. (150–250 F)
Sky-high restaurant—but the prices won't make you dizzy.

121

LA CLOSERIE DES LILAS **32** N5 Ⓔ (line B) Port-Royal
171, boulevard du Montparnasse (6th); tel. 43.26.70.50. Service brasserie noon–1 a.m. non-stop (100–120 F); restaurant noon–3 p.m. and 7 p.m.–1 a.m. (300 F), American bar noon–1.30 a.m.
Has always been a favourite of the literary crowd.

LA COUPOLE **31** M5 Ⓜ Vavin
102, boulevard de Montparnasse (14th); tel. 43.20.14.20. Service 7 a.m.—2 a.m. (200 F)
Simone de Beauvoir and Jean-Paul Sartre's local has been renovated but fortunately retained its Art Deco character. Popular in the morning with businessmen who meet over brunch. At lunchtime or in the evening, you're bound to recognize at least one famous name in the sea of 1,500 faces.

DROUANT **16** N8 Ⓜ Quatre-Septembre
18, rue Gaillon (2nd); tel. 42.65.15.16. Service noon–2.30 p.m. and 7.30–10.30 p.m. (500 F, grill room 200–300 F)
Refurbished in its original traditional style. The members of the Goncourt jury always deliberate and announce the year's prize-winner here. The vast menu includes *huîtres au bœuf gros sel* (oysters with salt beef) and *cuisses de grenouilles à la fricassée de homard des Goncourt* (frogs' legs with lobster fricassee).

FOUQUET'S **14** J12 Ⓜ George-V
99, avenue des Champs-Elysées (8th); tel. 47.23.70.60. Service noon–3 p.m. and 7 p.m. to half-past midnight. Closed Saturday, Sunday, and from 20 July to 20 August. (200–400 F)
Inside or outside, *the* place to be seen on the Champs-Elysées. Set menu 190 F, wine extra. The bar is open non-stop.

GRAND CAFÉ CAPUCINES **15/16** N12 Ⓜ Opéra
4, boulevard des Capucines (9th); tel. 47.42.75.77. 24-hour service. (150–350 F)
Another superb Belle Epoque brasserie, specializing in shellfish.

LA GRANDE CASCADE Ⓜ Porte Maillot
Bois de Boulogne (16th); tel. 45.27.33.51. Bus no. 244 to Carrefour de Longchamp. Service 12.30–2.45 p.m. and 7–10.30 p.m. Closes at 6 p.m. November to April. (500 F)
In the Bois de Boulogne, near the Longchamp racecourse. In summer, a shady terrace; in winter, a Napoleon III setting for high-quality classic cuisine.

JULES VERNE **21** H9 ⓇⒺⓇ (line C) Champ-de-Mars
2nd floor of the Eiffel Tower (7th); tel. 45.55.61.44. (private lift). Service 12.30–4 p.m. and 7.30–11 p.m. Reserve four weeks in advance for dinner; three to four days for lunch. (500 F)
Paris at your feet and a fine meal at your fingertips. One floor below, and a notch lower in prices, **La Belle France** has a more intimate atmosphere (tel. 45.55.20.04; service noon–2.30 p.m. and 7–9 pm. Reserve in advance. (250 F)

JULIEN **17** Q2 Ⓜ Strasbourg–Saint-Denis
16, rue du Faubourg Saint-Denis (10th); tel. 47.70.12.06. Service noon–3 p.m. and 7 p.m.–1.30 a.m. (250 F)
An authentic "bouillon"—a 19th-century sawdust-strewn restaurant that served boiled beef and the stock (*bouillon*) it was cooked in—now elevated to brasserie standard with the same kind of food as the Brasserie Flo (see page 121).

LIPP (BRASSERIE)   **23/24** N8   Ⓜ Saint-Germain-des-Prés
151, boulevard Saint-Germain (6th); tel. 45.48.53.91. Service 11.45–2 a.m. (250–300 F)
Everyone who's anyone in Saint-Germain-des-Prés has his own table here. Not to be missed for the front-row view of the neighbourhood eccentrics—if you're let in.

MAXIM'S   **15** L11   Ⓜ Concorde
3, rue Royale (8th); tel. 42.65.27.94. Service until 1 a.m. (600–800 F)
The most famous restaurant in the world. It's the done thing to roll up in your chauffeur-driven Rolls-Royce.

PAVILLON MONTSOURIS   **38** O2   🚇 (line B) Cité Universitaire
20, rue Gazan (14th); tel. 45.88.38.52. Service noon–2.30 and 7–10.30. (225 F, wine extra)
A country-like setting for this 1930s pavilion, where the choice of appetizers, main dishes and desserts is almost *too* bewildering.

LE PIED DE COCHON   **24** O/P10   Ⓜ Les Halles
6, rue Coquillière (1st); tel. 42.36.11.75. 24-hour service. (200–300 F)
Night-owls love to prowl the district of Les Halles, like in the good old days when the market was at its most hectic at 3 a.m. It's never too early to sample the shellfish or a grilled pig's trotter....

PRÉ CATALAN   **12** D11   ·   Ⓜ Porte Dauphine
Bois de Boulogne, route de Suresnes (16th); tel. 45.24.55.58. Service noon–2.30 p.m. and 7.30–10 p.m. Closed Sunday evening, Monday and February holidays. (550–600 F)
A very chic restaurant in the middle of the Bois. Out-of-doors dining in summer, in the Orangerie garden; in winter, a wood fire burns in the big dining-room. The renowned pâtissier Lenôtre presides over the Pré Catalan—so whatever you do, leave room for dessert.

123

LE PROCOPE   **24** O8   Ⓜ Odéon
13, rue de l'Ancienne-Comédie (6th); tel. 43.26.99.20. Service until 2 a.m. (200 F)
A literary café founded in 1686. Classic cuisine—but people come for the witty conversation, more memorable than the food.

LE TRAIN BLEU   **34** T6   Ⓜ Gare de Lyon
Gare de Lyon, 20, boulevard Diderot (12th); tel. 43.43.09.06. Service noon–2.15 p.m. and 7–9.45 p.m. (250 F)
Traditional cuisine in an amazing setting of ornately gilded stucco.
   Set menus: lunch 200 F including wine; dinner 200 F, wine extra. Same menus in the restaurant l'Astrée; country-style self-service at the **Buron**, inside the station.

ETHNIC

Round the world in 20 arrondissements. Should you ever tire of French cuisine, there's plenty more to choose from—African or Indian, Japanese or Spanish or the many different kinds of Chinese. Or even American—the Parisians are intrigued and amused by Stateside-style restaurants.

African/Antilles

CHEZ CHALOMÉ **16** P13   Ⓜ Cadet
9, rue de Trévise (9th); tel. 47.70.91.03/48.24.12.65. Service 7 p.m.–midnight. (130 F)
Excellent couscous—simple or royal—as well as paella.

LE FLAMBOYANT **37** L3/4   Ⓜ Pernety
11, rue Boyer-Barret (14th); tel. 45.41.00.02. Service noon–1.45 p.m. and 7.45–10.45 p.m.; closed Sunday evening, Monday and Tuesday lunch and all August. (150 F)
Splendid food in the sunny West Indies style. The *féroce*, a purée of avocado and cassava, is ferocious in name only. Try the pork with coconut.

LE MASAÏ **7** M15   Ⓜ La Fourche
11, rue Dautancourt (17th); tel. 42.28.94.05. Service 8 p.m.–2 a.m. Closed Monday. (200–250 F)
This unusual restaurant blends gastronomy and culture—*nouvelle cuisine* African and West Indies style, such as quail with kiwi sauce, and art exhibitions.

LE PETIT CHARTIER **18** T11   Ⓜ Parmentier
103, avenue Parmentier (11th); tel. 43.57.72.35. Service noon–3.30 p.m. and 7 p.m.–1.30 a.m. (150 F)
A marriage of African and Antilles specialities, from the entrée of *beignet de fiançailles* ("engagement fritters"—spicy meatballs) to *Soir de noces sur nid de crème d'orange* ("wedding night on an orange cream nest"). Set menu 50 F, including wine.

American

JOE ALLEN **24** P10   Ⓜ Etienne Marcel
30, rue Pierre Lescot (1st); tel. 42.36.70.13. Service noon–1 a.m. (150–200 F)
The oldest American restaurant in town; good hamburgers, like the New York original. Weekend brunch from noon, 95 F.

CACTUS CHARLY   **14** K12   Ⓜ Franklin-D.-Roosevelt
68, rue de Ponthieu (8th); tel. 45.62.01.77. Service noon–1.15 a.m. (80 F)
Where nostalgic Americans come for their hamburgers. Music groups on Friday and Saturday nights; brunch Sundays.

CHICAGO MEATPACKERS   **24** O/P10   Ⓜ Les Halles
8, rue Coquillière (1st); tel. 40.28.02.33. Service 11.30 a.m.–3 p.m. and 6.30 p.m.–1.30 a.m. (200 F)
As you might expect, the accent is on meat. Classic US delicacies such as baby back ribs.

Asian

HAWAÏ   **39** S2   Ⓜ Porte d'Ivry
87, avenue d'Ivry (13th); tel. 45.86.91.90. Service 10.30 a.m.–3 p.m. and 6–10.30 p.m. Closed Thursday. (80 F)
Speedy service. The Vietnamese soups in huge bowls make almost a complete meal.

LE PRÉSIDENT   **18** T12   Ⓜ Belleville
120–124, rue du Faubourg du Temple (11th); tel. 47.00.17.18. Service noon–2.30 p.m. and 7 p.m.–1.30 a.m. (120 F)
Two hundred Chinese dishes to choose from, in an exuberantly oriental setting.

Brazilian

PAU BRASIL   **13/14** H12   Ⓜ Charles-de-Gaulle–Etoile
32, rue de Tilsitt (17h); tel. 42.27.31.39. Service 8 p.m.–1 a.m., weekend until 2–3 a.m. Reserve a week in advance. (190 F; children under 13 120 F)

125

The tables are set at the bottom of a converted Thirties' swimming pool. No choice of menu—only *rodizio*, a brochette of 12 different kinds of meat. Unlimited quantities served with salad. Carnival atmosphere guaranteed at night.

Central European

JO GOLDENBERG   **25** R9   Ⓜ Saint-Paul
7, rue des Rosiers (4th); tel. 48.87.20.16. Service noon–11 p.m.; closed for Yom Kippour. (150 F)
Walk through the delicatessen to the restaurant. Russian, Hungarian, Polish and Yiddish specialities in a joyous Jewish atmosphere. Nostalgic music in the evening.

Indian

RAVI   **23** M9   Ⓜ Rue du Bac
*50, rue de Verneuil (7th); tel. 42.61.17.28. Reserve the previous day;
service noon–2 p.m. and 8–11 p.m. (350 F).*
A small room seating around 25, with a discreet Indian décor. The first
time you come, the cheery *patron* will regale you with his succulent
tandoori specialities—unforgettable. And let yourself be tempted by
an extravagant dessert—pistachio ice cream topped with *vark*, edible
silver leaf.

Italian

LE FLORENCE   **22** J8/9   Ⓜ Ecole Militaire
*22, rue du Champ-de-Mars (7th); tel. 45.51.52.69. Service noon–
2.30 p.m. and 7.30–10.30. p.m. Closed Sunday and Monday. (250–
270 F)*
Unpretentious, delicious Italian food (ravioli with lobster; carpaccio
of angler-fish with basil; mouth-watering zabaglione). Set menu
210 F: an entrée, main dish and dessert.

Japanese

KINUGAWA   **15/23** M11   Ⓜ Tuileries
*9, rue du Mont-Thabor (1st); tel. 42.60.65.07. Service noon–2.30 and
6.30–10 p.m. Closed Sunday. (150–300 F)*
Beautifully presented traditional dishes—pictures on a plate. Stark
Japanese environment, very much in fashion.

Lebanese

FAKHR EL DINE   **13** G10   Ⓜ Iéna
*30, rue de Longchamp (16th); tel. 47.27.90.00. Service noon–1.30 a.m.
(200–250 F)*
In opulent surroundings, Middle-Eastern food, with tempting, varied
mezze (small starters), and *chawarma*—marinated, spit-roast lamb.
There's another Fakhr el Dine at 3, rue Quentin-Bauchard (8th), tel.
47.23.74.24, métro George-V. Same opening hours. Specializes in fish.

Mexican

MEXICO MAGICO 25 R9 Ⓜ Saint-Sébastien–Froissart
105, rue Vieille-du-Temple (4th); tel. 42.72.77.37. Service noon–3 p.m. and 8 p.m.–midnight. (100 F)
Deliciously spicy specialities—*ceviche acapulqueño* and *puntas caippolte.*

Pakistani

PALAIS DU KASHMIR 8 O16 Ⓜ Jules Joffrin
77, rue du Poteau (18th); tel. 42.59.40.86. Service noon–2.30 p.m. and 7–11.30 p.m. (100–200 F)
A décor fit for a maharajah. The cuisine is as colourful as the waiters' costumes: Punjab chicken, tandoori shrimp.

Portuguese

SAUDADE 24 P9 Ⓜ Châtelet
34, rue des Bourdonnais (1st); tel. 42.36.30.71. Service noon–2 p.m. and 7.30–10.30 p.m.; closed August and 23–28 December. (180–200 F)
Salt cod and lots more. Surprisingly good wines, and, of course, superlative port.

Russian

ANNA KARENINA 25 Q10 Ⓜ Rambuteau **127**
176–178, rue Saint-Martin (3rd); tel. 48.04.03.63. Service 8.30 p.m.– 2 a.m. (150–250 F)
Zakouski, pielemienis, goulash—to the sound of the balalaika. You can come just for a glass of vodka or two, and to soak up the atmosphere.

Spanish

LA LUNA 24 O8 Ⓜ Odéon
12, rue Dauphine (6th); tel. 46.33.85.85. Service noon–2 p.m. and 7.30–11.30 p.m. (250–300 F)
Paella and fish dishes prevail, as you might expect. Two bars, one with *tapas* for a sunny apéritif.

The haunts of *Tout-Paris*—film stars, models, pop singers, rock idols and anyone else who wants his photo in the glossies....

BERMUDA ONION **21/29** F/G7   Ⓜ Charles Michels
16, rue Linois (15th); tel. 45.75.11.11. Service 8–11.30 p.m. Reserve in advance. (250 F)
Freaky setting with legs sticking out of the walls...and an up-to-date cuisine much appreciated by journalists and admen.

CAFÉ DE LA JATTE **5** F16   Ⓜ Pont de Levallois-Bécon
60, boulevard Vital-Bouhot, 92 Neuilly-sur-Seine; tel. 47.45.04.20. Service noon–3 p.m. and 8 p.m.–midnight. Closed Saturday lunch. (200 F)
Popular with the trendy crowd from the neighbouring advertising agencies, who come to savour an equally trendy, light cuisine.

CITY ROCK CAFÉ **14** K12   Ⓜ George-V
13, rue de Berri (8th), tel. 43.59.52.09. Service noon–2 a.m., later at the weekend. (100–200 F)
All-American setting, complete with an effigy of Marilyn Monroe and a pink Cadillac. Excellent T-bone steak.

NIOULLAVILLE **18** U12   Ⓜ Belleville
32–34, rue de l'Orillon (11th); tel. 43.38.30.44. Service noon–3.30 and 7 p.m.–1 a.m. (80 F)
Chinese, Vietnamese, Thai...lots of specialities, a warm welcome, and rapid service.

128 **LE PETIT POUCET** **5** F16   Ⓜ Pont de Levallois-Bécon
1, boulevard de Levallois, Neilly-sur-Seine; tel. 47.38.61.85. Service noon–2.30 and 8–11 p.m. Closed Saturday lunch, Sunday, and Monday evening from 1 October to 15 April. (170–200 F)
Pleasant covered terrasse overlooking the Seine.

PLANET DINNER HALL **5** F13   Ⓜ Les Sablons
6, rue du Commandant-Pilot, Neuilly-sur-Seine; tel. 46.40.08.88. Service noon–1 a.m. Closed Sunday evening. (100–150 F)
Good food in trendy Sixties' style.

PUZZLE **24** N8   Ⓜ Mabillon
15, rue Princesse (6th); tel. 46.34.55.80. Service until 3 a.m.; closed Sunday. (165 F)
Classic cuisine in an ultra-modern décor in black and white marble and pale green by designer Philippe Starck.

EASY-GOING

Though the Parisians always seem to be in a hurry, the idea of relaxing over a lengthy breakfast or an afternoon tea has caught on. Saturday and Sunday brunches are all the rage, with salmon and pastrami, scrambled eggs and sausages, salads, fruit, flapjacks and maple syrup—the lot. Tea rooms are also "in", but don't expect to find a good old English cuppa—the French like their tea weak, with a delicate, refined flavour, spicy, fruity, smoky or whatever, and no milk. The cakes served with it are usually home-made and very good—cheesecake, brownies, pecan pie, lemon chiffon pie, lots of variations on the chocolate theme.

JOE ALLEN: brunch (see page 124)

CACTUS CHARLY: brunch (see page 125)

LA CHARLOTTE DE L'ISLE   **25** R7   Ⓜ Sully-Morland
24, rue Saint-Louis-en-l'Île (4th); tel. 43.54.25.83. 2–8 p.m. closed Monday and Tuesday.
Delicious home-made cakes of chocolate and spices, thirty varieties of tea, in a Victorian dolls' house setting.

THE COCKNEY TAVERN   **7** N14   Ⓜ Blanche
39, boulevard de Clichy (9th); tel. 48.74.36.71. 11 a.m.–4 p.m.
When you're dying for a pint of bitter...or a real English breakfast.

LES ENFANTS GÂTÉS   **25** R9   Ⓜ Saint-Paul
43, rue des Francs-Bourgeois (4th); tel. 42.77.07.63. 9 a.m.–7 p.m. Closed 9–19 May and 10–20 August.
Comic-strip menu to help you choose a quiche or savoury tart. On Sunday, from noon to 7 p.m., four brunches: 70 F, 100 F, 135 F, and 170 F (with champagne). Popular with American and Swedish students.

129

LA FOURMI AILÉE   **24** P7   Ⓜ Maubert-Mutualité
8, Rue du Fouarre (5th), tel. 43.29.40.99. Noon–7 p.m. Closed Tuesday.
A cosy tea room at the back of a bookshop. Boiled eggs with bread soldiers, buns, scones and muffins. Saturday and Sunday, noon–6.30 p.m., three different brunches, small 75 F; medium 85 F and large 100 F.

L'HEURE GOURMANDE   **24** O8   Ⓜ Odéon
22, passage Dauphine (6th); tel. 46.34.00.40. 11 a.m.–7 p.m. Closed Sunday, one week at Easter, three weeks in August, Christmas–New Year.

Artists and writers appreciate the cosy, "British" atmosphere of this tea room. A large variety of teas and English cakes. Brunch is served every day except Sunday from 11.15 a.m. to 4 p.m. for 95 F.

MARIAGE: tea and brunch (see page 96)

PERRAUDIN: brunch (see page 120)

ROYAL-MONCEAU **14** J14 Ⓜ Charles-de-Gaulle–Etoile
39, avenue Hoche (8th), tel. 42.25.06.66. 9 a.m.–9.30 p.m.
Four or five kinds of health-food brunches, 180 F, beside the swimming pool. Sunday 11.30 a.m.–3.30 p.m. Reserve in advance.

TEA FOLLIES **16** O13 Ⓜ Saint-Georges
6, place Gustave-Toudouze (9th); tel. 42.80.08.44. Noon–10 p.m. (Sunday 7 p.m.)
An art gallery-cum-restaurant. Delicious pâtisseries at tea-time; brunch on Sundays (12.30–4 p.m.) 49 and 89 F.

EATING ALL NIGHT

Paris never sleeps. If you tend to feel peckish in the middle of the night, rest assured, there's something open somewhere.

From midnight to...

...1 a.m.

LA BRASSERIE DE L'ÎLE SAINT-LOUIS **25** Q8
55, quai de Bourbon (4th); tel. 43.54.02.59; closed Wednesday. Sauerkraut and beer in a cosmopolitan atmosphere.

LE SEPT **16** N11
7, rue Sainte-Anne (1st); tel. 42.96.25.82; closed Tuesday. Salmon in papillote, fruit gratins. Sophisticated gay scene.

...2 a.m.

LES BAINS **25** Q10
7, rue du Bourg-l'Abbé (3rd); tel. 48.87.01.80 (closes at 3 a.m. Friday and Saturday). From 9 p.m. onwards, sample Olympe's exquisite cuisine. Then dance it all off in the disco downstairs.

BASTILLE CORNER **26** T7
47, rue de Charenton (12th); tel. 43.47.12.17; closed Saturday. New York in the heart of the Bastille (French, American and Mexican food).

CHORUS CAFÉ   **16** O12
*23, rue Saint-Marc (2nd); tel. 42.96.81.00; closed Saturday lunch and
Sunday*. Hot meals until midnight, then cold. Jazz and rock music.

CITY ROCK CAFÉ (see page 128)

LA COUPOLE (see page 151)

1929   **26** T8
90 bis, rue de la Roquette (11th); tel. 43.79.71.55. Good food, great
wines, low prices.

...2.30 a.m.

L'ALDIANA   **25** R/S8
7, rue Saint-Paul (4th); tel. 48.87.15.51. Succulent Senegalese specialities.

...3 a.m.

LE BAYERNE   **24** P9
Place du Châtelet (1st); tel. 42.33.48.44. Pork and sauerkraut.

CACTUS BLEU   **26** T8
8, rue de Lappe (11th); tel. 43.38.30.20. Exotic food, drink and décor.

LA CHAMPAGNE   **7** M14
10 bis, place Clichy (9th); tel. 48.74.44.78. A ship-shape restaurant
where the fish is caught before your very eyes.

KING OPÉRA   **15** N11
21, rue Daunou (2nd); tel. 42.60.99.89. A real American home-away-
from-home.

131

LE MUNICHE   **24** N/O8
27, rue de Buci (6th); tel. 46.33.62.09. Oysters galore.

...5 a.m.

L'ENTR'ACTE   **16** P12
*25, boulevard Poissonnière (2nd); tel. 46.26.01.93. Closed Monday
evening*. Prolong your night out at the theatre without changing the
scenery, with a tasty tournedos or sole meunière.

LE VERRE BOUTEILLE   **13** G13
*85, avenue des Ternes (17th); tel. 45.74.01.02. Closed Saturday, Sun-
day and Christmas*. Lively atmosphere. Last orders for night owls—
for salads, pasta, sandwiches, wine by the glass—just when the
early-morning workers nip in for their breakfast.

Day and night, but specially busy in the early hours

LE BOUGNAT 24 O8
15, rue Séguier (6th); tel. 43.54.31.55; closed Sunday. Traditional cuisine. Favourite haunt of literary and political personalities.

LE PIED DE COCHON (see page 123)
LA TOUR DE MONTLHÉRY 24 P10
5, rue des Prouvaires (1st); tel. 42.36.21.82. Closed Sunday. Stuffed cabbage and mutton stew, beneath garlands of sausage and cured hams.

WINE BARS

They are springing up all over, much to the delight of wine lovers and those who'd like a good snack or hot dish without a hefty bill.

AUX NÉGOCIANTS 8 P15 Ⓜ Château-Rouge
27, rue Lambert (18th); tel. 46.06.15.11. Service noon–8 p.m., Tuesday, Thursday and Friday until 10 p.m. Closed Saturday, Sunday, public holidays and August. Glass of red or white wine under 15 F; *terrine persillée* (parsleyed terrine) 48 F.

LES BACCHANTES 15 M12 Ⓜ Havre-Caumartin
21, rue Caumartin (9th); tel. 42.65.25.35. 11.30 a.m.–2 a.m., closed two weeks in August. Glass of red or white wine under 20 F; *assiette de campagne* (plate of ham, paté, sausage with bread 35 F, *andouillette de Duval pommes au four* (tripe sausage with baked potato) 46 F.

132 ## BISTROT-CAVE DES ENVIERGES 19 V12 Ⓜ Pyrénées
11, rue des Envierges (20th); tel. 46.36.47.84. Service noon–8.30 p.m., Wednesday, Thursday and Friday until 2 a.m., closed Monday and Tuesday. Glass of red or white wine under 10 F; *cake aux olives* (olive bread) 18 F, *coq au vin* 48 F.

BISTROT DU SOMMELIER 15 L12 Ⓜ Saint-Lazare
97, boulevard Haussmann (8th); tel. 42.65.24.85. Service noon–3 p.m. and 7.30–10.30 p.m. Closed Saturday evening, Sunday and holidays. Glass of red or white wine 15–50 F; *entrée* 50 F, main dish 100 F.

MA BOURGOGNE 14 K12 Ⓜ Miromesnil
133, boulevard Haussmann (8th); tel. 45.63.50.61. Service 7 a.m.– 8 p.m. Closed Saturday, Sunday, public holidays and July or August. Glass of red or white wine under 15 F; snack of Morvan ham and bread 20 F.

DAME TARTINE　　**25** Q9　　　　　　　　Ⓜ Hôtel-de-Ville
2, rue Brisemiche (4th); tel. 42.77.32.22. Service noon–11 p.m. Glass of
red or white wine under 20 F, open salmon sandwich 32 F, chocolate
tart 15 F.

DUC DE RICHELIEU　　**16** O12　　　　　Ⓜ Richelieu-Drouot
110, rue de Richelieu (2nd); tel. 42.96.38.38. Service 7 a.m.–5 a.m. Glass
of red or white wine under 15 F; hot dish 60 F (good country-style
cooking).

L'ÉCLUSE　　**24** O8　　　　　　　　　Ⓜ Saint-Michel
*15, quai des Grands-Augustins (6th); tel. 46.33.58.74. Service noon–
2 a.m.* Glass of red or white wine under 20 F; goose foie gras 96 F;
chocolate cake 33 F. Five other wine bars of the same name, all easily
recognizable by their green façade, in the 1st, 8th, 9th arrondissements and in Neuilly.

JACQUES MÉLAC　　**27** V8　　　　　　　Ⓜ Charonne
*42, rue Léon-Frot (11th); tel. 43.70.59.27. Service 9 a.m.–7.30 p.m.,
Tuesday and Thursday until 10.30 p.m. Closed Saturday, Sunday and
14 July–August 15.* Glass of red or white wine under 15 F; cheese plate
46 F, *tripoux* (tripe and sheep's trotters) 44 F.

LE PÈRE TRANQUILLE　　**31** L5　　Ⓜ Montparnasse-Bienvenüe
*30, avenue du Maine (15th); tel. 42.22.88.12. Service 10 a.m.–8 p.m.
Closed Sunday and Monday.* Glass of red or white wine under 15 F;
terrine du patron (home-made pâté) and hot *plat du jour* (day's
special) 45 F.

LE RUBIS　　**15/23** N11　　　　　　　Ⓜ Pyramides
*10, rue du Marché-Saint-Honoré (1st); tel. 42.61.03.34. Service
7 a.m.–10 p.m. Closed Saturday and Sunday.* Glass of red or white
wine under 15 F, plate of cold cuts 38 F, day's special 45 F.

LE SAUVIGNON　　**23** M8　　　　　　Ⓜ Sèvres-Babylone
*80, rue des Saints-Pères (7th), tel. 45.48.49.02. Service 9 a.m.–10 p.m.
Closed Sunday and all August.* Glass of red or white wine under 20 F;
plate of goat cheese and butter with bread 39 F.

LE VAL D'OR　　**14** K11　　　　　　Ⓜ Franklin-D.-Roosevelt
*28, avenue Franklin-D.-Roosevelt (8th); tel. 43.59.95.81. Service
7.30 a.m.–9 p.m. (Saturday 11 a.m.–6 p.m.). Closed Sunday and
Christmas–New Year.* Glass of red or white wine under 15 F. Sandwich
with Poilâne wholemeal bread and salad 29 F.

Paree is as gay as ever—it still hasn't lost any of the glitter and bounce that Toulouse-Lautrec made famous at the turn of the century. From boisterous floor shows to select jazz clubs, there's entertainment for all tastes, from traditional to the most eccentric. The only problem is that there's so much to choose from—it's enough to make your head spin.

Whereas bars and discotheques don't liven up until around 11 p.m., theatre performances begin quite early (8.30 or 9 p.m.). There are plenty of restaurants open late for supper after the show, mainly in the more animated quarters like the Champs-Elysées, les Halles, the Grands Boulevards, Montmartre, Saint-Germain-des-Prés or Montparnasse. Cinema performances generally start in the afternoon.

The streets of Paris are reasonably safe at night—you just need to know which places to avoid. Don't tempt fate by flashing wads of banknotes around, or wearing ostentatious jewellery. Hot spots like Pigalle and the Bois de Boulogne are taken over by prostitutes and drug-pushers as soon as daylight starts to fade—go there at your own risk.

Public transport closes down at half past midnight; unaccompanied women should avoid it at night and take a taxi.

CINEMA

There's no doubt about it, Paris offers the largest variety of films shown at any one time anywhere in the world. Every week, you can choose from among 300 titles—first-runs, reruns, foreign films, art and experimental films, documentaries, not to mention those shown in the city's cinémathèques. Foreign films are shown in at least one cinema in the original language (v.o.); the dubbed French version is indicated by v.f. Programmes, which change on Wednesday, and hours can be found in the "what's on" magazines, *l'Officiel des Spectacles, Pariscope, 7 à Paris*, and the daily newspapers.

Most of the big cinemas are split up into smaller ones, so make sure you are waiting in the right queue. When you buy your ticket, say the

Dance the night away... or watch others do it.

name of the film you want to see. Some cinemas accept Visa cards; seats are about 40% cheaper on Monday, and reductions are usually accorded to holders of student cards.

English films are shown at the **British Council**, 9, rue de Constantine (7th); tel. 45.55.95.95.

The cinemas mentioned below are all something special—either because of the quality of the films shown or the originality of the building.

CINÉMATHÈQUE FRANÇAISE   **21** G10   ⓜ Trocadéro
Musée du Cinéma, Palais de Chaillot, corner of avenues Albert-de-Mun and Président-Wilson (16th); tel. 47.04.24.24.
The masterpieces of cinema; they change at each showing. French and v.o.

LE GRAND REX   **16** P12   ⓜ Bonne-Nouvelle
1, boulevard Poissonnière (2nd); tel. 42.36.83.93. v.f. Continuous programme from 1.30 p.m. to midnight.
Built between the World Wars by John Eberson, the theatre can seat 2,800 and has fanciful murals of an old Spanish town under a starry ceiling. Extra-wide screen.

MAX LINDER PANORAMA   **16** P12   ⓜ Rue Montmartre
24, boulevard Poissonnière (9th); tel. 48.24.88.88. v.o.
Ultra-modern theatre with big screen. Some 70-mm, THX system films.

LA PAGODE   **23** K8   ⓜ Saint-François-Xavier
57 bis, rue de Babylone (7th); tel. 47.05.12.15. v.o.
The first manager of the Bon Marché department store had this real pagoda built for his wife. It served as an experimental cinema for more than 50 years. Most of its old splendour has gone, but the walls of the ground-floor theatre still have the original ornately carved and embroidered décor.

136

There's also a tiny Japanese tea garden, lovely in summer for tea and cakes after the film. (Weekdays 4–10 p.m.; Sunday 2–8 p.m.)

TRIANON   **8** P14   ⓜ Anvers
80, boulevard de Rochechouart (18th); tel. 46.06.63.66. v.f. Continuous programme 10 a.m.–midnight.
An old-time cinema showing spaghetti westerns and kung-fu films.

VENDÔME OPÉRA   **16** N11   ⓜ Opéra
32, avenue de l'Opéra (2nd); tel. 47.42.97.52. v.o. Continuous showing 2 p.m.–midnight.
Films of dance and opera.

THEATRE

Paris claims some 100 theatres—not counting those of the suburbs and the café-théâtres. From one-man-shows to light drawing-room comedies in the *théâtres de boulevard* to grandiose superproductions, there's something for all tastes.

The high standards of French classical drama—Molière, Racine and Corneille—are upheld by the **Comédie Française**, though the troupe is slowly expanding its repertory (Beckett's *Endgame*, for example). On the Left Bank, the **Odéon** is the home of the "Theatre of Europe"—modern and classical plays by prestigious guest companies performing in all European languages.

In the contemporary theatre the stars are generally the directors, not the actors. Look for the innovators—Ariane Mnouchkine who directs the Théâtre du Soleil troupe at the **Cartoucherie** in Vincennes, Patrice Chéreau in Nanterre at the **Théâtre des Amandiers**, and Peter Brook, who is based at **Bouffes du Nord**. Robert Hossein puts on spectacular plays on historical themes, with audience participation. Other theatres specializing in drama by contemporary authors are the **Théâtre Renaud-Barrault**, run by the famous French actors Madeleine Renaud and Jean-Louis Barrault, the **Splendid Saint-Martin**, the **Est parisien**, and the ultra-modern **Théâtre de la Colline.**

If your French is up to it, you might enjoy the tiny *cafés-théâtres*, where you can sip a drink—or sometimes have a meal—while watching satirical cabaret or an avant-garde play; these little "theatre workshops" are generally showcases for new talents. It all began, and still carries on, at the **Café de la Gare**, one of the best. The **Tintamarre**, Rue des Lombards, is another café-théâtre guaranteeing good entertainment. For the witty political satire of the *chansonniers*, the right venues are the **Caveau de la République** and the **Deux Anes**—though you have to be really fluent in French and very up-to-date with the news to understand the jokes.

We have provided the addresses and phone numbers of all these theatres below, but for details of performances you'll have to rely on the listings in the "what's on" press, which cover all the theatres in Paris and the suburbs. The English-language monthly magazine *Paris Passion* features interesting articles on all things cultural, and contains a calendar of events giving details on everything from debates to rock concerts. To procure tickets, see pages 138–139.

137

BOUFFES DU NORD   **9** R14   Ⓜ Porte de la Chapelle
37 bis, boulevard de la Chapelle (10th); tel. 42.39.34.50. Bookings noon–7 p.m., except Sunday. No performance Monday or Thursday.

How to book seats

Tickets are usually put on sale 13 or 14 days before the performance. If you haven't arranged seats in advance through your travel agent, try one of the following possibilities:

Your **hotel concierge** might be able to get hold of tickets—but you'll have to pay commission.

Call at the **box office** of the venue itself—cancellations are returned directly to the theatre, so you might be able to get tickets for shows supposed to be sold out.

By **Minitel**: call up **Spectamatic** (36 15 MATIC) or **Ticketel** (36 15 TICK) to reserve and pay at the same time with your credit card (Visa or Eurocard). Your ticket will be waiting for you at the theatre—just mention your credit card number. There's a surcharge of 10–15% for these services.

Billetel terminals work on the same principle as the Minitel, but they deliver the tickets at the same time. They are strategically placed throughout Paris, in the FNAC stores (Etoile, Forum and Montparnasse), in the RER stations Auber and Châtelet–Les Halles, the Gare de Lyon, the Cité des Sciences, the Centre Pompidou, Galeries Lafayette and BHV. You can reach the Billetel through a personal Minitel (36 15 BILLETEL); you'll be given a password so you can pick up your ticket from a Billetel machine.

Ticket agencies charge a commission of 22%; they can also book seats on the bateau-mouche or other excursions.

   Chèque-Théâtres, 33, rue Le Peletier (9th); tel. 42.46.72.40. Map 16 O12; métro Le Peletier.

CAFÉ DE LA GARE   **25** Q9   Ⓜ Rambuteau/Hôtel-de-Ville
41, rue du Temple (4th); tel. 42.78.52.51. Entrance and first drink 100 F. No performance Sunday or Monday.

CARTOUCHERIE   Ⓜ Château de Vincennes
Route du Champ-de-Manœuvres, Vincennes (94); tel. 43.74.99.61, 43.28.36.36, 43.74.24.08 and 43.28.97.04. Bookings every day except Monday, 2–7 p.m. No performance Sunday evening or Monday. From the métro station, take bus no. 112 or the free shuttle bus to the Cartoucherie stop.

CAVEAU DE LA RÉPUBLIQUE   **17** R11   Ⓜ République
1, boulevard Saint-Martin (3rd); tel. 42.78.44.45. Bookings from 11 a.m., six days in advance. No performance Sunday evening or Monday.

Gefco, 69, avenue de la Grande-Armée (16th); tel. 45.02.13.90. Map 13 G12/13; métro Argentine.

S.O.S. Théâtres, 73, avenue des Champs-Elysées (8th); tel. 42.25.67.07/42.25.03.18. Map 14 J12; métro Franklin-D.-Roosevelt.

Kiosque Théâtre (opposite no. 15, place de la Madeleine (8th); map 15 M11; métro Madeleine) sells theatre tickets at half price for performances the same day. The seats available are among the most expensive; 11 F commission per ticket. Open Tuesday to Friday 12.30–8 p.m.; Saturday 12.30 p.m. for matinées and 2–8 p.m. for evening performances; Sunday 12.30–4 p.m. Closed Monday.

As seats at the Opéra de Paris-Garnier are largely filled by subscribers, only 300 tickets are available, 13 days before each performance. The cheapest ones go almost as soon as the box office is opened, so be there early (or phone 47.42.53.71, Monday to Saturday, noon–6 p.m.). You can also book in writing: Théâtre de l'Opéra, Service de location par correspondance, 8, rue Scribe, 75009 Paris.

The back seats of the boxes are put on sale from 1.30 p.m. the day before the performance; any seats left are sold off cheaply to students just before the performance is due to begin.

The Comédie Française puts 112 cheap seats on sale before each performance (usually 18 F, but 32 F for exceptional plays). Join the queue at 7.45 p.m. (You might end up on a foldaway seat *(strapontin)* in the gods.)

The Odéon offers 99 seats at 28 F and 46 F, half an hour before the show.

COMÉDIE FRANÇAISE　　24 N10　　　　　　Ⓜ Palais-Royal
2, rue de Richelieu (1st); tel. 40.15.00.15. Bookings 11 a.m.–6 p.m., 14 days in advance.

139

DEUX ÂNES　　7 N14　　　　　　　　　Ⓜ Blanche
100, boulevard de Clichy (18th); tel. 46.06.10.26. Bookings 11 a.m.–7 p.m., 14 days in advance. No performance Sunday evening or Monday.

ODÉON　　32 O7　　　　　　　　　Ⓜ Odéon
Place Paul-Claudel (6th); tel. 43.25.70.32. Bookings 14 days in advance. No performance Sunday or Monday.

LE SPLENDID **17** R12 Ⓜ Strasbourg-
SAINT-MARTIN Saint-Denis
48, rue du Faubourg Saint-Martin (10th); tel. 42.08.21.93. Bookings
1–7 p.m. No performance Sunday.

THÉÂTRE DES AMANDIERS Ⓡ Nanterre-Université
7, avenue Pablo Picasso, Nanterre (92); tel. 47.21.18.81. Bookings
noon–7 p.m., Tuesday to Saturday. Shuttle bus from RER station.

THÉÂTRE DE L'EST PARISIEN **19** X11 Ⓜ Saint-Fargeau
159, avenue Gambetta (20th); tel. 43.64.80.80. Bookings 10.30 a.m.–
7 p.m. (Sunday 10.30 a.m.–5 p.m.). No performance Sunday evening
or Monday.

THÉÂTRE NATIONAL DE LA COLLINE **19** W10 Ⓜ Gambetta
15, rue Malte-Brun (20th); tel. 43.66.43.60. Bookings 11 a.m.–7 p.m.
(Monday 3–7 p.m.), 14 days in advance.

THÉÂTRE **14** K11 Ⓜ Franklin-D.-Roosevelt
RENAUD-BARRAULT
*2 bis, avenue Franklin-D.-Roosevelt (8th); tel. 42.56.60.70 and
42.56.08.80.* Bookings 11 a.m.–6 p.m., 14 days in advance. No performance Sunday evening or Monday. Concerts Sunday morning.

LE TINTAMARRE **25** Q9 Ⓜ Châtelet–Les Halles
10, rue des Lombards (4th); tel. 48.87.33.82. Bookings 2–7 p.m. No
performance Sunday or Monday.

CLASSICAL MUSIC, OPERA AND MODERN DANCE

Music lovers are spoiled in Paris—there's a vast choice of high-
quality concerts and recitals. As you're more likely to choose a show
for the performers rather than for the venue, we have listed only the
better-known theatres here. Many of these theatres are polyvalent,
and can be used for music hall, plays, operettas, classical concerts or
modern dance; some opera performances are held in unlikely places
such as the Palais des Sports (see page 143). Just to confuse matters,
the old Opéra is now used only for ballet, and is now known as Opéra
de Paris-Garnier. The Opéra Bastille, inaugurated for the Bicenten-
nial celebrations on 14th July 1989, will open for performances in
February 1990. Except for the free recitals in churches (see page 9)
and at Radio France (see below), you should book in advance.

  Modern dance is enjoying a revival, with a new wave of tiny,
imaginative young companies stepping in the wake of successful

choreographers Régine Chopinot, Claude Gallotta and Karine Saporta. They start off in a small way at the Café de la Danse, the Déjazet, the Espace Kiron, Théâtre Gémier and the Centre Pompidou, before reaching the great heights of the Théâtre de la Bastille and final consecration at the Théâtre de la Ville.

AUDITORIUM DES HALLES   24 P10   Ⓜ Châtelet
Porte Sainte-Eustache (1st) tel. 42.36.13.90.
Concerts every day—all kinds of music—and dance.

AUDITORIUM DU LOUVRE   24 N/O10   Ⓜ Palais-Royal
Passage Richelieu (beneath the Pyramid), Louvre museum (1st); tel. 40.20.51.86. Reservations Monday to Friday, 2–5 p.m., on 40.20.52.29, or by Minitel: 36 15 code THOA.
Chamber music recitals in the evening; also one Thursday a month, 12.30–1.30 p.m., as part of the "Midis du Louvre" programme (see page 36).

CAFÉ DE LA DANSE   26 T8   Ⓜ Bastille
5, passage Louis-Philippe (11th); tel. 48.05.57.22.
An alternative approach to modern dance and musicals.

CENTRE GEORGES-POMPIDOU—IRCAM   25 Q10   Ⓜ Châtelet
19, rue Beaubourg (4th); tel. 42.78.79.95.
Contemporary, experimental music (see page 37).

CHÂTELET THÉÂTRE MUSICAL DE PARIS   24 P9   Ⓜ Châtelet
Place du Châtelet (1st); tel. 42.33.00.00 (answering machine). Reservations on 40.28.28.40, 11 a.m.–7 p.m. daily except Sunday, or by Minitel: 36 15 CHÂTELET, 14 days in advance.
Ballet (choreographer William Forsythe shares his time between here and Frankfurt), opera, classical and chamber music, and music hall.
  Special recitals in the theatre foyer—Monday, Wednesday and Friday at 12.45 p.m. *("midis musicaux")*; Sunday at 4 p.m. *("dimanche à 16 heures")*.

141

ÉGLISE DES BILLETTES   25 Q9   Ⓜ Hôtel-de-Ville
24, rue des Archives (4th); tel. 42.33.43.00.
Sacred and classical music.

MAISON DE LA RADIO   21 F8   Ⓜ Passy
116, avenue du Président-Kennedy (16th); tel. 42.30.15.16.
Performances by the New Philharmonic Orchestra (NOP), which can adapt itself to many styles—symphony music, chamber music, opera, etc.

OPÉRA COMIQUE   **16** O12   Ⓜ Richelieu-Drouot
(SALLE FAVART)
5, rue Favart (9th); tel. 42.96.06.11.
Light opera and operettas, but also plays.

OPÉRA DE PARIS-GARNIER   **15** N12   Ⓜ Opéra
*Place de l'Opéra (9th); tel. 47.42.57.50. Bookings on 47.42.53.71, every
day except Sunday and holidays, noon–6 p.m.*
The French national ballet, directed by Nureyev. Classics like *Swan
Lake* and *Giselle,* and some experimental ballet.

OPÉRA BASTILLE   **26** T8   Ⓜ Bastille
2–6, place de la Bastille (12th).
The brand-new headquarters of the National Opera Company, directed by a young Korean, Myung-Whun Chung. Architect Carlos
Ott's functional, multi-purpose building has caused a lot of controversy—Parisians find it ugly, and the music-lovers are indignant that
opera has been taken away from the Opéra. But the acoustics are
superb.

PALAIS DE L'UNESCO   **30** J7   Ⓜ Ségur
125, avenue de Suffren (7th); tel. 45.68.10.00.
Music and dance by international companies.

SALLE GAVEAU   **14** K12   Ⓜ Miromesnil
45, rue La Boétie (8th); tel. 49.53.05.07.
Classical music.

SALLE PLEYEL   **14** J13   Ⓜ Ternes
*252, rue du Faubourg Saint-Honoré (8th); tel. 45.63.88.73 (reserva-
tions for the Orchestre de Paris on 45.63.07.96).*
Top soloists perform here with the country's most prestigious sym-
142 phony orchestra, l'Orchestre de Paris. Celebrated jazz artists such as
Oscar Peterson appear at the Pleyel, too.

THÉÂTRE DES CHAMPS-ÉLYSÉES   **14/22** J11   Ⓜ Alma-Marceau
15, avenue Montaigne (8th); tel. 47.20.36.37.
Classical music, ballet, opera. Many international dance or music
festivals take place in the theatre recently renovated in the grand old
velvet-and-gilt tradition.

THÉÂTRE 14   **36** K2   Ⓜ Porte de Vanves
JEAN-MARIE SERREAU
20, avenue Marc Sangnier (14th); tel. 45.45.49.77.
Music, dance, plays—all with a modern accent.

POP AND ROCK MUSIC

French pop singers, rock groups and international superstars perform at the following venues—advertised by posters all over the city. Tickets can be obtained from the FNAC shops and Virgin Megastore, or by phoning the numbers given.

BATACLAN   **18** T10   Ⓜ Saint-Ambroise
50, boulevard Voltaire (11th); tel. 47.00.30.12.
One of the trendiest music halls.

OLYMPIA   **15** M12   Ⓜ Madeleine
28, boulevard des Capucines (9th); tel. 47.42.25.49. Bookings 10 a.m.–7 p.m. Well-known pop singers (mainly French) perform in this old-fashioned music hall.

PALAIS DES CONGRÈS   **13** G13   Ⓜ Porte-Maillot
Porte Maillot (17th); 42.66.20.75.
All kinds of music, and trade fairs.

PALAIS OMNISPORTS PARIS BERCY   **34** U5   Ⓜ Bercy
8, boulevard de Bercy (12th); tel. 43.46.12.21.
A multi-purpose building, with adjustable walls to hold from 3,500 to 17,000 spectators. From operas to rock concerts to judo tournaments.

PALAIS DES SPORTS   **29** G4   Ⓜ Porte de Versailles
Porte de Versailles (15th); tel. 48.28.40.10.
Huge echoing hall—hard to see who's singing.

LE ZÉNITH   **11** W15   Ⓜ Porte de Pantin
211, avenue Jean-Jaurès (19th); tel. 42.00.22.24/42.40.60.00.
Intended as a temporary structure, it ended up a permanent auditorium for 6,300 spectators. Exclusively for pop and rock concerts.

143

DISCOS, BARS AND NIGHTCLUBS

Nothing changes so fast as what is in or out on the disco scene—keeping in step with the latest boîte is a full-time job for the night owl. Most disco music is British or American; the best live sounds are Brazilian, Caribbean or West, Central and North African. You won't be disappointed by the jazz, which the French have always taken seriously.

LES BAINS   **25** Q10   Ⓜ Etienne Marcel
7, rue du Bourg-l'Abbé (3rd); tel. 48.87.01.80. 11.30 p.m.–dawn. Entrance and first drink 120 F.
A Turkish bath-house décor for immersing yourself in the steamy crowd that still counts a few hopeful models and photographers. First-floor restaurant: count 250 F for dinner (service 9 p.m.–2 a.m.).

LE BAISER SALÉ   **25** Q9   Ⓜ Châtelet
58, rue des Lombards (1st); tel. 42.33.37.71. 8 p.m.–5 a.m.
Live music for a young crowd, and videos in the bar. Rhythm and blues on Monday, jazz the rest of the week. Trendy, relaxed atmosphere.

BALAJO   **26** T8   Ⓜ Bastille
9, rue de Lappe (11th); tel. 47.00.07.87. 10 p.m.–4.30 a.m. Friday and Monday matinées at 3 and 6.30 p.m. Closed Tuesday. Entrance and first drink: 100 F in the evening, 50 F afternoon.
Old-time dance hall with old-time tango, waltz and cha-cha; but Monday and Thursday the in-crowd comes for disco dancing.

BAR DU POTAGER   **25** Q10   Ⓜ Les Halles
9–11, rue de la Grande-Truanderie (1st); tel. 40.26.50.96. 6 p.m.–4 a.m.
Trendy bistrot with a billiards room.

BARS OF THE RITZ HOTEL   **15** M11   Ⓜ Opéra
15, place Vendôme (1st); tel. 42.60.38.30.
Vendôme side lounge (11 a.m.–1 a.m.), piano at cocktail time. **Hemingway** on Rue Cambon side (11 a.m.–1 a.m.), tiny, very chic—jacket and tie required. **Club Ritz,** 38, rue Cambon: 9 p.m.–dawn. Jacket and tie. A vodka costs 150 F.

LE BILBOQUET   **23/24** N8   Ⓜ Saint-Germain-des-Prés
13, rue Saint-Benoît (6th); tel. 45.48.81.84. 10.30 p.m.–3 a.m. Drinks 100 F.
Good live jazz in the bar. Count 250 F for dinner in the restaurant, 7.30 p.m.–midnight.

144

LES BOUCHONS   **24** P9   Ⓜ Châtelet
19, rue des Halles (1st); tel. 42.33.28.73. Noon–2 a.m. Entrance free.
From 8 p.m., live American jazz in the wine cellar.

BOY   **15** M12   Ⓜ Havre-Caumartin
6, rue Caumartin (9th); tel. 47.42.68.05. 11 a.m.–dawn. Entrance and first drink 50 F.
House music for gay men. Boy's Tea Dance, Sunday 5–10.30 p.m. Entrance 10 F. Monday, theme night.

BUS PALLADIUM   **16** N8   Ⓜ Blanche
6, rue Fontaine (9th); tel. 48.74.54.99. 11.30 p.m.–dawn. Closed Monday. Entrance and first drink 110 F.
Fairly tame and preppy nightclub compared to the days when it was a nest of Hell's Angels.

CAVEAU DE LA HUCHETTE   **24** P8   Ⓜ Saint-Michel
5, rue de la Huchette (5th); tel. 43.26.65.05. 9.30 p.m.; Thursday and Sunday until 2.30 a.m.; Friday 3 a.m.; Saturday and eves of holidays 4 a.m. Entrance 45 F, weekend 55 F, drinks (optional) 15 F.
Traditional jazz cellar, with dancing every night.

CHAPELLE DES LOMBARDS   **26** T8   Ⓜ Bastille
19, rue de Lappe (11th); tel. 43.57.24.24. 10.30 p.m.–dawn; Sunday 5 p.m.–1 a.m.; Monday 8.30 p.m.–dawn. Entrance 60 F, Thursday 70 F, Friday and Saturday 80 F.
Salsa and reggae, for a swinging night out.

CLUB 79   **14** J12   Ⓜ George V
79, avenue des Champs-Elysées (8th); tel. 47.23.68.75. Friday and Saturday 10 p.m.–dawn; Sunday to Thursday 9.30 p.m.–3 a.m. Afternoons 4–7 p.m.; Sunday 3.45–7 p.m. Entrance and first drink: nights 90–110 F; evenings 60 F; afternoons 50 F, Sunday afternoon 55 F.
Two disco nights, old-time evenings and afternoon dance—jitterbug, waltz, foxtrot....

CONCORDE-LAFAYETTE   **13** G13   Ⓜ Porte Maillot
3, place du Général-Koenig (17th); tel. 47.58.12.84. 11 a.m.–2 a.m.
A bar on the 33rd floor, looking out over the west of Paris. Green Jack, one of the barman's 40 cocktails, 56 F before 9.30 p.m., 85 F after.

L'ENTREPÔT   **26** U8   Ⓜ Ledru-Rollin
14, rue de Charonne (11th); tel. 48.06.57.04. 7 p.m.–2 a.m. (3 a.m. Thursday, Friday, Saturday).
Quietly sophisticated bar, for trendy jazz-lovers. Drinks 33–46 F.

145

FORUM   **15** M12   Ⓜ Madeleine
4, boulevard Malesherbes (8th); tel. 42.65.37.86. 11.30 a.m.–2 a.m.; Saturday and Sunday 5.30 p.m.–2 a.m.
This bar has become an institution. Glass of champagne 53 F.

LE GARAGE   **14** J12   Ⓜ George V
41, rue Washington (8th); tel. 45.63.21.27. 11 p.m.–dawn; drinks 100 F.
Very trendy, classy disco. Once or twice a week, top fashion models are invited to dinner.

HARRY'S BAR   **15** N11   Ⓜ Opéra
5, rue Daunou (2nd); tel. 42.61.71.14. 10.30 a.m.–4 a.m.
Animated and fun, piano music at night. Since the Twenties, a
favourite haunt of Americans and Americanophile French.

LA JAVA   **18** T12   Ⓜ Belleville
*105, rue du Faubourg du Temple (10th); tel. 42.02.20.52. Tuesday to
Sunday 9.30 p.m.–5 a.m. Sunday, Monday and holidays 2.30–7 p.m.
Closed Wednesday. Entrance 55–80 F, matinée 35 F.*
Sixties' music for a student audience; afternoon dancing—waltz,
tango and cha-cha-cha.

JAZZ CLUB LIONEL HAMPTON   **13** G13   Ⓜ Porte Maillot
*Hôtel Méridien Paris Etoile, 81, boulevard Gouvion-Saint-Cyr (17th);
tel. 47.58.12.30. 6 p.m.–2 a.m. Drinks 50 F until 10 p.m.; 110 F after.*
Pleasant piano bar until 10 p.m., then prestigious names in the
mainstream jazz world.

KITTY O'SHEA'S PUB   **15** M/N11   Ⓜ Opéra
*10, rue des Capucines (2nd); tel. 40.15.00.30. Noon–1.30 a.m. (2 a.m.
Friday and Saturday).*
As Irish as a shamrock. Business lunch 95 F; jazz brunch Sunday
11.30 a.m. and 2.30 p.m. 130 F.

LÀ-BAS   **14** J12   Ⓜ George V
*Corner of rues Balzac and Lord-Byron (8th); tel. 45.63.12.39. 11 p.m.–
dawn; closed Sunday. Drinks 90 F.*
A white door opens onto a décor signed Philippe Starck—but only if
the doorman likes the look of you. Rock music.

LA LOCOMOTIVE   **8** N14   Ⓜ Pigalle
*90, boulevard de Clichy (18th); tel. 42.57.37.37. 11.30 p.m.–6.30 a.m.
(weekend 7.00 a.m.); closed Monday. Entrance Tuesday to Thursday
50 F; Friday and Saturday 90 F, Sunday 50 F (free for women).*
Modern rock music.

146

LE MEMPHIS   **17** Q12   Ⓜ Bonne-Nouvelle
*3, impasse Bonne-Nouvelle (10th); tel. 45.23.34.47. 11 p.m.–6 a.m.;
Sunday matinée 2.45–7 p.m. Entrance and first drink: weekdays 70 F,
weekend 90 F, Sunday matinée 40 F.*
Disco and video screens in a deep-south setting. Exclusive disco in
basement "submarine" Friday, Saturday and Sunday.

LA MOUSSON   **26** S8   Ⓜ Bastille
*9, rue de la Bastille (4th); tel. 42.71.85.20. 8 p.m.–1 a.m. Closed Sunday
and Monday.*

Trendy and intimate bar in a neo-colonial décor; cocktails from 45 F. Dining upstairs (count 180 F).

LE NEW MORNING   **17** Q12   Ⓜ Château d'Eau
7–9, rue des Petites-Ecuries (10th); tel. 45.23.51.41 (temperamental answering machine); hours change according to performers. Advance reservation advised.
Good jazz club, attracting all the major American and European musicians.

LA PAILLOTE   **31/32** O7   Ⓜ Odéon
45, rue Monsieur-le-Prince (6th); tel. 43.26.45.69. 9 p.m.–dawn; closed Sunday.
A good bar for jazz-lovers. Dusky lighting; exotic décor; tropical punch. Drinks 20–40 F.

LE PALACE   **16** O/P12   Ⓜ Rue Montmartre
8, rue du Faubourg Montmartre (9th); tel. 42.46.10.87. 11 p.m.–dawn. Entrance weekdays 100 F; Friday, Saturday, Sunday 120 F.
Theme nights with fancy dress, great fun. Count 200 F for dinner in the restaurant, 9 p.m.–2 a.m.

LE PETIT OPPORTUN   **24** P9   Ⓜ Châtelet
15, rue des Lavandières-Sainte-Opportune (1st); tel. 42.36.01.36. 11 p.m.–3 a.m. Entrance and first drink 120 F.
A cellar club for jazz addicts.

LA PLANTATION   **16** O11   Ⓜ Palais-Royal
45, rue de Montpensier (1st); tel. 49.27.06.21. 11 p.m.–dawn, except Monday. Entrance and first drink 80 F.
Intimate nightclub with excellent African and Caribbean music. Wednesday and Saturday, matinée at 2.30 p.m. for the under-18s. Boys 30 F, girls 10 F.

147

LE REX CLUB   **17** Q12   Ⓜ Bonne-Nouvelle
5, boulevard Poissonnière (2nd); tel. 42.36.83.98. Tuesday 10 p.m.– 5 a.m.; Wednesday, Friday and Saturday 11.30 p.m.–5 a.m.; Sunday 7 p.m.–1 a.m.; closed Monday and Thursday. Entrance Tuesday, Wednesday and Friday 60 F; Saturday 70 F; Sunday 30 F.
Eclectic choice of live music—new wave, pop, rock, funk, rap, varieties, and theme nights.

LE SAINT   **24** P8   Ⓜ Saint-Michel
7, rue Saint-Séverin (5th); tel. 43.25.50.04. 11 p.m.–5 a.m. Admission free.
Tiny, crowded nightclub; music from the Forties to Eighties.

LE SLOW-CLUB   **24** P9   Ⓜ Châtelet
130, rue de Rivoli (1st); tel. 42.33.84.30. Tuesday to Thursday
9.30 p.m.–2.30 a.m.; Friday 9.30 p.m.–3 a.m.; Saturday 9.30 p.m.–
4 a.m. Drinks 50 F; Friday and Saturday 62 F.
One of the oldest jazz clubs in Paris. New Orleans jazz, bebop and
rock.

LE TOIT DE PARIS   **21** H8   Ⓡ (line C) Champ-de-Mars
Hôtel Hilton, 18, avenue de Suffren (15th); tel. 42.73.92.00. 6 p.m.–
2 a.m. Closed Sunday.
Cocktails named after the monuments visible from this bar on the
10th floor of the Hilton: Trocadéro, Eiffel, Opéra: all at 55 F. Glass of
champagne 55–70 F, snacks served until 11.30 p.m.

LES TROTTOIRS DE BUENOS AIRES   **24** P9   Ⓜ Châtelet
37, rue des Lombards (1st); tel. 42.33.58.37. Opens 8.30 p.m.; closed
Monday. Entrance 90 F, drinks from 25 F.
French varieties at 8.30 p.m.; professionals dance the Argentinian
tango at 10.30. Sunday, 5.30 p.m.–midnight, dance. Entrance fee 70 F,
includes first drink.

LE VILLAGE   **23/24** N8   Ⓜ Saint-Germain-des-Prés
7, rue Gozlin (6th); tel. 43.26.80.19. 10 p.m.–3 a.m.; Friday, Saturday,
Sunday 10 p.m.–5 a.m. Drinks 60 F, 70 F and 80 F; menu 79 F, 130 F,
180 F.
Alcoholic and soft drinks at the bar; good restaurant (8 p.m.–
0.30 a.m.), and piano jazz.

WHISKY À GOGO   **24** N8   Ⓜ Mabillon
57, rue de Seine (6th); tel. 43.29.60.01. Wednesday 10.30 p.m.–
4.30 a.m.; Friday and Saturday 10.30 p.m.–dawn; Sunday 3–8 p.m.
Closed Monday and Tuesday. Entrance and first drink, 50 F, 80 F
and 40 F, respectively.
The biggest discothèque in Saint-Germain-des-Prés.

148

CABARET AND VARIETIES

Constantly updated with new material, fast-paced and glittery shows
have more panache than ever.

ALCAZAR   **24** O8   Ⓜ Odéon
62, rue Mazarine (6th); tel. 43.29.02.20. Bookings by telephone from
10 a.m. Dinner and show 8.30 p.m., 510 F, 680 F and 900 F according
to menu; 10 p.m. show and half-bottle champagne 350 F.
Brassy, tongue-in-cheek and fun.

AU LAPIN AGILE   8 O15   Ⓜ Lamarck-Caulaincourt
22, rue des Saules (18th); tel. 46.06.85.87. 9 p.m.–2 a.m. Closed Monday. Show and drink 90 F.
One of the great old Montmartre cabarets, still showing off new talents—musicians and satires in racy French.

BAL DU MOULIN ROUGE   7/8 N14   Ⓜ Blanche
82, boulevard de Clichy (9th); tel. 46.06.00.19. 8 p.m. dinner dance, champagne and floor show, 530 F, 575 F and 645 F according to menu; 10 p.m. and midnight, champagne and floor show 365 F.
The good old Montmartre mill is still churning out glitz by the barrel.

CRAZY HORSE SALOON   14 J11   Ⓜ George V
12, avenue George-V (8th); tel. 47.23.32.32. 9 p.m. and 11.30 p.m.; Friday and Saturday 8.20 p.m., 10.35 p.m., 0.45 a.m. One drink in bar 195 F; two drinks on floor 290 F, 370 F or 470 F depending on how close you are to performers.
The world's most sophisticated striptease show—a play of light and shadow.

FOLIES BERGÈRE   16 P12   Ⓜ Cadet
32, rue Richer (9th); tel. 42.46.77.11. On-the-spot bookings 11 a.m.–6.30 p.m. Seats 72 F–361 F; evening 9 p.m.; Sunday matinée 3 p.m.; closed Monday.
The music hall that launched the careers of Josephine Baker and Mistinguett. Hasn't changed much since the Good Old Days—the high-stepping chorus girls in sequins and feathers keep up a crackling pace.

    Before the show you can dine (menu at 135 F, service 7.30–8.30 p.m.); or have a drink at the bar (open 7.30–9 p.m.).

LE LIDO   14 J12   Ⓜ George V
116 bis, avenue des Champs-Elysées (8th); tel. 45.63.11.61. Dinner dance, champagne and show 8 p.m., 530 F; champagne and show 10 p.m. and 0.15 a.m., 365 F.
Bluebell Girls in fishnet stockings.

149

MICHOU   8 O14   Ⓜ Pigalle
80, rue des Martyrs (18th); tel. 46.06.16.04/42.57.20.37. From 9 p.m.; dinner and show 470 F. Drink in bar 160 F.
Transvestites parody the big stars.

LE MILLIARDAIRE   14 J11   Ⓜ Franklin-D.-Roosevelt
68, rue Pierre-Charron (8th); tel. 42.25.25.17. Show at 10.30 p.m. and 0.30 a.m., "night show" at 2.30 a.m. Two drinks 310 F.
A handful of charming dancers comprise its treasures.

PARADIS LATIN   **33** Q7   Ⓜ Cardinal Lemoine
28, rue du Cardinal-Lemoine (5th); tel. 43.25.28.28. 8 p.m. dinner and
show 530 F, 680 F and 780 F depending on menu. 10 p.m. show and
champagne 365 F.
Musical, witty and peppy parodies.

LATE-NIGHT CAFÉS

A few "institutions" for a drink after the show. Le Fouquet's, Lipp and
the brasserie Mollard have so long been part of Parisian life they have
been listed as National Historic Monuments.

LE BRÉBANT   **16** P12   Ⓜ Bonne-Nouvelle
32, boulevard Poissonnière (9th); tel. 47.70.75.33. 8 a.m.–2 a.m.
In the last century, literary dinners flourished here, but now it's just a
cheery brasserie.

CAFÉ BEAUBOURG   **25** Q9   Ⓜ Hôtel-de-Ville
45, rue Saint-Merri (4th); tel. 48.87.63.96. 8 a.m.–2 a.m.
Warm, friendly atmosphere in a temple of modernity by architect
Christian de Portzamparc.

CAFÉ COSTES   **24** P10   Ⓜ Les Halles
4, rue Berger (1st); tel. 45.08.54.39. 8 a.m.–2 a.m.
A popular modern café famous for its "design" in plastic, imitation
leather and formica, by Philippe Starck. They serve alcohol, but
everyone comes for the hot chocolate.

CAFÉ DE FLORE   **23/24** N8   Ⓜ Saint-Germain-des-Prés
172, boulevard Saint-Germain (6th); tel. 45.48.55.26. 7 a.m.–1.30 a.m.
Once the haunt of intellectuals, now everyone's favourite. Snacks are
served, such as omelettes and sandwiches.

CAFÉ DE LA PAIX   **15/16** N12   Ⓜ Opéra
12, boulevard des Capucines (9th); tel. 42.68.12.13; 10 a.m.–1.30 a.m.
A national historic monument, designed by the same architect as the
Opéra, in the same opulent style.

LA CLOSERIE DES LILAS   **32** N5   Ⓡ (line B) Port-Royal
171, boulevard du Montparnasse (6th); tel. 43.26.70.50. Noon–
1.30 a.m.
It started life as a coaching station, and has been going strong ever
since. Strindberg, Modigliani, André Breton and Lenin scratched their

names on the tables, while a copper plaque honours Hemingway at the spot where he wrote *The Sun Also Rises*. Today's clientele is a mixture of writers, artists, yuppies and people who want to be seen.

LA COUPOLE **31** M5 Ⓜ Vavin
102, boulevard du Montparnasse (14th); tel. 43.20.14.20. 7 a.m.–2 a.m.
Famous old café-restaurant, a bastion of intellectuals and artists. Despite recent renovation, the Art Deco pillars are the originals, protected as historic features.

Next door at no. 100, there's a dance hall where all ages of singles and couples meet and mix. All styles of dancing, lots of coloured light effects. Saturday and Sunday 3–7 p.m.; Friday and Saturday 9 p.m.–3 a.m. Entrance and first drink 80 F; Friday evening 90 F.

LES DEUX MAGOTS **23/24** N8 Ⓜ Saint-Germain-des-Prés
170, boulevard Saint-Germain (6th); tel. 45.48.55.25; 7.30 a.m.–1.30 a.m.
Not quite the intellectual spot it once was, nevertheless its terrace and view on the church haven't lost their charm.

LE DÔME **31** M5 Ⓜ Vavin
108, boulevard du Montparnasse (14th); tel. 43.35.25.81. 8 a.m.–2 a.m. closed Monday.
Old-fashioned décor, with an interesting collection of photos of Montparnasse at the height of its glory. Jean-Paul Sartre used to spend his afternoons here.

LE FOUQUET'S **14** J12 Ⓜ George V
99, avenue des Champs-Elysées (8th); tel. 47.23.70.60; 9 a.m.–2 a.m.
It has long been the most famous rendezvous spot on the Champs-Elysées. Stylish restaurant, as well as the terrace café and bar indoors.

151

LIPP **23/24** N8 Ⓜ Saint-Germain-des-Prés
151, boulevard Saint-Germain (6th); tel. 45.48.53.91. 11 a.m.–2 a.m.
This celebrated brasserie attracts its share of celebrities.

MOLLARD **15** M13 Ⓜ Saint-Lazare
115, rue Saint-Lazare (8th); tel. 43.87.50.22. noon–1 a.m.
The opulent Art Moderne décor is worth a detour.

LE SELECT **31** M5 Ⓜ Vavin
99, boulevard du Montparnasse (6th); tel. 45.48.38.24. 8.30 a.m.–3 a.m.
Popular with admen and their acolytes.

Thousands of hotels cater to the annual throng of several million visitors. Officially they are divided into five categories, from one-star to four-star luxury, according to the amenities offered and the degree of comfort. In drawing up our list we took into account value for money (not indicated by the official classification), special charm...or high quality.

By law, tariffs should be posted outside each establishment, at the reception desk and behind the door of every room. Breakfast is not always included in the room rate, and it is only served in the room in hotels with three or four stars. It is usually "continental"—the hot drink of your choice, a roll or croissant or slices of baguette, butter and jam.

It may be hard to find a room in Paris during trade fairs and exhibitions, so you'd be well advised to book as soon as you can. Even in the middle of the winter, whole regiments of furniture salesmen or booksellers might descend on the capital, taking all the hotels by storm. Rooms also fill up quickly at Easter, May weekends, September and October, and Christmas.

You can obtain a complete list of hotel addresses from the **French National Tourist Office,** 178 Piccadilly, London W1V 0AL; tel. (01) 493-6594.

UNDER 300 F

All the rooms in the hotels mentioned in this section have bath or shower, and toilet.

AUX TROIS PORTES★★   **26** T9   Ⓜ Bréguet-Sabin
44, boulevard Richard-Lenoir (11th); tel. 47.00.52.77. 22 rooms. Single or double 230 F, breakfast 22 F.

BONNE-NOUVELLE★★   **17** Q11   Ⓜ Bonne-Nouvelle
17, rue Beauregard (2nd); tel. 45.08.42.42. 20 rooms. Single 200–240 F, double 280–300 F, breakfast 22 F.

153

CROISÉS★★   **15** N12   Ⓜ Chaussée d'Antin
14, rue Joubert (9th); tel. 48.74.38.68. 32 rooms. Double 205–245 F, breakfast 20 F.

Hotels from the bland to the blasé, to welcome the flow of visitors.

HÔTEL DE L'EXPOSITION★★   **17** S11   Ⓜ République
4, boulevard de Magenta (10th); tel. 46.07.61.42. 27 rooms. Single 184–209 F, double 219–229 F, breakfast 18 F.

LE LAUMIÈRE★★   **10** U14   Ⓜ Laumière
4, rue Petit (19th); tel. 42.06.10.77. 54 rooms. Room 130–225 F; breakfast 20 F.

Panic Stations

If you have been unable to book a hotel room in advance, you can turn to the following organizations for help.
   Paris Néotel: tel. 40.44.81.81
   Resatel: tel. 45.26.60.69
   Paris Séjour Réservation: tel. 42.56.30.00
Or call at the **Paris Tourist Office**, 127, avenue des Champs-Elysées (8th); tel. 47.23.61.72. Map **13/14** H12; métro Charles-de-Gaulle–Etoile. Daily 9 a.m.–8 p.m. (no reservations by phone).

You may be able to find a studio or furnished flat through **Paris-Bienvenue:** 10, avenue de Villars (7th); tel. 47.53.80.81. Map **22** K8; métro Saint-François Xavier. Weekdays 9 a.m. to 7 p.m.

Young people can obtain clean, cheap accommodation through the AJF—**L'Acceuil des Jeunes en France**, which offers rooms for 1 to 6 people in hostels, university halls of residence and a certain number of 1- to 3-star hotels. Just call at one of the offices:

AJF-Beaubourg: 119, rue Saint-Martin (4th); tel. 42.77.87.80. Map **25** Q10; métro Châtelet. Monday to Saturday 9.30 a.m.–7 p.m. in winter, 8 p.m. in summer.

AJF-Saint-Michel: 139, boulevard Saint-Michel (5th); tel. 43.54.95.86. Map **32** O5; RER Port-Royal. Monday to Friday 10 a.m.–7 p.m.

AJF-Gare du Nord: Gare du Nord, Passage 4, 4, rue de Dunkerque (10th); tel. 42.85.86.19. Map **17** Q–R14; métro Gare du Nord. End May to mid-October open daily 7.30 a.m.–10 p.m.; outside these months open only during school holidays, Monday–Friday, 9 a.m.–6 p.m.

AJF-Hôtel de Ville: 16, rue du Pont-Louis-Philippe (4th); tel. 42.78.04.82. Map **25** R8; métro Pont-Marie/Saint-Paul. Monday to Friday 9.30 a.m.–6.30 p.m., June, July, August.

You can also book rooms through the AJF by writing, at least a month in advance, to one of the addresses listed above.

LE LIONCEAU★★   **37** M4   Ⓜ Denfert-Rochereau
22, rue Daguerre (14th); tel. 43.22.53.53. 9 rooms. Double 220–230 F, breakfast 20 F.

PARIS-BRUXELLES★★   **17** R11   Ⓜ République
4, rue Meslay (2nd); tel. 42.72.71.32. 38 rooms. Single or double 225 F, breakfast 18 F.

RÉSIDENCE ALHAMBRA★★   **18** S11   Ⓜ République
13, rue de Malte (11th); tel. 47.00.35.52. 50 rooms. Single or double 200–230 F, breakfast 20 F.

RÉSIDENCE DE BRUXELLES★★   **9** Q14   Ⓜ Barbès-Rochechouart
88, boulevard de la Chapelle (18th); tel. 46.06.87.40. 25 rooms. Single 140 F, double 180–210 F, breakfast 20 F.

ROYAL MONTMARTRE★★   **8** N14   Ⓜ Blanche
68, boulevard de Clichy (18th); tel. 46.06.22.91. 50 rooms. Doubles only, 140–240 F, breakfast 23 F.

SAINT-PIERRE★★   **24/32** O7   Ⓜ Cluny–La Sorbonne
4, rue de l'Ecole-de-Médecine (6th); tel. 46.34.78.80. 50 rooms. Single 210–250 F, double 226–266 F (breakfast included).

SELECT RASPAIL★★   **31** N4   Ⓜ Raspail
259, boulevard Raspail (14th); tel. 43.35.34.03. 20 rooms. Single or double 150–210 F, breakfast 17 F.

AGORA★★   **24/25** P10   Ⓜ Les Halles
7, rue de la Cossonnerie (1st); tel. 42.33.46.02. 29 rooms with bath or shower and toilet. Single 290–428 F, double 290–450 F, breakfast 28 F. Double-glazed windows muffle the murmur from the Forum des Halles and Centre Pompidou. The rooms are impeccably clean, and decorated with exquisite taste.

155

ALLIGATOR★★★   **31** M5   Ⓜ Edgar Quinet
39, rue Delambre (14th); tel. 43.35.18.40. 35 rooms with bath or shower and toilet. Single 295 F, double 395–445 F, breakfast 30 F. With a Roman-style atrium where you can lounge like a lizard on fine days.

L'AVENIR★★★   **31** N6   Ⓜ Saint-Sulpice
65, rue Madame (6th); tel. 45.48.84.54. 35 rooms, with bath or shower and toilet. Single or double room 310–370 F, breakfast 25 F. Well-run.

CLARET* **34** U5 Ⓜ Bercy
44, boulevard de Bercy (12th); tel. 46.28.41.31. 52 rooms with bath or shower and toilet. Single 290 F, double 380–500 F, breakfast 30 F. Each room is named after a Bordeaux, and you'll even find a bottle by your bedside.

DU COLLÈGE DE FRANCE **32** P7 Ⓜ Maubert-Mutualité
7, rue du Thénard (5th); tel. 43.26.78.36. 29 rooms with bath or shower and toilet. Double room 390–450 F, breakfast 25 F. On a quiet street just off Saint-Germain-des-Prés.

DES DUCS D'ANJOU **24** P9 Ⓜ Châtelet
1, rue Sainte-Opportune (1st); tel. 42.36.92.24. 38 rooms—34 with bath or shower and toilet and 4 with toilet only. Single 357–377 F, double 404 F, breakfast 27 F. Small rooms looking onto a little square.

ETOILE* **13/14** H13 Ⓜ Charles-de-Gaulle–Etoile
3, rue de l'Etoile (17th); tel. 43.80.36.94. 25 rooms with bath or shower and toilet. Single 450 F, double 470 F, breakfast 30 F. Deserves three stars for its excellent location, modern comforts and library-sitting room.

FAMILY **15** M11 Ⓜ Madeleine
35, rue Cambon (1st); tel. 42.61.54.84. 26 rooms with shower or bath and toilet. Single 300–450 F, double 350–450 F, breakfast 22 F. Great value in a posh neighbourhood.

KENSINGTON **22** J8 Ⓜ Ecole Militaire
79, avenue de la Bourdonnais (7th); tel. 47.05.74.00. 26 rooms, with bath or shower and toilet. Single 190–220 F, double 220–350 F, breakfast 24 F. Unaffected décor in cork and jute.

LENOX* **23** N9 Ⓜ Solférino/Saint-Germain-des-Prés
9, rue de l'Université (7th); tel. 42.96.10.95. 34 rooms with bath or shower and toilet. Single 360–450 F, double 450–490 F, breakfast 30 F. Touches of refinement—and Left-Bank charm.

156 **LENOX-MONTPARNASSE*** **31** M5 Ⓜ Vavin
15, rue Delambre (14th); tel. 43.35.34.50. 52 rooms with bath or shower and toilet. Single or double 410–550 F, breakfast 30 F. Newer than the Lenox, above, but with similar amenities.

LA LOUISIANE* **24** N8 Ⓜ Mabillon
60, rue de Seine (6th); tel. 43.29.59.30. 79 rooms—75 with bath or shower and toilet, 4 with separate washbasin and toilet. Single 250–300 F, double 350–450 F, breakfast 25 F. Tiny, attractive, but you'll have to reserve well in advance.

MAGELLAN★★ **5** H14 Ⓜ Péreire
17–19, rue Jean-Baptiste-Dumas (17th); tel. 45.72.44.51. 75 rooms with bath or shower and toilet. Single 265–367 F, double 367 F, breakfast 23 F. Not far from the Défense.

DES MARRONNIERS★★★ **23/24** N8 Ⓜ Saint-Germain-des-Prés
21, rue Jacob (6th); tel. 43.25.30.60. 37 rooms with bathrooom or shower and toilet. Single 265–285 F, double 380–455 F, breakfast 25 F. The building is a historic monument. Charming courtyard garden, rustic décor and quiet atmosphere.

MODERN HOTEL LYON★★★ **26** T6 Ⓜ Gare de Lyon
3, rue Parrot (12th); tel. 43.43.41.52. 52 rooms with bath or shower and toilet. Single 295–410 F, double 450–470 F, breakfast 32 F. Sound-proofed against the train station bustle.

NOUVEL HÔTEL★★ **27** W6 Ⓜ Nation
24, avenue du Bel-Air (12th); tel. 43.43.01.81. 28 rooms—22 with bath or shower and toilet, 6 with separate washbasin and toilet. Single 185–295 F, double 295–385 F, breakfast 35 F. Has retained its charm and its little garden, despite frequent modernization.

OUEST HÔTEL★★ **7** L14 Ⓜ Rome
165, rue de Rome (17th); tel. 42.27.50.29. 50 rooms—48 with bath or shower and toilet, 2 with separate washbasin and toilet. Single 190–260 F, double 210–280 F, breakfast 23 F. Cosy and comfortable.

PASSY EIFFEL★★★ **21** F9 Ⓜ Passy
10, rue de Passy (16th); tel. 45.25.55.66. 50 rooms with bath or shower and toilet. Single 420–450 F, double 450–480 F, breakfast 30 F. The classic décor is an indication of its quality.

LE PAVILLON★★ **22** K9 Ⓜ Invalides/Latour-Maubourg
54, rue Saint-Dominique (7th); tel. 45.51.42.87. 19 rooms—17 with bath or shower and toilet, 2 with separate washbasin and toilet. Single 305 F, double 325–440 F, breakfast 29 F. There's nothing monastic about this one-time convent except for the cell-sized rooms!

157

PERREYVE★★ **31** N6 Ⓜ Saint-Placide/Rennes
63, rue Madame (6th); tel. 45.48.35.01. 30 rooms with bath or shower and toilet. Single 270–325 F, double 307 F, extra bed 150 F, breakfast 26 F. Just a few steps from the peaceful Luxembourg gardens.

PLAISANT★★ **33** Q7 Ⓜ Maubert-Mutualité
50, rue des Bernardins (5th); tel. 43.54.74.57. 24 rooms—14 with bath or shower and toilet, 10 with separate washbasin and toilet. Single or double 140–300 F, breakfast 20 F. As pleasant as its name.

QUEEN'S★★   **20** D/E7   Ⓜ Michel-Ange–Auteuil
4, rue Bastien-Lepage (16th); tel. 42.88.89.85. 22 rooms with bath or shower and toilet. Single 210–310 F, double 310–410 F, breakfast 22 F. Attractive, comfortable rooms, modern paintings on the walls.

RENNES-MONTPARNASSE★★★   **31** M6   Ⓜ Montparnasse-Bienvenüe
151, rue de Rennes (6th); tel. 45.48.97.38. 41 rooms with bath or shower and toilet. Single or double 350–450 F, breakfast 30 F. Ask for a room at the back—the front ones are on a noisy street.

RIBOUTTÉ-LAFAYETTE★★   **16** P13   Ⓜ Cadet
5, rue Riboutté (9th); tel. 47.70.62.36. 24 rooms with bath or shower and toilet. Single 320 F, double 324 F, 3-bed 450 F, breakfast 20 F. Tiny rooms.

SAINT-LOUIS★★   **25** Q8   Ⓜ Pont Marie
75, rue Saint-Louis-en-l'Ile (4th); tel. 46.34.04.80. 21 rooms with bath or shower and toilet. Double 430–590 F, breakfast 30 F. A beautiful old house with simple, refined rooms. But five storeys high and no lift.

SAINT-THOMAS-D'AQUIN★★   **23** M8   Ⓜ Rue du Bac
3, rue du Pré-aux-Clercs (7th); tel. 42.61.01.22. 21 rooms with bath or shower and toilet. Single 320–382 F, double 415 F (breakfast included). A friendly welcome.

SOLFÉRINO★★   **23** M9   Ⓜ Chambre des Députés
91, rue de Lille (7th); tel. 47.05.85.54. 33 rooms—27 with bath or shower and toilet, 6 with separate washbasin and toilet. Single 215–362 F, double 388–525 F (breakfast included). Calm and relaxing setting, near the Orsay Museum.

DE VARENNE★★★   **23** L9   Ⓜ Varenne
44, Rue de Bourgogne (7th); tel. 45.51.45.55. 24 rooms with bath or shower and toilet. Single 320 F, double 370–470 F, breakfast 30 F. Very popular—book well in advance.

158 **DU VIEUX MARAIS★★**   **25** Q9   Ⓜ Rambuteau
8, rue du Plâtre (4th); tel. 42.78.47.22. 30 rooms with bath or shower and toilet. Single 250–375 F (without breakfast), double 400–425 F (breakfast included), breakfast 22 F. In the heart of old Paris, its rooms are kept spotlessly clean.

WELCOME★★   **24** N8   Ⓜ Odéon
66, rue de Seine (6th); tel. 46.34.24.80. 30 rooms with bath or shower and toilet. Single 225 F, double 320–380 F, breakfast 24 F. Where it's all happening in Saint-Germain-des-Prés.

UP TO 1,500 F

ALEXANDER★★★★   **13** G11   Ⓜ Victor Hugo
102, avenue Victor-Hugo (16th); tel. 45.53.64.65. 62 rooms with bath or shower and toilet. Single 655 F, double 830 F, suite 119 F (breakfast included). Tasteful, comfortable, quiet, and a courteous welcome.

D'ANGLETERRE★★★   **23/24** N8   Ⓜ Saint-Germain-des-Prés
44, rue Jacob (6th); tel. 42.60.34.72. 29 rooms with bath or shower and toilet. Single 350–440 F, double 500–700 F, breakfast 28 F. A historic staircase takes you to quality rooms.

BRADFORD★★★   **14** K12   Ⓜ Saint-Philippe-du-Roule
10, rue Saint-Philippe-du-Roule (8th); tel. 43.59.24.20. 46 rooms with bath or shower and toilet. Single 490 F, double 520 F, suites 630 F, breakfast included. A specially pleasant, quiet hotel near the Champs-Elysées.

CAYRÉ★★★   **23** M8   Ⓜ Rue du Bac
4, boulevard Raspail (7th); tel. 45.44.38.88. 130 rooms with bath or shower and toilet. Single 870 F, double 900 F. Huge rooms, much favoured by artists and writers.

CLARIDGE-BELLMAN L★★★★   **14** J11   Ⓜ Franklin-D.-Roosevelt
37, rue Francois-1er (8th); tel. 47.23.54.42. 42 rooms with bath or shower and toilet. Single 970 F, double 1150 F, breakfast 63 F. A new look to the old Claridge.

DES DEUX-ÎLES★★★   **25** R7   Ⓜ Pont Marie
59, rue Saint-Louis-en-l'Ile (4th); tel. 43.26.13.35. 17 rooms with bath or shower and toilet. Single 500 F, double 600 F, breakfast 35 F. Exquisite rooms, but dolls'-house size.

DUMINY-VENDÔME★★★   **15/23** M11   Ⓜ Tuileries
3–5, rue du Mont-Thabor (1st); tel. 42.60.32.80. 79 rooms with bath or shower and toilet. Single 450 F, double 595–715 F, breakfast included. Brass beds and flowery wallpaper, but modern amenities.

ÉDOUARD-VII★★★★   **15/16** N11   Ⓜ Opéra **159**
39, avenue de l'Opéra (2nd); tel. 42.61.56.90. 100 rooms—93 with bath or shower and toilet, 7 with separate washbasin and toilet. Single 700 F, double 880 F. A stone's throw from the Opéra.

ÉLYSÉES-MAUBOURG★★★   **22** K9   Ⓜ La Tour-Maubourg
35, boulevard de La Tour-Maubourg (7th); tel. 45.56.10.78. 28 rooms, 2 suites, all with bath or shower and toilet. Single or double 450–650 F, suite 700 F, breakfast included. Friendly, attractive. Tiny indoor courtyard for tea.

HOLIDAY INN L****   **17** S11   Ⓜ République
10, place de la République (11th); tel. 43.55.44.34. 333 rooms with bath
or shower and toilet. Single 950 F, double 1,200–1,250 F. A very comfortable modern hotel behind a 19th-century façade.

HÔTEL FOREST HILL***   **29** F5   Ⓜ Balard
1, boulevard Victor (15th); tel. 40.60.16.16. 125 rooms and 5 suites,
with bathrooms. Single 450 F and 650 F, double 590 F and 790 F, suite
950 F, breakfast buffet 50 F. It looks like a ship sailing off into the
night.

LE MÉRIDIEN-MONTPARNASSE PARIS***   **31** L5   Ⓜ Gaieté
19, rue du Commandant-René-Mouchotte (14th); tel. 43.20.15.51. 950
rooms with bath or shower and toilet. Single 1,100 F, double 1,250 F,
breakfast 58 F. Big and comfortable, but low ceilings make it seem a
bit claustrophobic.

REGENT'S GARDEN***   **13/14** H13   Ⓜ Ternes
6, rue Pierre-Demours (17th); tel. 45.74.07.30. 40 rooms with bath or
shower and toilet. Single 450–700 F, double 560–800 F, breakfast 30 F.
The garden is indeed splendid enough for royalty.

Forest Hill Aquaboulevard
4, rue Louis-Armand (15th); tel. 40.60.10.00; métro Balard. The
Aquaboulevard, as everyone calls it, is a low building at the foot of
the Sofitel hotel, with two lopped-off pyramids at one end.
   Inside, it's a sportsman's dream. Tennis, golf and shooting clubs,
swimming pools and water chutes, billiards, bowling, pétanque—
everything you can imagine. Even sport-haters can have a quiet
game of bridge, bet on the races, or relax in a seaweed bath.
   Children from 2 to 6 years can be parked in a playgroup
(halte-garderie); their big brothers and sisters (6 to 13 years) are
welcome to visit the "Archipel des Enfantaisies", a kind of youth
club, where qualified monitors will keep an eye on them. There's a
juniors' bar, a mini-disco, games, video arcades and a library.
   Not to mention the four restaurants, ten bars, banquet halls and
an auditorium seating 2,000 spectators for tennis tournaments,
concerts or seminars.

BRISTOL L★★★★   **14** K12   Ⓜ Saint-Philippe-du-Roule
112, rue du Faubourg Saint-Honoré (8th); tel. 42.66.91.45. 200 rooms with bath or shower and toilet. Single 1,635–2,265 F, double 2,767–3,330 F, breakfast 95 F. A true palace—marble halls, antiques, garden, rooftop swimming pool.

INTER-CONTINENTAL PARIS★★★★   **15/23** M11   Ⓜ Tuileries
3, rue de Castiglione (1st); tel. 42.60.37.80. 500 rooms with bath or shower and toilet. Single 1,900 F, double 2,200 F, breakfast 90 F, American breakfast 130 F. Modern amenities in a historic building designed by Charles Garnier, architect of the Opéra.

L'HÔTEL L★★★★   **24** N9   Ⓜ Saint-Germain-des-Prés
13, rue des Beaux-Arts (6th); tel. 43.25.27.22. 27 rooms with bath or shower and toilet. Single 850–1,300 F, double 850–1,700 F, breakfast 70 F. Every room has a different décor. Oscar Wilde died in one of them in 1900.

PLAZA-ATHÉNÉE L★★★★   **14/22** J11   Ⓜ Alma-Marceau
25, avenue Montaigne (8th); tel. 47.23.78.33. 220 rooms with bath or shower and toilet. Single 1,700–2,100 F, double 2,370–3,070 F, suite 3,740–4,950, breakfast 100 F. There's no place more chic than this.

RAPHAËL L★★★★   **13** H12   Ⓜ Kléber
17, avenue Kléber (16th); tel. 45.02.16.00. 88 rooms with bath or shower and toilet. Single 1,200–1,400 F, double 1,400–1,600 F, suite 1,900–2,300 F, breakfast 70 F. Preferred by many cinema stars as much for its quiet as for its elaborate furnishings.

RÉSIDENCE MAXIM'S   **14** K11   Ⓜ Champs-Elysées
DE PARIS L★★★★   –Clemenceau
42, avenue Gabriel (8th); tel. 45.61.96.33. 43 rooms with bath or shower and toilet. Single or double 2,000 F, breakfast 90 F, American breakfast 145 F. The décor is signed Cardin.

RITZ L★★★★   **15** M11   Ⓜ Opéra
15, place Vendôme (1st); tel. 42.60.38.30. 164 rooms with bath or shower and toilet. Single 1,995 F, double 2,460 F, suite 3,700 F, breakfast 110 F. A legend. Beautiful terrace garden, excellent restaurant, cooking school, nightclub-discotheque, pool, health club and squash court.

A BREATH OF FRENCH AIR

When Paris is buzzing all round you, when you can't take another minute of pavement pounding—slow down, get off the boulevards and take a deep breath. There are, indeed, quiet ways of seeing the city.

Paris is quite different (and perhaps even more lovely) seen from the water. The high seats of a sightseeing coach give another dimension to streets you may have trodden many times before. You can get a bird's-eye view from a helicopter—or a worm's-eye view from below. But nothing can compare with a leisurely stroll to see the details, to get the real feel of Paris. And wherever you go, there's always a café terrace, a park or garden to rest your weary feet.

BOAT RIDES

BATEAUX-MOUCHES   22 J10   Ⓜ Alma-Marceau
Landing stage of the Pont de l'Alma, right bank (7th); tel. 42.25.96.10.
Boat trip lasting 75 minutes, departure every half hour, daily 10 a.m.–noon and 1.30–7 p.m. Adults 30 F, children 4–12 years 10 F.
Illuminated cruise, 75 minutes, departure every half hour, daily 8 p.m.–10 or 11 p.m. (in winter, one cruise only at 9 p.m.). Adults 30 F, children 4–12 years 15 F.
Lunchtime cruise, daily except Monday, 1–2.45 p.m. Adults 300 F, children 150 F.
Dinnertime cruise, daily 8.30–10.45 p.m., 500 F (black tie; children not admitted).
Afternoon tea cruise, Saturday and Sunday 3.45–5.15 p.m., adults 60 F, children 40 F.

The usual tour leaves from the Pont de l'Alma, turns round the Pont Mirabeau, then goes up the Seine to Pont de Sully and to the end of the Ile Saint-Louis, returning from there. Outdoor and indoor seating.

CANAUXRAMA
Tel. 46.07.13.13. Reservation advised.
Canal Saint-Martin: from La Villette dock to the Port de l'Arsenal, daily 9.15 a.m. and 2.30 p.m. Departure 5 bis, quai de la Loire (19th);

Once you've taken pictures of all the sights, try to spot who's who in the faces on the wall.

map **10** T14; métro Jaurès. From Port de l'Arsenal to La Villette, daily 9.30 a.m. and 2.30 p.m. Departure opposite 50, boulevard de la Bastille (12th); map **26** T7; métro Bastille. Price 70 F; children under 12 45 F (70 F on Saturday and Sunday afternoons and public holidays); under 6 free.

Canal de l'Ourcq: full-day cruise from La Villette dock to Meaux, return by coach; daily except Wednesday, 8.30 a.m.–7 p.m. Departure 5 bis, quai de la Loire (19th); map **10** T14; métro Jaurès. Price: 180 F (no meals included).

The Canal Saint-Martin goes through Paris, while the Canal de l'Ourcq takes you through the Ile de France region, with a stop for a lunch break. Either take a picnic or opt for a restaurant near the stop.

PARIS CANAL   **23** M10   Ⓜ Solférino
Embark at Quai Anatole-France, at the foot of the musée d'Orsay (7th); or at the Centre d'information du Parc de la Villette (19th); map **11** W16; *métro Porte de Pantin.* Tel. 48.74.75.30. Reservation advised. From 25 March to 12 November, 3-hour cruises twice a day in each direction. Departure from Quai Anatole-France at 9.30 a.m. and 2 p.m.; from La Villette 9.45 a.m. and 2.30 p.m. Adults 90 F, children 6–12 50 F.

The two boats–*la Patache Eautobus* and *le Canotier*—take you through Paris along the Seine and the Canal Saint-Martin. The same company also offers day trips along the Seine and the Marne.

VEDETTES PARIS ILE-DE-FRANCE   **21** G9   Ⓜ Passy
Landing stage of the Port de Suffren, right bank (7th); tel. 47.05.71.29. Trips last 60 minutes; departures every half hour, daily 10 a.m.–11 p.m. (1–5 p.m. in winter). Prices: adults 30 F, children 15 F.

There are several different kinds of cruises—with lunch, dinner, or on special themes. A typical one leaves from the foot of the Eiffel Tower and ends at the Ile Saint-Louis.

VEDETTES DU PONT-NEUF   **24** O9   Ⓜ Pont-Neuf
Landing stage of the Pont-Neuf, Square du Vert-Galant (1st); tel. 46.33.98.38.
Trips last 60 minutes; departure every half hour, daily 10 a.m.–noon and 1.30–6.30 p.m. (in winter 10.30 a.m., 11.15 a.m., noon, and every half hour from 2 to 5 p.m.). Illuminated cruise every half hour from 9–10.30 p.m. Adults 30 F, children under 10 12 F.

The boats glide past the Eiffel Tower, round the islands and back to their departure point.

COACH TOURS

CITYRAMA   **23** N10   Ⓜ Palais-Royal
4, place des Pyramides (1st); tel. 42.60.30.14. Departures from the same address. Half-price for children 4–10 years, under 4 free.

Tour Cityrama: this 2-hour tour, taking in the main sights, is a good way to become familiar with the layout of Paris. Departure every day at 9.30 a.m., 11 a.m., 1.30 p.m., 2 p.m. Extra departure at 10 a.m. Saturday and Sunday. 100 F. Double-decker coach, taped commentary in 8 languages, individual headphones.

Illuminations: from Place Vendôme to the Opéra, including the Louvre, Saint-Germain-des-Prés, Notre-Dame, the Champs-Elysées, the Arc de Triomphe, the Eiffel Tower and Place Pigalle. Departure every evening at 8.30 p.m. Reservation compulsory; 585 F.

Paris ''X'': for adults only. A naughty night out, including a ride through the city, strip-tease in a Pigalle cabaret, and a live show. Departure every evening at 8.30 p.m. Reservation compulsory; 465 F.

PARIS VISION   **23** N10   Ⓜ Tuileries
214, rue de Rivoli (1st); tel. 42.60.30.01/42.60.31.25. Tours depart from the same address. Half-price for children 4–12 years, under 4 free.

Découverte Paris Vision, a 2-hour discovery of Paris, its history and great monuments. Leaves daily at 9.30 a.m., 11 a.m., 1.30 p.m., 2 p.m. Extra departure Saturday and Sunday, 10 a.m. 100 F. Taped commentary and background music.

Illuminations, the "City of Light" at night-time. Every evening at 9 p.m. 120 F.

Paris interdit, adults only: a sexy revue and an erotic show. Every evening at 9 p.m. 440 F.

PARIS FROM THE AIR

HÉLICAP   **29** F4   Ⓜ Balard **165**
Héliport de Paris, 4, avenue de la Porte-de-Sèvres (15th); tel. 45.57.75.51.
Monday to Friday, 22-minute tour of Paris 510 F per person (minimum 4 people). 8-minute flight over the Défense 210 F per person. 12-minute flight over Versailles 310 F per person.

HÉLI-FRANCE   **29** F4   ⓜ Balard
*Héliport de Paris, 4, avenue de la Porte-de-Sèvres (15th); tel.
45.57.53.67.*
Daily, 20–22-minute flight over Paris 530 F per person (minimum
4 people). Departure times vary according to availability of hel-
icopters and pilots.

Puffing round Paris
Once or twice a month, the railway buffs of the **International
ferroviaire club** organize unusual train rides round the periphery
of the city, drawn by a steam engine dating from 1922. It's best to
reserve your seat in advance.
   They also arrange trips into the outskirts in an old platform bus,
a Thirties' métro train or a barge—with commentary and photo
stops.
46, avenue de Savigny, 93600 Aulnay-sous-Bois; tel. 43.84.78.17.

PARIS UNDERGROUND

THE CATACOMBS   **37** N4   ⓜ Denfert-Rochereau
*1, place Denfert-Rochereau (14th); tel. 43.22.47.63 (answering ma-
chine outside office hours, in French). Tuesday to Friday 2–4 p.m.;
Saturday and Sunday 9–11 a.m. and 2–4 p.m. Guided tour Wednesday at 2.45 p.m. (maximum 4 people). Visits for groups (maximum 30)
can be arranged.*
An underground attraction for those with a taste for the macabre.
This vast network of corridors was scooped out to provide building
materials above ground and a mass burial place down below. The
remains of 6 million unidentified dead lay here, transferred from
overcrowded cemeteries across the city or buried in times of mass
deaths. Skulls and bones are sometimes laid out in gruesomely
decorative arrangements. You'll need a flashlight.

THE SEWERS   **22** J10   ⓜ Alma-Marceau
*Les égouts de Paris, Place de la Résistance (7th); tel. 47.05.10.29.
Wednesday to Sunday, 3–8 p.m. The visit (unguided) lasts 30–
60 minutes.*
See Paris from underneath—through the sewers tracing a parallel
network of streets. They cover 2,100 kilometres (you won't have to
walk quite that far), evacuating 1,500,000 cubic metres of waste
waters per day. Conditions are perfectly hygienic.

LEISURELY WALKS

We have included here a few well-known quarters, such as the Marais, and others that visitors to Paris rarely venture into—the colourful "outer" arrondissements, mainly inhabited by immigrants who have conferred their own special atmosphere to these old working-class districts.

Bonne Journée, the brainchild of an American lady in Paris, Laurie Lesser-Chamberlain, organizes walking tours in English of specific quarters, such as the Marais, or tours on special themes, like Hemingway's Paris (the places he lived in and the bars he propped up) or the History of Crime (from the prisons of Châtelet to the gallows at Place Maubert). Reservations essential. Each walk lasts 2–3 hours. 6, place Charles-Dullin (18th); tel. 46.06.24.17, map **8** O14; métro Anvers/Abbesses.

THE BANKS OF THE SEINE

The river embankments used to be the domain of Paris's *clochards,* or tramps, until they were chased away by the *voie express Georges-Pompidou,* rapid transit lanes conceived to relieve through-traffic. But some space has been left for strollers and sunbathers round the two islands, in particular the Square du Vert-Galant at the western tip of the Ile de la Cité.

The *bouquinistes* and their 230 "wagon green" stalls along the parapets of the Seine are a familiar sight for both casual strollers and book lovers, who often unearth an interesting old edition from the mass of books, posters, prints and postcards. The *bouquinistes* originally set up on the Pont-Neuf in the 17th century, selling old books and pamphlets out of boxes. Established booksellers on the Ile de la Cité were enraged and drove them off to the banks of the Seine, where they have remained ever since—though they did not become a permanent fixture until after World War I.

The City of Paris grants concessions for stalls located mainly on the Quai des Grands-Augustins (music criticism and artistic bindings), Quai Saint-Michel (antiquarian editions), Quai de Montebello (novels, history, engravings, old objects, postcards) and Quai de la Tournelle (royal edicts) on the left bank; Quai de la Mégisserie, Quai de Gesvres and Quai de l'Hôtel-de-Ville on the right.

167

BELLEVILLE   18 U12   Ⓜ Belleville

This one-time village was incorporated into Paris in the 1860s. It became a working-class district, and has now been taken over almost entirely by immigrants—Rue de Belleville serves as a frontier between the Asian and North African communities. Most of the old houses have been demolished and replaced by anonymous-looking high-rises, though a few narrow, picturesque streets and passageways remain.

The sugary fragrance of Far-Eastern sweets hits you as you walk past the bakeries and exotic restaurants of Rue de Belleville, Boulevard de la Villette, rues Civiale and Louis-Bonnet. Whereas rues Ramponneau and de l'Orillon, or Boulevard de Belleville, could be the back streets of Tunis or Marrakesh.

CHINATOWN   39 Q/R3   Ⓜ Place d'Italie

Though it's called the Quartier Italie, this part of the 13th arrondissement has a distinctly Asian air. During the 1970s, hundreds of new apartment blocks were built south of Place d'Italie to accommodate the refugees from South-east Asia. Close-knit communities of Cambodians, Laotians, Vietnamese and Chinese have created a real home-from-home, complete with pagoda-like boutiques, Chinese groceries and exotic restaurants.

To get an idea of the district as it used to be, look around Rue de la Butte-aux-Cailles. Its swimming pool has been supplied with natural ferruginous water since 1924.

The 13th arrondissement also has some spectacular examples of contemporary architecture—the *Hautes-Formes,* Rue de Tolbiac (see page 57); and buildings along Avenue de Choisy. Note, too, Richard Serra's sculpture in the Square de Choisy, installed in 1985.

LA GOUTTE-D'OR   8/9 Q15   Ⓜ Barbès-Rochechouart

This district in the 18th arrondissement is the most cosmopolitan of Paris—at least 30 nationalities mingle with the basic French population, very much attached to the neighbourhood, and many of them young craftsmen. Rue de la Goutte-d'Or runs through the middle of the area delimited by Boulevard Barbès, Rue Myrha, Rue Stephenson and Boulevard de la Chapelle. Its name, "Golden Drop", came from the wine produced there in the 15th century when it was a vineyard.

Poor peasants from the countryside settled here in the 19th century; Emile Zola relates the sad life of one of them in his novel *L'Assommoir* (Drunkard). Waves of immigrants followed—Arabs, Africans and West Indians. The district always had a rather seedy reputation, but in the last few decades the buildings have been cleaned up and commerces have started to thrive. There's a preponderance of shops selling exotic fabrics—Addad, Toto-Soldes, Super-Afrique, El Fouta—in rues de la Goutte-d'Or and Polonceau, and on Sunday, several colourful markets attract crowds.

LE MARAIS   **25/26** Q/S8/9   Ⓜ Saint-Paul

The Marais has bravely withstood the onslaught of real estate developers over the years, providing a remarkably authentic record of the city's development from Henri IV at the end of the 16th century up to the Revolution. Built on land reclaimed from the swamps, it contains some of Europe's most elegant Renaissance-style houses, now transformed into museums and libraries. After a visit to Beaubourg or the superb Place des Vosges (see page 31), take the time to stroll through the old Jewish quarter along Rue des Rosiers and the neighbouring streets. It's a very lively district (except on Saturdays), and becoming ever more cosmopolitan with the arrival of Asian, Yugoslavian and Pied-noir communities. On Rue des Rosiers you'll discover the oldest Turkish baths *(hammam)* in Paris (dating from the 12th century). Don't miss Jo Goldenberg's deli (see page 95), the Chat perché (page 184) or Izraël (page 95).

PASSAGE BRADY   **17** Q/R12   Ⓜ Château d'Eau

This covered street in the 10th arrondissement has become a "Passage to India", a wonderful bazaar offering silks and brocades, embroidered cottons, heady spices, basmati rice and chapatis. Immigrants—mostly from Pondicherry—have opened up a succession of groceries, boutiques, restaurants and video clubs, spreading to neighbouring streets—Rue du Faubourg Saint-Denis and Rue Jarry.

LEAFY RETREATS

BOIS DE   **12** D11   Ⓜ Porte d'Auteuil
BOULOGNE   or Les Sablons

More blithely known as *Le Bois*, the forest on the western edge of Paris was left completely wild until 1852, when Napoleon III turned it into a place of recreation and relaxation for the people of Paris. Baron Haussmann's transformations were among his happier achievements. There are roads and paths for cycling and rambles, horse-trails, two boating lakes, restaurants and cafés, and the Longchamp and Auteuil racecourses. The Bois is not safe to wander at night (see page 135).

169

   One of the main attractions is the **Parc de Bagatelle,** with the city's most magnificent display of flowers and a famous rose garden with 8,000 plants. The little castle was the residence of Marie-Antoinette. Recently restored, it's an 18th-century gem.

Parc de Bagatelle, route de Sèvres (16th); métro Pont de Neuilly; tel. 40.67.97.00. Guided tours Saturday and Sunday at 2 and 4 p.m.

BOIS DE VINCENNES
M Porte Dorée

To the east of Paris, the Vincennes forest was the favourite hunting ground of Philippe Auguste and Saint Louis. It includes the Vincennes racecourse, the zoo (see page 174), and a flower garden.

The 15th–17th-century **château** (métro Château de Vincennes) is open from 10 a.m. to 5.15 p.m. (4.15 p.m. in winter).

CIMETIÈRE DE MONTMARTRE   7 N15
M Blanche

20, avenue Rachel (18th); tel. 43.87.64.24. 16 March to 5 November 7.30 a.m.–6 p.m.; Saturday 8.30 a.m.–6 p.m.; Sunday 9 a.m.–6 p.m. Winter 8 a.m.–5.30 p.m.; Saturday 8.30 a.m.–5.30 p.m.; Sunday 9 a.m.–5.30 p.m.

Several illustrious figures are buried in this tranquil little cemetery—Degas, Berlioz, Offenbach, Stendhal, Nijinski, Heine, Sacha Guitry—and Alphonsine Plessis, who inspired Alexandre Dumas's *La Dame aux camélias.*

CIMETIÈRE DU   27 W9
PÈRE-LACHAISE
M Philippe-Auguste

16, rue du Repos (20th); tel. 43.70.70.33. 16 March to 6 November 7.30 a.m.–6 p.m.; winter 8 a.m.–5.30 p.m.

This vast "City of the Dead" is an inspiring pilgrimage for tourists and Parisians alike. Named after Louis XIV's confessor, a member of the Jesuits who previously owned the land, the cemetery has long been renowned as the resting place for the heroes of the country's revolutions. You'll find many of the city's artists: Colette, Alfred de Musset, Rossini, Chopin, Ingres, Corot, La Fontaine, Molière, Sarah Bernhardt, Balzac, Delacroix, Bizet, Proust, Apollinaire, Isadora Duncan, Oscar Wilde, Gertrude Stein, and Edith Piaf, who still draws crowds here. And among them, Jim Morrison of the Doors. To find your way among the maze of tombs, ask for a map at the entrance.

ENCLOS BABYLONE   23 N8
M Sèvres-Babylone

7, rue de Babylone (7th).

A little country garden with espaliered apple and pear trees, donated to the city by the congregation of the Sisters of Charity.

JARDIN DU LUXEMBOURG   32 N6
RER (line B) Luxembourg

This park was created in 1613 along with the Palais du Luxembourg—today the seat of the Senate, beyond the pond where well-behaved children sail their boats. It is quite formal, with neat gravel avenues, though not as rigidly geometric as Versailles. To one side of the palace are statues of queens and princesses of France, to the other a monument to Eugène Delacroix by Dalou. The 17th-century Medicis fountain is the work of Salomon de Brosse.

You can play tennis or chess, roller-skate, join in a game of *boules*, or watch Punch and Judy. There's a playschool, a miniature car track, and donkey rides. Or you might just like to dream under the shade of the horse chestnuts, beeches and plane trees that were a major inspiration for the bucolic paintings of Watteau; there's a statue of him on the southern side.

JARDIN DES TUILERIES   23 M10   Ⓜ Concorde

A classical 17th-century garden by Le Nôtre, framed by the Terrasse des Feuillants on the Rivoli side and the Terrasse du Bord de l'Eau to the south, facing the Seine. The old Jeu de Paume museum occupies one corner at the Concorde side, with the Orangerie museum opposite. Behind the octagonal pond, geometrical arrangements of trees and paths lead up to the Carrousel arch and garden displaying several female nude statues by Maillol (1861–1944). The pilasters of the main gate at the Concorde end are topped by two equestrian statues by Coysevox, *Fame* and *Mercury*, brought from Marly in 1719.

For children there's a merry-go-round, puppet shows, donkey rides and a pond for sailing boats.

PARC DES   10 U13   Ⓜ Buttes-Chaumont
BUTTES-CHAUMONT

One of the city's most beautiful parks, created by Baron Haussman on a rubbish dump near the infamous Montfaucon gallows. The entrance is on Avenue J.-de-Liniers (19th). Children find it quite adventurous, with its grassy slopes, lake, waterfalls, and eery cavern.

PARC GEORGES BRASSENS   36 J3   Ⓜ Porte de Vanves

A fairly recent creation, named after the singer-poet, on the site of the old Vaugirard slaughterhouses, Rue Brancion (15th). A second-hand book market is held every Saturday and Sunday in the iron Baltard halls transferred from the old Halles.

PARC MONTSOURIS   38 O2   Ⓡ (line B) Cité Universitaire

Baron Haussman had the idea of transforming the wastelands and quarries along Boulevard Jourdan (14th) into a recreation ground, complete with lake and hillocks. There are swings, slides and a sandpit, and a handy restaurant, the Pavillon Montsouris. An unusual feature is the Bardo palace, a reproduction after a postcard of the bey's palace in Tunis.

171

SQUARE GEORGES CAIN   25 S9   Ⓜ Saint-Paul

14, rue Payenne (3rd).

A charming little garden, scattered with ancient sculpted stones discovered during renovations in the district.

WHAT TO DO WITH THE CHILDREN

Don't think twice about bringing your offspring to Paris—they'll love it. Even when the novelty of being abroad has worn off, even when they've been up the Eiffel Tower, down the Catacombs and round the Cité des Sciences, they'll find something fascinating to do—once they know where to look.

We have listed here the parks and gardens, museums, shows, boutiques and toyshops specially intended for children. They will, of course, also enjoy many of the museums, monuments and excursions described elsewhere in this book. We have included workshops wherever fluent French is not an absolute necessity to join in the fun.

And if you want a night out without the kids, leave them in the good hands of a baby-sitter from one of the reliable agencies mentioned on page 189. Your hotel may also have baby-sitting facilities.

OUTDOORS

Most of the city parks, and also the Bois de Boulogne and de Vincennes, have playgrounds, cycle trails, boat ponds, Punch and Judy, donkey rides and such. But the following offer a little bit more.

JARDIN D'ACCLIMATATION **12** E13 Ⓜ Les Sablons
Bois de Boulogne (16th); tel. 46.24.10.80. 10 a.m.–7 p.m. (6 p.m. in winter); Wednesday, Saturday, Sunday and holidays 2–5.30 p.m. Miniature train, doll's house, clockwork toys' village, enchanted river. Entrance fee plus extra charge for almost every activity.
You can take a little train at the Porte Maillot to get to the main entrance. A children's paradise, with playgrounds, merry-go-rounds, open-air circus, wild and tame animals, aviary. And the **Musée en Herbe**, an educational museum with creative workshops (see page 178).

JARDIN DES ENFANTS DES HALLES **24** P10 Ⓜ Les Halles
105, rue Rambuteau (1st); tel. 45.08.07.18. Tuesday, Wednesday, Thursday and Saturday 10 a.m.–7 p.m., Sunday 2–7 p.m. (from October to May 9 a.m.–noon and 2–6 p.m.)
For non-accompanied children from 7 to 12 years. Professional child-minders will take them into the heart of a volcano and onto a desert island. Adventure games on Wednesday at 2 p.m.

Toothy dragon delights thousands of children at La Villette.

JARDIN DES PLANTES   **33/34** S6   Ⓜ Gare d'Austerlitz
Place Valhubert (5th). Daily 8 a.m. (7.15 a.m. in summer) until nightfall.
Admission free, except for the menagerie.
Children can run about freely—as long as they don't trample the lawns. The gardens are planted out to represent typical country landscapes, every species neatly labelled.

Exotic plants thrive in the steamy heat of the glasshouses—mostly from Australia and Mexico. Don't miss the labyrinth, made up of many rare species, including the oldest cedar in France.

The **menagerie** is open from 9 a.m. to 6 p.m. (5 p.m. in winter). Close-up view of wild beasts, birds, cuddlies and creepy-crawlies.

PARC FLORAL DE PARIS   Ⓜ Château de Vincennes
Bois de Vincennes, 16, route de la Pyramide (12th); tel. 43.43.92.95.
Spring and autumn 9.30 a.m.–6 p.m.; summer 9.30 a.m.–8 p.m. week-
days, 9 p.m. Saturdays; winter 9.30 a.m.–5 p.m.
A vintage train, playgrounds, an old merry-go-round, miniature golf, boating lake, woods for picnicking and beautiful flowerbeds. The **Maison de la Nature** (tel. 43.28.47.63) presents the secrets of nature in a town environment, suitable for children of school age.

PARC ZOOLOGIQUE DE PARIS   Ⓜ Porte Dorée
53, avenue de Saint-Maurice (12th); tel. 43.43.84.95. 9 a.m.–6 p.m.
(5.30 p.m. in winter)
In the Bois de Vincennes, a spacious zoo with more than a thousand animals. Don't forget to take a bag of carrots and dry bread to feed the bears and monkeys.

AMUSEMENT PARKS

PARC MIRAPOLIS   Train from Gare Saint-Lazare to
Cergy-Saint-Christophe
Ⓡ (line A) Nanterre-Université
A free shuttle bus takes you from the station to Mirapolis. This is France's first attempt at a leisure theme park, based on Rabelais's outsize character Gargantua. Lusty, thumping fun for all, from the twistiest of hair-raising helter-skelters and Gargantua's gigantic roasting spits to the slightly more demure "Belle Epoque garden" or the "Land of Legends".

174
Mirapolis: Paris-Parc, route de Courdimanche, Cergy-Pontoise; tel.
34.43.20.00. Open mid-May to mid-October, daily from 10 a.m. to
7 p.m. (Saturday 9 p.m.). Reduced admission fee for large families.

PARC ASTÉRIX
Ⓜ Fort d'Aubervilliers

Uderzo's comic-strip character Asterix is France's answer to Mickey Mouse. And just as Mickey Mouse has his Magic Kingdom, so Asterix now has his own theme park, 40 km north of Paris in the heart of the "Gaul's Forest". Take the shuttle bus from the métro station or leave your chariot outside the gates (8,500 parking spaces).

Walk through the entrance, and you'll find yourself at the top of the Via Antica, lined with buildings inspired by Asterix's adventures in the Roman Empire—from Britain to Egypt. In the Gaul's village you'll meet indomitable Asterix and Obelix, as large as life—still holding out stubbornly against Roman invasion with a little help from the venerable druid Getafix (Panoramix, to the French) and his magic potion. There's a Roman city, complete with an arena where comic gladiator fights are staged, the Julius Caesar merry-go-round, and Ben Hur's dodgem chariots. You can take a Viking longship to sail across to the helter-skelter and roller-coaster on the far side of Dolphin Lake, or stay on dry land and watch the dolphins and sea-lions perform. Then walk along the Rue de Paris to see how the capital has evolved from Lutetia to today's city.

Attractions, shows, shops, snack bars, restaurants, currency exchange, nursery, and so on. Information office at entrance. Parc Astérix, Plailly; tel. 44.62.31.31. Open 30 April to 1 October, daily 10 a.m.–6 p.m.; Saturday and eves of holidays 10 a.m.–10 p.m. Free entrance for children under 3.

AQUARIUMS

AQUARIUM DU TROCADÉRO   **21** G10
Ⓜ Trocadéro

Jardin du Trocadéro (16th); tel. 47.23.62.95. 10 a.m.–5.30 p.m. (6.30 p.m. in summer).
All the freshwater fish of France.

AQUARIUM TROPICAL
Ⓜ Porte Dorée

Musée des Arts africains et océaniens, 293, avenue Daumesnil (12th); tel. 43.43.14.54. 10 a.m.–noon and 1.30–5.30 p.m., except Tuesday, Saturday afternoon and holidays. Free admission for children under 18.

175

Fish from all the seas and rivers in the world, in a hundred tanks.

CENTRE DE LA MER ET DES EAUX   **32** O6   Ⓡ Luxembourg

19, rue Saint-Jacques (5th); tel. 46.33.08.31. Tuesday to Friday 10 a.m.–12.30 p.m. and 1.15–5.30 p.m.; Saturday and Sunday 10 a.m.–5.30 p.m.

The finest specimens of tropical fauna, a permanent exhibition, and projections of Commandant Cousteau's films on Wednesdays, Saturdays and Sundays at 3 and 4 p.m.

CENTRE OCÉANIQUE   **24** P10   Ⓡ Châtelet–Les Halles
COUSTEAU   Ⓜ Louvre–Rue de Rivoli

Nouveau Forum des Halles (1st); tel. 40.26.13.78. Entrance Porte du Louvre or Porte du Jour. Daily, except Monday, noon–7 p.m. (ticket office closes at 5.30 p.m.)

An hour and a half is enough to descend 10,000 metres to the depths of the ocean and explore a sunken ship and a seaweed jungle, just as if you were with Commandant Cousteau and his team. But you won't feel a drop of water, or see a living fish. Thanks to the most sophisticated techniques, you get the impression that you're a real deep-sea diver. You'll discover marine animals, see how they see us, and learn to interpret the whales' song. Like Jonas, you can walk around inside a whale. There's a film and an exhibition on oceanography throughout the ages, and computer games and videos to answer all your questions.

WORKSHOPS

Cultural or educational workshops are organized by several museums (in French, unless otherwise mentioned). They are described below, but please refer to the museum section (pages 33–59) for the relevant addresses.

CENTRE GEORGES-POMPIDOU (see page 37)

Daily 2–6 p.m., except Tuesday, Sunday and holidays.

Park-a-kid free of charge while you visit the museum. Play group with organized activities such as dancing, painting, games, with English-speaking monitors. For children from 5 to 12 years old. Wednesday and Saturday (and every day during holidays) from 2.30–4 p.m. (Reserve in advance, the same day, from 2 p.m.)

CITE DES SCIENCES ET DE L'INDUSTRIE (see page 39)

The Inventorium takes in children Tuesdays, Thursdays and Fridays at 2 p.m. and 3.30 p.m.; Saturdays and Sundays 12.30, 2, 3.30 and 5 p.m.; sessions last 1½ hours.

Magic in the air
Every day, between 10 a.m. and 6 p.m., the **Musée Grévin** invites children from 4 years to a half-hour show of magic and mystery. *10, boulevard Montmartre (2nd); tel. 47.70.85.05. Map 16 O12; métro Montmartre.*

Two age groups, 3–6 and 6–12, for fascinating leisure activities including videos, Lego construction, and an introduction to the world of robots.

INSTITUT DU MONDE ARABE (see page 56)
Wednesday and Saturday at 2 p.m.
Children from 5 to 15 can learn all about the Arab world.

MÉDIATHÈQUE DES ENFANTS   **11** V16   Ⓜ Porte de la Villette
Wednesday, Saturday and Sunday, from 2 to 6.30 p.m. Admission free.
The resources centre on floor S1 of the Villette is devoted to children. All kinds of activities are proposed, from reading to participating in scientific experiments. There's a "story time" (in French), and cartoons on Saturday at 5 p.m.

MUSÉE D'ART MODERNE DE LA VILLE DE PARIS (see page 42)
Talks about the exhibitions, with painting or drawing. Wednesday 2.30–4 p.m., children from 8 years.
   The **Musée des Enfants** (16, avenue de New-York) holds temporary exhibitions designed specifically for children, and recreational workshops on artistic themes. Wednesday, Saturday and Sunday at 3 p.m.

MUSÉE DES ARTS AFRICAINS ET OCÉANIENS (see page 46)
Three workshops:
L'Afrique, la couleur, la métamorphose: Wednesday 10 a.m.–noon, free admission, 8–16 years. Load your children up with empty egg boxes, yoghourt pots, washing powder drums or any other salvaged material, and they'll transform them into a work of art.
Calligraphie: Saturday 2.30–4.30 p.m., from 14 years. Arab and Latin calligraphy.
Contes et légendes du bassin méditerranéen: Wednesday 2.30–4.30 p.m., 4–16 years, admission free. Tales and legends from Egypt, the Lebanon, Turkey, Greece, Spain, North Africa, Corsica and Sicily.

MUSÉE DU CHÂTEAU DE VERSAILLES (see page 198)
Lecture tours of the castle based on various themes, such as How the castle was built, A day in the life of the king, Louis XIV's family, etc.

177

Wednesday and Saturday at 2.30, free admission. For children up to 10 and from 10 to 15.

Lectures on more specialized themes—Marquetry, Personal hygiene, and so on—Wednesday 2 p.m., 8–15 years. Reserve in advance by phone (30.84.75.57).

MUSÉE GUIMET (see page 43)
Wednesday and Saturday at 3 p.m. Talks on the art and culture of the Far East, for different age groups—5 to 8 years, 9 to 11 and 12 to 18.

MUSÉE EN HERBE   **12** E13   Ⓜ Les Sablons
Jardin d'Acclimatation, Bois de Boulogne (16th); tel. 40.67.97.66. Daily 10 a.m.–6 p.m.; Saturday 2–6 p.m.
Workshops and leisure activities: outdoor games, from 4 years. Museum visit and written game (in English), from 7 years. Museum visit and show, from 7 years, 10.15 a.m. and 2.45 p.m.

MUSÉE NATIONAL DES MONUMENTS FRANÇAIS (see page 44)
Wednesday and Saturday, 2–4 p.m., 8–12 years. Exploratory visit, with sculpture, architecture and wall-painting workshops.

MUSÉE D'ORSAY (see page 38)
Workshop: discussion with monitors about artistic creation in the 19th century. Wednesday and Saturday 2.30–4.30 p.m., reserve in advance.

Where to Find Out More
For complete information on all the activities available for children in Paris, contact the following:

Les Affaires culturelles de la Ville de Paris: Hôtel d'Albret, 31, rue des Francs-Bourgeois (4th) and Hôtel Coulanges, 37, rue des Francs-Bourgeois; tel. 42.76.67.00/42.76.67.87. Map **25** R9; métro Saint-Paul. Open 9 a.m.–noon and 2–5.30 p.m.; closed Saturday and Sunday. Here you can obtain a brochure edited by the principal museums of Paris, which includes a list of activities organized specially for children.

La Direction des Musées de France: 34, quai du Louvre (1st); tel. 42.60.39.26. Map **24** O9; métro Louvre–rue de Rivoli. Open 9.45 a.m.–6.30 p.m., closed Tuesday. This association publishes a brochure entitled *Objectif Musées*, which describes all the workshops organized for children in the different museums.

Visits of discovery: exploratory visits based on specific themes. For 8–13 years and 13–16, Wednesday and Saturday 2.30–4.30 p.m. Free admission.

MUSÉUM NATIONAL D'HISTOIRE NATURELLE (see page 51)
Birds and bees, flowers and trees...nature study for children from 7 to 15, Wednesday at 2.30 p.m. Reserve in advance by phoning 43.36.54.26.

PALAIS DE LA DÉCOUVERTE (see page 51)
Chemistry made fun. Wednesday and Saturday at 2.30 p.m., 12–16 years.
Astronomy: Wednesday and Saturday 2.30 and 4.30 p.m., 12–18 years.

MAGIC AND PUPPET SHOWS

CENTRE D'ANIMATION   **7** L15   Ⓜ Brochant
DES BATIGNOLLES
75 bis, rue Truffaut (17th); tel. 47.37.30.75 (reservation compulsory). Wednesday 2.30 p.m., Sunday and school holidays 3 p.m.
For children from 3 to 12. Clowns, ventriloquists, conjuring tricks and Guignol—the French Punch and Judy.

CENTRE JEAN VERDIER   **17** R11   Ⓜ Jacques Bonsergent
11, rue de Lancry (10th); tel. 60.16.45.41/42.03.00.47. Wednesday 2.30 p.m.
String puppets, animated by the Vagabond Theatre.

GUIGNOL ANATOLE   **10/18** U18   Ⓜ Buttes-Chaumont
Parc des Buttes-Chaumont (19th); tel. 43.98.10.95. Saturday and Sunday 3 and 4 p.m.
Open-air Punch and Judy show for warm days.

GUIGNOL DU SQUARE   **29/30** H5/6   Ⓜ Vaugirard
SAINT-LAMBERT
Square Saint-Lambert (15th). Monday, Tuesday, Thursday, Friday 5 p.m., Wednesday, Saturday, Sunday 3.30 p.m.
Punch and Judy show for all the family.

LES JARDINS   **31** M6   Ⓜ Montparnasse-Bienvenüe
D'HOLLYWOOD   **179**
55 bis, boulevard de Montparnasse (6th); tel. 45.44.19.18/40.49.00.72
Party time—lunch and show with clowns, ventriloquists, conjurors,

trained dogs...for 5–10-year-olds, Saturday and Sunday. Children's menu, parents à la carte. Mini rave-up for kids 10–15, Wednesday and Saturday 3 and 6 p.m.

MARIONNETTES **22** H9 Ⓜ Ecole Militaire
DU CHAMP-DE-MARS
Champ-de-Mars, near Place du Général Gouraud (7th); tel. 46.37.07.87. Wednesday, Saturday, Sunday, and every day during school holidays, 3.15 and 4.15 p.m.
Two different, alternating puppet shows.

MARIONNETTES **14** K11 Ⓜ Franklin-D.-Roosevelt
DES CHAMPS-ÉLYSÉES
Rond-Point des Champs-Elysées (8th); tel. 42.57.43.34. Wednesday, Saturday and Sunday, 3, 4 and 5 p.m.
Traditional Punch and Judy.

MARIONNETTES **32** O6 Ⓡ (line B) Luxembourg
DU LUXEMBOURG
Jardin du Luxembourg (6th); tel. 43.26.46.47/43.50.25.00. Wednesday and Sunday 2.30, 3.30 and 4.30 p.m., Saturday 3 and 4 p.m.
Indoors Punch and Judy.

MARIONNETTES **38** O1 Ⓡ (line B) Cité Universitaire
DE MONTSOURIS
Parc Montsouris (14th); tel. 46.65.45.95. Wednesday, Saturday and Sunday 3 and 4 p.m.
You can wander round the pretty park while the children watch the show in a warm little theatre.

MARIONNETTES DE VAUGIRARD **36** J3 Ⓜ Porte de Vanves
Parc Georges-Brassens (15th); tel. 46.07.45.69. Wednesday, Saturday, Sunday 3, 4 and 5 p.m.

SALLE MARGUERITE GAVEAU **15** L12 Ⓜ Miromesnil
45, rue La Boétie (8th); tel. 45.63.20.30. Wednesday 2.30 p.m.
Clowns, music, songs, magic and puppet shows, and the children join in (3–9 years). With a tea party at the end.

THÉÂTRE DU FOYER **21** G10 Ⓜ Trocadéro
Palais de Chaillot, 1, place du Trocadéro (16th); tel. 47.04.86.80. Tuesday, Thursday, Friday 10 a.m. and 2.30 p.m., Wednesday 2.30 p.m., Saturday 3 p.m. Reduction for children, but reserve well in advance.
Puppets, theatre and fairy tales.

THE CIRCUS

CIRQUE NATIONAL GRUSS
Ⓜ Porte de la Villette

Tel. 40.36.10.72; in Paris from October to mid-February. It changes location every season, but the phone number is always the same.
A real, old-fashioned circus, sawdust and all.

CIRQUE DE PARIS
ⓇⒺⓇ (line A) Nanterre-Ville

Corner of avenue de la Commune-de-Paris and avenue Hoche, Nanterre (92), tel. 47.24.11.70. Wednesday, Sunday and school holidays 3 p.m.
The wonderful world of the circus: clowns, jugglers, ponies, wild animals.

DIANA MORENO BORMANN

Tel. 64.05.36.26; in Paris from end March to end June and mid-September to end December (changes location each year).
Royal Bengal tigers, elephant football, parrots, cockatoos, clowns, magic show.

STUDIO A   **14** J12
Ⓜ Franklin-D.-Roosevelt

Galerie Point Show, 66, avenue des Champs-Elysées (8th); tel. 42.25.12.13/42.25.69.25. Wednesday 3–6 p.m.
A circus with a difference: from 3 to 4 p.m., **Elysées Circus** offers jugglers, tightrope walkers, clowns; from 4 to 4.30 p.m. tea party; from 4.30 to 6 p.m. everyone dons theatre makeup for a mini rave-up.

CINEMA

CINÉMA LOUIS LUMIÈRE   **11** V16
Ⓜ Porte de la Villette

At the Villette; phone 40.35.79.40 (answering machine, in French) for the day's programme.
Daily showings of cartoons, documentaries, science-fiction films, all based on a theme such as oceanography, botany, fauna etc. After the film, the children can join in work groups or a debate.

THÉÂTRE DE L'EST PARISIEN   **19** X12
Ⓜ Saint-Fargeau

159, avenue Gambetta (20th); tel. 43.63.20.96. Wednesday and Saturday, 2 and 4 p.m.; Fridays during school holidays.
American cartoons—Mickey Mouse, Felix the Cat, and so on—but usually dubbed in French.

AU BEC FIN **16** N11 ⓂPyramides
6, rue Thérèse (1st); tel. 42.96.29.35. Wednesday and school holidays 2 and 3.30 p.m.
Performances for 3–7-year-olds.

BLANCS-MANTEAUX **25** R9 ⓂRambuteau
15, rue des Blancs-Manteaux (4th); tel. 43.63.51.37. Wednesday 2.15 and 3.30 p.m., Saturday 3 p.m., Sunday and school holidays 4 p.m.
For young children, with audience participation.

POINT VIRGULE **25** R9 ⓂHôtel-de-Ville
7, rue Sainte-Croix-de-la-Bretonnerie (4th); tel. 43.71.43.48. Wednesday and school holidays 2.15 and 3.30 p.m., Saturday and Sunday 4 p.m.
Musicals, comedies, ballets, with audience participation.

SENTIER DES HALLES **16** P11 ⓂSentier
50, rue d'Aboukir (2nd); tel. 42.36.37.27. Monday to Friday 2 p.m. Wednesday 2.30 p.m., Saturday 3.30 p.m.
The children (from 4 years) join in the songs, music and dancing.

THÉÂTRE ASTRAL ⓂChâteau de Vincennes
Parc floral de Paris (12th); tel. 48.08.79.06/43.55.78.33. Wednesday, Thursday, Friday 3 p.m., Sunday and holidays 3.30 and 7 p.m.
For children from 3 years.

THÉÂTRE BON'MIN' **12** E11 ⓂPorte Dauphine
Le Relais du Bois, route de Suresnes, Bois de Boulogne (16th); tel. 45.25.49.05. Wednesday, Saturday, Sunday and holidays 10.30 a.m.–6 p.m.
Clowns, jugglers, conjurors. On Saturdays at 4 p.m., Sundays and holidays at 4.30 p.m., the children can join in a stage makeup class.

THÉÂTRE DE LA MAINATE **18** S12 ⓂGoncourt
36, rue Bichat (10th); tel. 42.08.83.33. Wednesday 1.45 and 3 p.m., every weekday during holidays 9.45 a.m. and 2.30 p.m.
Two actors bring fairy tales to life with splendid costumes and stage sets (for children up to 12).

THÉÂTRE DE LA **17** R11 ⓂStrasbourg-Saint-Denis
PORTE SAINT-MARTIN
16, boulevard Saint-Martin (10th); tel. 46.07.37.55/42.08.00.01. Every weekday 2.30 p.m.
Classic performances.

THÉÂTRE 13   **38** P3   Ⓜ Glacière
*24, rue Daviel (13th); tel. 45.80.18.60. Wednesday, Thursday, Saturday
3 p.m. Admission free.*
Singing and dancing.

BOOKS

The English bookshops, W.H. Smith, Brentano's and Galignani all
have a good choice of children's books. See pages 106–109. The
shops listed below may also please baby bookworms.

CHANTELIVRE   **31** M7   Ⓜ Sèvres-Babylone/Saint-Sulpice
*13, rue de Sèvres (6th); tel. 45.48.87.90. Tuesday to Saturday
10 a.m.–6.50 p.m.*
Thousands of books, and reading corner.

LIBRAIRE DU MUSÉUM   **33** R5   Ⓜ Monge
D'HISTOIRE NATURELLE
*36, rue Geoffroy-Saint-Hilaire (5th); tel. 43.36.30.24. Monday to Sat-
urday 10 a.m.–6.30 p.m.; Sunday 11 a.m.–6 p.m.*
Nature books, mainly in French and English.

RIBAMBELLE   **14** H13   Ⓜ Ternes
*46, rue Poncelet (17th); tel. 42.27.96.54. Tuesday to Friday 10.15 a.m.–
2 p.m. and 3–7 p.m.; Saturday 10.15 a.m.–1.15 p.m. and 2.15–7 p.m.*
On the ground floor, books, scale models, cut-outs and party decorations; upstairs, wooden toys designed for outdoors.

TOYS

The big stores have wonderful toy departments (see pages 69–70),
but you'll also find the following shops hard to resist.

ALI BABA   **22** J8   Ⓜ Ecole Militaire
29, avenue de Tourville (7th); tel. 45.55.10.85, open 10 a.m.–1 p.m. and
2–7 p.m.
Three floors of toys and games. Fathers will love the collection of
hand-painted tin soldiers.

AU NAIN BLEU   15 M11   Ⓜ Concorde/Madeleine
406–410, rue Saint-Honoré (8th); tel. 42.60.39.01. Monday to Friday 9.45 a.m.–6.15 p.m.; Saturday 9.45 a.m.–6.30 p.m.
This toy paradise, more than 100 years old, inspired Baudelaire to pen ''La Morale du joujou''.

BOOMERANG   16 P13   Ⓜ Poissonnière
Lots of games and toys at reasonable prices.
79, rue du Faubourg-Poissonnière (9th); tel. 42.47.04.03. 10 a.m.– 6.30 p.m.; Monday noon–5.30 p.m.

BOUTIQUE D.A.C.   33 Q7   Ⓜ Cardinal-Lemoine
10, rue du Cardinal-Lemoine (5th); tel. 43.54.99.51. 10 a.m.–7.30 p.m.; Monday 2.30–7 p.m.
String puppets, china dolls, music boxes and clockwork toys, and a fabulous collection of dolls' houses and furniture.

CHAT PERCHÉ   25 R9   Ⓜ Saint-Paul
54, rue du Roi-de-Sicile (4th); tel. 42.77.20.48. Tuesday to Saturday 11 a.m.–7 p.m.
A wide range of toys from 10 to 4,000 F, from kaleidoscopes to clockwork. And lovely little stars that shine when you turn out the light.

LE CIEL EST A TOUT LE MONDE   16 P4   Ⓜ Anvers
7, avenue Trudaine (9th); tel. 48.78.93.40. Tuesday to Saturday 10.30 a.m.–7 p.m.
Superb kites, jumping jacks and wooden puppets.
*Also 10, rue Gay-Lussac (5th); tel. 46.33.21.50, Map **32** 06*—one shop full of kites, and another next door, with toys.

ÉOL   31 P7   Ⓜ Maubert-Mutualité
*62/70, boulevard Saint-Germain (5th); tel. 43.54.01.43. 8 a.m.–8 p.m. Also 10, rue Erard (12th); tel. 43.47.21.06, Map **27** V6.*
Model aeroplanes and the like.

184 **JOUETS AND CO   24** P9   Ⓜ Châtelet
11, boulevard de Sébastopol/16, rue Saint-Denis (1st); tel. 42.33.67.67. 10.30 a.m.–7.30 p.m.
Toy hypermarket with kindergarten.

MAGIE MODERNE   **32** P7   Ⓜ Maubert-Mutualité
HATTE MAYETTE
8, rue des Carmes (5th); tel. 43.54.13.63. Tuesday to Saturday
10 a.m.–7 p.m.
Jokes and novelties, like stink bombs, squeaking camemberts, whoopee cushions; also some good conjuring tricks.

LA MAISON DES TRAINS   **15** M13   Ⓜ Gare Saint-Lazare
24, passage du Havre (9th); tel. 48.74.55.29, Tuesday to Saturday
9.15 a.m.–7 p.m.; Monday 9.15–noon and 1.15–7 p.m.
Electric trains.

MULTICUBES   **25** R8   Ⓜ Saint-Paul
5, rue de Rivoli (4th); tel. 42.77.10.77. 10 a.m.–7 p.m.
*Also 110, rue Cambronne (15th), tel. 47.34.25.97, Map **30** J5.*
Specializes in wooden toys.

PAIN D'ÉPICES   **16** O12   Ⓜ Richelieu-Drouot
29–31, passage Jouffroy (9th); tel. 47.70.82.65. Tuesday to Saturday
10 a.m.–7 p.m.; Monday 12.30–7 p.m.
Everything in miniature, from tiny fishing rods to dolls'-house furniture. A few collector's items.

LA PELUCHERIE   **14** J12   Ⓜ George-V
84, avenue des Champs-Elysées, galerie "Les Champs" (8th); tel.
43.59.49.05. Daily 10 a.m.–midnight; Monday early closing 8 p.m.;
Sunday 11.30 a.m.–7.30 p.m.
Cuddly stuffed toys—incredibly lifelike. And babywear.

LA POUPÉE MERVEILLEUSE   **25** Q9   Ⓜ Hôtel-de-Ville
9, rue du Temple (4th); tel. 42.72.63.46. 10 a.m.–6.30 p.m.
A dolls' hospital, where you can hire fancy dress costumes, and buy fireworks, jokes and novelties.

SI TU VEUX   **16** O11   Ⓜ Bourse
68, galerie Vivienne (2nd); tel. 42.60.59.97. 11 a.m.–7 p.m.
Mail order catalogue. Lots of games at reasonable prices. Fancy dress—ready-made or in sewing kits, and all you could possibly want for a children's tea party.

LE TRAIN BLEU   **20** E9   Ⓜ La Muette **185**
2, avenue Mozart (16th); tel. 42.88.34.70. 10 a.m.–7 p.m. Other branches in the 6th and 15th arrondissements.
A huge shop with classic and sophisticated toys and games.

BOUTIQUES

Fashion-consciousness comes to Parisian kids at an early age—
even Dior has a baby boutique! Apart from the children's sections
in the big department stores, don't miss these boutiques for the
trendiest toddlers in town. Children's sizes are based on height, in
centimetres.

BABY DIOR   **14/22** J11   Ⓜ Alma-Marceau
28, avenue Montaigne (8th); tel. 40.73.55.14. 10 a.m.–6.30 p.m.
If price is no object.... For your little treasures, from pram to school
age.

BASTIEN BASTIENNE   **31** L6   Ⓜ Vaneau/Sèvres-Babylone
*71, rue du Cherche-Midi (6th); tel. 45.48.71.84. 11 a.m.–7 p.m.; Monday
2.30–7 p.m.*
Shoes for all sizes, from tiny-toed tots to big-footed teenagers.

CACHAREL   **14** J12   Ⓜ Franklin-D.-Roosevelt
*74, avenue des Champs-Elysées, galerie du Claridge (8th); tel.
45.63.23.09. 10 a.m.–7.30 p.m.; Monday 11.30 a.m.–7.30 p.m.*
Classy, classic clothes for 4 to 18-year-olds: Liberty prints for the girls,
smart stripes for the boys. Blazers and pleated skirts....

LA CHÂTELAINE   **13** F11   Ⓜ Victor-Hugo
*170, avenue Victor-Hugo (16th); tel. 47.27.44.07. Tuesday to Friday
9.30 a.m.–6.30 p.m.; Saturday 9.30 a.m.–12.30 p.m. and 2.30–6.30 p.m.*
Ultra-chic—the "in" place for children's clothes. High quality, tasteful
design, and expensive. (For girls and boys from birth to 12 years).

CHERCHEMINIPPES ENFANTS   **31** L6   Ⓜ Duroc
*21, rue Mayet (6th); tel. 45.67.04.81. 10.30 a.m.–7 p.m. (until January
1990.) Then: 110, rue du Cherche-Midi (6th), tel. 42.22.33.89, Map 31
L6, same hours.*
Impeccable second-hand clothes for children from birth to 10 years.

CYRILLUS   **6** J14   Ⓜ Pereire
*104, avenue de Villiers (17th); tel. 47.66.43.17. 10 a.m.–7 p.m.; Monday
2–7 p.m.*
Well-made, hard-wearing clothes at reasonable prices.

JACADI   **15/23** N11   Ⓜ Villiers
186 *77, rue du Rocher (8th); tel. 45.22.03.89. 10 a.m.–5 p.m. Branches all
over Paris.*
Smart fashions for schoolchildren (up to 16). Competitive prices,
classic style with trendy trimmings.

MARALEX   **20** E/F9   Ⓜ La Muette
*1, rue de la Pompe (16th); tel. 42.88.92.90. Tuesday to Saturday
9.30 a.m.–12.30 p.m. and 2–7 p.m.*
Sensible shoes of reliable quality.

NUAGE ROUGE   **23/24** N8   Ⓜ Mabillon
*26, rue des Canettes (6th); tel. 43.26.52.32. 11 a.m.–7 p.m.; Monday
2–7 p.m.*
Inexpensive clothes of the "back to nature" type. See also **Le Mouton
à Cinq Pattes** (page 82).

PETIT FAUNE   **23/24** N8   Ⓜ Saint-Germain-des-Prés
33, rue Jacob (6th); tel. 42.60.80.72. 10.30 a.m.–7.15 p.m.
Irresistibly attractive...but big price-tags.

POM' D'API   **24** P10   Ⓜ Les Halles
*13, rue du Jour (1st); tel. 42.36.08.87. 10.30 a.m.–7 p.m.; Saturday until
7.30 p.m.*
Colourful, unusual shoes.

NINA RICCI   **14/22** J11   Ⓜ Franklin-D.-Roosevelt
*39, avenue Montaigne (8th); tel. 47.23.78.88. 10 a.m.–6.30 p.m.; Sat-
urday 10 a.m.–1.15 p.m. and 2.15–6.30 p.m.*
One section devoted to lucky babies.

SONIA RYKIEL ENFANTS   **23** M8   Ⓜ Sèvres-Babylone
*8, rue de Grenelle (6th); tel. 42.22.43.22. 10 a.m.–7 p.m.; Monday
2–7 p.m.*
The inimitable stamp of Rykiel. Three months to 14 years.

TARTINE ET CHOCOLAT   **14** K12   Ⓜ Miromesnil
*89, rue du Faubourg Saint-Honoré (8th); tel. 42.66.36.39. 10 a.m.–
6.45 p.m.*
Lovely children's clothes (6–10 and 14–16 years), accessories and fun
gadgets. And maternity wear.

TATI   **9** Q14   Ⓜ Barbès-Rochechouart
*2–4, boulevard Barbès (18th); tel. 42.55.13.09. 9.30 a.m.–7 p.m.; Mon-
day 10 a.m.–7 p.m. Other branches in the 3rd and 6th arrondissements (see page 83).*
Very cheap. Good underwear, jeans and track suits.

TILL   **21** F19   Ⓜ La Muette   **187**
*54, rue de Passy (16th); tel. 42.88.11.50. 9.30 a.m.–7 p.m.; Monday 2–
7 p.m. Other branches in the 6th, 8th, 14th and 15th arrondissements.*
Three hundred types of shoes, and qualified advisors.

CHARLES CHEVIGNON   **23/24** N8   Ⓜ Saint-Germain-des-Prés
4, rue des Ciseaux (6th); tel. 43.26.06.37. 10.15 a.m.–7 p.m.
Sportswear in worn leather, cotton and hessian, liberally encrusted with badges and insignia. For those who like designer labels splashed all over their backs. Accessories in the same vein. Expensive.

CHIPIE   **24** P9   Ⓜ Châtelet
31, rue de la Ferronnerie (1st); tel. 45.08.58.74. 10 a.m.–7 p.m., Monday 11 a.m.–7 p.m. Other branches in the 6th and 16th arrondissements.
Expensive sportswear for juniors who like to show off the labels. Footwear in the boutique next door.

FIORUCCI   **24** P9   Ⓜ Châtelet
34, rue Saint-Denis (1st); tel. 42.33.85.08. 10.30 a.m.–7.30 p.m.
The trendy Italian look. No jeans. High prices.

MARIE COQUINE   **8** P15   Ⓜ Château-Rouge
20, rue Custine (18th); tel. 42.55.80.84. 10 a.m.–7 p.m.; Monday 11 a.m.–7 p.m.
An amusing boutique which sells or hires all kinds of disguises and costumes for fancy dress parties. Made to measure, on request (children and adults).

NEW MAN   **24** O8   Ⓜ Odéon
10, rue de l'Ancienne-Comédie (6th); tel. 43.54.77.54. 10 a.m.–7.30 p.m.
Gabardine and denim for men. Reasonable prices, and sizes to fit the slimmest to the most muscular he-men.

OPOX   **23** N8   Ⓜ Saint-Sulpice
64, rue de Rennes (6th); tel. 45.44.23.75. 10.30 a.m.–7.30 p.m.
Fashion New York style, and amazing accessories. Reasonable prices.

TWINS   **25** Q10   Ⓜ Rambuteau
27, rue de Quincampoix (4th); tel. 42.77.72.22. 10.30 a.m.–8 p.m.; Sunday noon–8 p.m.
High-class second-hand clothes, unusual accessories and gadgets.

188

WALTER   **19** V11   Ⓜ Ménilmontant
18, rue Etienne-Dolet (20th); tel. 46.36.03.63. Tuesday to Saturday 11 a.m.–7.30 p.m.

Where the rock stars find their boots. A fabulous collection—hand-tooled, high-heeled, square-toed, studded, spangled, leather, velvet....

WESTERN HOUSE   **23/24** N8   Ⓜ Mabillon
23, rue des Canettes (6th); tel. 43.54.71.17. 10 a.m.–7.15 p.m., Monday 2–7 p.m.
Also 13, avenue de la Grande-Armée (16th); tel. 45.00.06.05, Map 31 M12.
Everything and anything straight from Mexico and California. Cowboy boots, jeans, leather jackets (Schott, Perfecto, Bombers, Avirex).

BABYSITTERS

ALLÔ MÀMAN POULE
Tel. 47.48.01.01, 24-hour service. Agency fee 40 F; hourly rate 24 F. Between 8 p.m. and midnight, if the child is in bed, 22 F. All night 290 F (specialist), 220 F (student). Weekend 500 F, one week 1,900 F, 4 weeks 4,600 F.
Reputed for reliable service. English-speaking sitters.

BABY-SITTING SERVICE
Tel. 46.37.51.24, 24-hour service. Agency fee 48 F. Nine hours 240 F plus expenses; weekend 500 F plus expenses.
The personnel is recruited among women students.

CENTRE RÉGIONAL DES ŒUVRES UNIVERSITAIRES ET SCOLAIRES
Tel. 47.21.48.50 (ext. 247), 46.61.33.04 (ext. 748) or 49.41.70.56
Students' babysitting service.

KID SERVICE
Tel. 42.96.04.16. Monday to Friday 9 a.m.–8 p.m., Saturday 10 a.m.–8 p.m. Agency fee 47 F (or annual subscription 1,800 F). Qualified nanny: 40 F per hour during the day; flat rate for 10 hours 300 F; 8 p.m.–8 a.m. 280 F; 24 hours (for babies under 3 months) 400 F; flat rates for weekends. Babysitter: 25 F per hour; flat rate for 10 hours 220 F: 8 p.m.–8 a.m. 150 F; weekend Saturday morning to Sunday evening 400 F; Friday to Sunday 450 F.
The oldest baby-sitting agency in Paris. Will go out of its way to please.

I t's difficult to talk about Paris without giving a mention to its *agglomération*—the suburbs. There's almost as much to be seen in the outskirts as in Paris itself, everything from magnificent castles with classical French gardens and romantic woods to futuristic urban development. The public transport network—métro, rapid-transit RER, train or bus—is extremely efficient, as long as you avoid rush hour (weekdays, 7–9 a.m. and 5–7 p.m.).

If you have time to venture beyond the suburbs, consider a trip to one of the charming old towns of the Ile-de-France, such as Chantilly, Chartres or Fontainebleau, made famous by their castle or cathedral—or dip your toes in the English Channel at Honfleur or Deauville.

BOULOGNE-BILLANCOURT   Ⓜ Boulogne–Pont de Saint-Cloud
On the south-west edge of Paris, the **Espace Albert Kahn** is the regional museum of the Hauts-de-Seine, harbouring a number of unexpected treasures. Albert Kahn was a diamond merchant, a financier and public benefactor. Between 1910 and 1930, he built up the "Archives of the Planet", a collection of thousands of photographs and films, now on view in his home. The house is in the middle of a park, the **Jardin Albert Kahn**, which has been divided up into a number of small gardens, each representative of the different landscapes that fascinated him. Growing side by side in total harmony: the clipped geometrical precision of a French formal garden; the smooth lines of Japanese yin and yang; the tangled disarray of English grasses, bushes and flowers; an orchard and rose garden; a pine forest; a golden forest; a blue forest....

Exhibitions relating to the environment are held in the **Maison de la Nature**, at the same address. Everything from solar energy to meteorology, from the forest to the oceans, from the country to the city. The subject changes every quarter. There's also a kitchen garden, welcoming children from 7 to 14 every Wednesday to see how things grow.

The Albert Kahn photo and film collections can be consulted by appointment at the **Photothèque-cinémathèque** (same opening

Von Spreckelsen designed the Grande Arche as "a window opening on the world".

hours as the park). This "film library" also holds exhibitions and shows films.

Jardin Albert Kahn: 1, rue des Abondances (can be reached through the Maison de la Nature); 15 March to 15 November, 9.30 a.m.–12.30 p.m. and 2–7 p.m. (6 p.m. in March, October and November). Free admission for children under 6.

Maison de la Nature: 9, quai du Quatre-Septembre; tel. 46.03.33.56. Open daily 9 a.m.–12.30 p.m. and 2–6 p.m. Admission free.

Photothèque-cinémathèque: 10, rue du Quatre-Septembre; tel. 46.04.52.80.

CERGY-PONTOISE

Ⓜ (line A3) Cergy-Saint-Christophe
Train from Gare Saint-Lazare to Gare de Pontoise
Situated 30 km north-west of Paris, Cergy-Pontoise is one of the more adventurous suburbs that have sprung up in the past twenty years, nestling in a curve of the Oise river. The architects were able to put into practice their post-1968 ideas for "humanizing" contemporary architecture. To avoid the problems of many dormitory towns, much thought was given to providing social facilities; Cergy-Pontoise has its fair share of theatres and cinemas, and there's a library, swimming pool, skating rink, an arts centre, even an academy of music. Half the population is under 20. Numerous industrial concerns have been attracted to the site, and a host of colleges for Higher Education—a campus is in the works. (For the amusement park, **Mirapolis,** see page 174.)

Cergy offered the town planners the chance to create one of those long perspectives the French are so fond of, similar to that of the Champs-Elysées: the 3-km-long **Axe majeur**, designed by the sculptor Dani Karavan. When it is finished, its grandiose span will link 12 "gateways". Coming out of the Cergy–Saint-Christophe railway station, distinguished by its gigantic clocks (the biggest in Europe), you reach the first of these, Ricardo Bofill's semi-circular **Place des Colonnes**, supposed to symbolize the earth. A gap in the building looks out over the landscape. In the centre of the square, Karavan's **Belvédère** tower (36 m high and 3.6 m wide) is a symbol of balance—even though it's slightly inclined in the direction of the Axe. A laser beam is to be installed at the summit; it will shoot right down the perspective to disappear in mid-air over the roundabout at the road entrance to Cergy. You can climb to the top of the tower for a panoramic view of the whole region.

To visit the Belvédère tower, borrow the key from the Cergy–Saint-Christophe Town Hall, rue de l'Abondance: Monday to Thursday 8.30 a.m.–noon and 1.30–6 p.m.; Friday until 5 p.m.; Saturday

8.30 a.m.–noon. Or from the Maison de Quartier, place du Marché: Monday to Friday 8.30 a.m.–12.30 p.m. and 1.30–7 p.m.; Saturday 9 a.m.–12.30 p.m. and 1.30–6 p.m. Or on Sunday, from the Boulangerie Maès, 10, rue des Frontons, during the shop opening hours.

The perspective continues towards the **Parc central** and the **Verger**, or orchard, reminders of Cergy's agricultural past, and on to the **Esplanade de Paris**, a little square outlined by paving stones from the Cour Napoléon in the Louvre. Continue to the **Terrasse**, where the plain suddenly dips to reveal the Oise valley, the Cergy-Neuville ponds, and Paris on the horizon. There, for the moment, stops the Axe majeur, for lack of funds.

LA DÉFENSE

(line A) La Défense

This haphazard conglomeration of shiny and brazenly futuristic business and residential buildings is a far cry from historical old Paris. The first construction was the **CNIT** building (National Centre of Industry and Technology) in 1958, with a huge vaulted roof spanning 283 m, anchored at three points. The vault is all that remains of the original CNIT, which has been completely remodelled to house exhibition and lecture halls, a shopping mall, radio and TV studios, a business centre, cafeteria and restaurant.

The first towers to go up were directly inspired by the straight, clean lines of American skyscrapers in the style of Mies van der Rohe—the **Esso** building (the first office block in France), which now seems tiny compared with its neighbours; and the **Tour Nobel** (now the Tour Roussel-Hoechst), at the end of the Esplanade near the Pont de Neuilly, built in 1966. The second generation towers were more ambitious in design, higher, less stark, with hollows and rounded corners—the triangular **Tour Assur**, opposite the Roussel-Hoechst; the cruciform **Tour GAN** (1974), by American architects Harrison and Abramowitz; the curvy **Tour Manhattan** (1975); and, with 44 floors the highest of all the Défense buildings, the polished black granite **Tour Fiat** (1974), designed by two French and three New York architects, Skidmore, Owings and Merill. Its neighbour, the **Tour Elf**, was built by the same architects ten years later, though with a completely new approach. Running costs were cut by two-thirds, thanks to the use of new materials, and the offices were designed on a more human scale, smaller, with natural daylight rather than harsh neon lighting, and windows that open. The Elf tower is now taken as the model of the third generation of towers.

In a desperate attempt to put some life and colour into this concrete jungle, the Défense promotion society commissioned a series of gigantic sculptures from world-famous artists. Bright plastic figures by Miró teeter across Place de la Défense, adding a bit of comic relief, along with a red iron stabile by Calder, and Rieti's mosaic face. A wall engraved by Guiro meanders along the Esplanade, opposite Agam's waterfall where 66 fountains play to the sound of laser discs. Round every turn, you'll come across a bas-relief, a "water mirror", a marble "moon woman", a "mechanical bird", constituting what the promoters like to call a Sculpture Park. All these sculptures are numbered on the Défense map on pages 2–3 of the map section. For the key, see below. The Défense has two art galleries: the **Galerie de l'Esplanade** (Esplanade du Général-de-Gaulle, La Défense 4; tel. 47.75.86.08; daily, noon–7 p.m.) which deals mainly with architecture, and the **Galerie Art 4** (15, place de la Défense, La Défense 4; tel. 49.00.15.96; daily except Tuesday noon–7 p.m.), displaying contemporary works of art.

The **Quatre-Temps** shopping centre was opened in 1981. With 240 shops and 20 restaurants, it's the most animated place in the whole district.

At the Tête-Défense (the prow of the Défense) is the **Grande Arche**, the late Johann-Otto von Spreckelsen's enormous monument that closes the perspective from the Arc de triomphe du Carrousel in front of the Louvre. It's on a slight bias in relation to the Champs-Elysées but directly in line with the Louvre's Cour carrée.

Key to map of La Défense (See map section facing p. 206)

1. **Prentice** Fontaine des Solstices
2. **Serra** Slat
3. **César** Icare
4. **Kowalski** La Porte de la Ville
5. **Torricini** La Colonne Oiseau
6. **Moretti** Le Pendule
7. **Lhoste** L'Envol
8. **Miró** (two figures)
9. **Rieti** (mosaic face)
10. **Rieti** (mural)
11. **Calder** (red stabile)
12. **Mitoraj** Grand Toscano
13. **Delfino** Les Lieux du Corps
14. **Deverne** (mosaic on ventilation chimneys)
15. **Casadeus** Les Points de Mire
16. **Barrias** La Défense de Paris
17. **Agam** La Fontaine de l'Esplanade
18. **Silva** Dame Lune
19. **Moretti** Monstre
20. **Guiro** (engraved wall)
21. **Clarus** (ventilation chimney in the Midi-Minuit pond)
22. **Leygue** La Fontaine des Corolles
23. **Atila** Le Sculpteur de Nuages
24. **Philolaos** L'Oiseau Mécanique
25. **Derbre** La Terre
26. **Selinger** La Danse
27. **Grataloup** (mosaic on a chimney)
28. **Torricini** La Grenouille devenue aussi grosse qu'un bœuf)
29. **Ben Jakober** BC1
30. **Venet** Doubles Lignes indéterminées
31. **Fenosa** Ophélie
32. **De Miller** Somnambule
33. **Deverne** (mosaic fountain)
34. **Takis** (traffic lights in pond)

A huge hollow cube, 110 m high and 106 m wide, the Grande Arche is big enough to enclose Notre-Dame and its spire, wide enough for the Champs-Elysées to pass through. The gables (visible if you approach from Paris or the west) are clad with white Carrara marble; the external façades with smooth grey marble and glass. The inside walls are faced with aluminium. The two sides of the Arche contain offices, while the roof has several conference rooms and four patios. Bubble lifts whoosh up to the terrace through the fibreglass and Teflon "cloud", floating on a web of fine steel cords stretching from one wall to the other.

JOUY-EN-JOSAS   Train from Gare Montparnasse
A four-minute walk from the station brings you to the **Fondation Cartier pour l'art contemporain**. On the lawn of a rather dainty-looking bourgeois house, a collection of outrageous or amusing contemporary works (such as a pile of compressed cars by César) steal the show.
3, rue de la Manufacture; tel. 39.56.46.46. Daily except Monday; November to May 11 a.m.–6 p.m., June to October 11 a.m.–8 p.m.

MARNE-LA-VALLÉE   (line A4) Noisy-le-Grand–Mont d'Est
A 20-minute RER ride from Châtelet, Marne-la-Vallée is a flourishing new town to the east of Paris, designed to integrate industries harmoniously into the landscape—a protected zone of forests, rivers, parks and châteaux. Shopping centres, offices and and tertiary industries cluster along the backbone of the RER line, eating ever further eastwards into the countryside to stop eventually at the Magic Kingdom of Euro Disneyland—still at the planning stage.
The town centre, at Mont d'Est, is a business district with a most hallucinating assortment of ultramodern architecture. Apartment buildings, shops and office blocks are set out round pedestrian precincts. The Arcades shopping centre is the nucleus of the new town, while Ricardo Bofill's high-flown blocks of flats, the **Palacio de Abraxas** and the **Théâtre**, on the model of Ancient Greek temples and amphitheatres, attract hordes of photographers. Manolo Nuñez' **Arènes de Picasso**, despite all appearances another apartment block, is decidedly Gothic in inspiration, complete with flying buttresses and enormous disks vaguely reminiscent of a rose window.

RUEIL-MALMAISON   (line A) Rueil-Malmaison
A peaceful-looking place, the 18th-century Château de Malmaison was Napoleon's favourite retreat before he became emperor, then Josephine's as she wasted away and died here after Napoleon divorced her. (Her tomb is in Rueil-Malmaison church.)

The château is a museum with a lived-in look to it, full of Napoleonic souvenirs and elegant Empire furniture. In Josephine's boudoir there's a superb dressing-table set and a harp; in Napoleon's apartments you can see an original (there are several in existence) of David's famous painting *Bonaparte au Grand-Saint-Bernard*.

Outside is a large park with Josephine's rose garden. The Château de Bois-Préau, close by, contains, among other treasures, souvenirs of Napoleon's exile on St. Helena—his uniform, his sword, his deathbed and a clock stopped at 5.49, the 5th May 1821, the moment his heart stopped beating.

Musée national des châteaux de Malmaison et de Bois-Préau, 1, avenue du Château; tel. 47.49.20.07. 10 a.m.–noon and 1.30 p.m.–4.30 p.m. (4.50 in summer); closed Tuesday. Park 10 a.m.–12.30 p.m.

SAINT-DENIS

(line D) Saint-Denis
Ⓜ Saint-Denis-Basilique

In the northern suburbs, the sanctuary and Benedictine abbey of Saint-Denis were erected round the tomb of Saint Denis, the first bishop of Paris. He had walked to this spot with his head in his hands after being decapitated on Montmartre hill in the year 250. In the 12th century, Abbot Suger began what was to become the model for the great Gothic cathedrals of the Ile-de-France. The cathedral lost its north tower after some unfortunate 19th-century restorations, and its main interest today is as the repository for monumental royal tombs, from Dagobert, who died in 639, to Louis XVIII (died 1824). The bodies were disposed of during the Revolution, but 79 recumbent statues have been preserved, including a mosaic for Clovis, brought from the church of Saint-Germain-des-Prés, and a double monument for François I and his wife. In the north transept, you can see two versions of Catherine de Médicis, one dead and one asleep. Louis XVI and Marie-Antoinette share the Bourbon family vault down in the crypt.

The **Théâtre Gérard Philipe** (59, boulevard Jules-Guesde, tel. 42.43.17.17) commemorates the great actor who was well known for plays such as *Le Cid, Caligula* and *Ruy Blas*, and films such as *Fanfan la Tulipe* and *Le Diable au corps*.

SAINT-GERMAIN-EN-LAYE

(line A1) Saint-Germain-en-Laye

Parisians like to go to Saint-Germain for a day out, for a meal in one of the many restaurants on the banks of the Seine, or a ramble through the ancient royal forest. Hunting lodges are still half-hidden among the fine old oaks, birches, beeches and pines. The forest provided sport for the court of the pentagonal **château** in which Louis XIV grew up and experimented with his architects before setting them to work on Versailles. The gardens, especially the **Grande Terrasse** north-east of the palace, affording a stunning view over the Seine Valley, represent the summit of Le Nôtre's landscaping genius.

Today, the palace houses the great **Musée des Antiquités nationales**, devoted to Stone Age art and the country's earliest history. With the 20,000-year-old *Vénus de Brassempouy*, the museum boasts the oldest known representation of a human face. Look out, too, for two marvellously expressive prehistoric horses, one leaping, the other whinnying, and a whole pantheon of Gallic, Celtic and Roman gods. *Musée des Antiquités nationales, place du Château; tel. 34.51.53.65. 9.45 a.m.–noon and 1.30–5.15 p.m. Closed Tuesday.*

VAUX-LE-VICOMTE   Train from Gare de Lyon to Melun, then taxi State financier Nicolas Fouquet's grandiose château (7 km from Melun station) offers a pleasant day trip out of Paris, along with an exquisite object lesson in the humiliation of the high and mighty. Following in the footsteps of Richelieu and Mazarin, Fouquet amassed a huge fortune from his job with the motto *Quo non ascendem?* ("What heights can I not scale?"). Louis XIV showed him. When the king was invited for dinner in 1661, he threw a tantrum at the extravagance of the reception and opulence of the place, tossed Fouquet in jail and appropriated his architect Le Vau, painter-decorator Le Brun and landscape architect Le Nôtre to build Versailles. As you can see by the unfinished splendour of the rotunda's Grand Salon, Le Brun had to leave in a hurry. But in Le Nôtre's gardens you can still appreciate the wonderful perspectives and surprise effects of the pools and canals. On summer weekends, there are illuminated fountain displays in the gardens and night-time tours of the castle by candlelight.
Château: tel. (1)60.66.97.09. Daily from 1 April to 31 October 10 a.m.– 6 p.m. From 1 November to 31 March 11 a.m.–5 p.m. Closed Christmas Day. Fountain displays at 3 and 6 p.m., the second and last Saturday of the month, April to October. Candlelight tours every Saturday, 8.30–11 p.m., May to September.

VERSAILLES   (line C5) Versailles-Rive gauche
You'll need a full day to do Versailles justice, with an early start. Organized coach tours leave from the Tuileries gardens, Rue de Rivoli.

Never could a piece of architecture more exactly express the personality of its builder than the Château de Versailles. Louis XIV's palace is as extravagant, pompous, dazzling, formidable and vainglorious as you might expect for someone who called himself the Sun King. Louis XIII had hoped to turn his favourite hunting ground into a modest **197** retirement home. For his son, Versailles became the centre of a universe, proclaiming his own grandeur in a sprawling edifice of brick, marble, gilt and crystal.

The central part of the building, where the royal family lived, was designed by Le Vau and completed by Hardouin-Mansart. Le Vau also designed the marble courtyard, decorated with 84 marble busts. Inside, the essential rooms to visit are the **Royal Chapel**, a gem of High Baroque; the **Grands Appartements**, named after the gods and goddesses whom Louis felt to be his appropriate companions; the glittering **Galerie des Glaces**, 73 m long, built to catch every ray of the setting sun in the 17 tall arched panels of mirrors. No less than 19 royal children were born in the **Queen's Bedroom**. The **King's Bedroom** is set at the exact centre of the sun's path from east to west. Louis XIV died here in 1715 of gangrene. And don't miss Louis XV's charming **Royal Opera**.

Lined with a multitude of statues, the formal **park**—along with Mansart's **Orangerie** and the pond called *la pièce d'eau des Suisses*—is one of Le Nôtre's finest achievements as a landscape architect. The central perspective of the **Tapis vert** sweeps down beyond the **Bassin d'Apollon** along the **Grand Canal**, where Louis used to keep his flotilla of Venetian gondolas.

North-west of the château, the **Grand Trianon**, surrounded by pleasantly unpompous gardens, was the home of Louis XIV's mistress, Madame de Maintenon, where the aging king increasingly took refuge. It's a lovely low palace with a peristyle and columns, beautifully restored and furnished inside (the restoration was paid for mainly by American groups and individuals). The **Petit Trianon** was Marie-Antoinette's favourite hideaway; in comparison with the rest of Versailles it's like a doll's house. The **Hameau**, in the same grounds, is a bucolic hamlet of thatched cottages where Marie-Antoinette

---

Versailles in depth

From October to March, lectures are given at lunchtime on specific works or themes to do with Versailles. Rendezvous at Entrance 1.

The history of the château is related every Saturday, at 9.45 a.m. and 2 p.m., from October to March. Rendezvous at Entrance 2.

From October to June, in-depth guided visits are held on Saturdays at 2.30. Rendezvous at Entrance 1.

For more details about these schedules and the subjects treated, write to:

Bureau d'action culturelle, Château de Versailles, 78000 Versailles.

dressed up to play milkmaid. You can rent a bicycle or take a little train to visit the Trianons.

Château and museum: tel. 30.84.74.00. 9.45 a.m.–5 p.m.; closed Monday and holidays. Free admission for anyone under 18.

Royal Chapel, Grands Appartements and Galerie des Glaces: self-guided tour.

King's bedroom and Royal Opera: 90-minute guided tours, first tour 9.45 a.m., last 3.30 p.m. Entrance 3. Saturday and Sunday closed 12.30–2 p.m.

Grand Trianon 9.45 a.m.–noon and 2–5 p.m. Petit Trianon 2–5 p.m. Self-guided tours (commented visits on request). The little train departs from the Grand Canal.

Turning on the Waterworks

To see the fountains of Versailles in all their glory, you have to be there on a Sunday. The **Grande Perspective** display takes place in the morning, from 11.15 to 11.35 a.m., while the **Grandes Eaux** are turned on in the afternoon, from 3.30 to 5 p.m. The show is quite spectacular, recapturing some of the splendour of festivities at the court of the Sun King. Some of the fountains play to music. At 5.20 p.m., they die down, leaving only Neptune to close the show with a magnificent finale.

There are also several special night-time floodlit displays with music and fireworks. Details (and reservations for the fireworks) from:

L'office de tourisme de Versailles, 7, rue des Réservoirs; tel. 39.50.36.22.

FURTHER AFIELD

CHANTILLY   Train from Gare du Nord

Chantilly is celebrated for its château, its elegant racecourse and stables, and for *crème chantilly*—whipped cream served at the château gates on hot waffles.

The **château**, which belonged to the powerful Condé dynasty in the 17th century, links a reconstruction of the Grand Château, destroyed during the Revolution, to the authentic Renaissance building known as the Petit Château. It houses the **Musée Condé**, a superb collection of Italian, French and Dutch masters, including Raphaël, Veronese and Fra Angelico, Poussin, Watteau, exquisite portraits by Clouet,   **199**

Van Dyck and Teniers. In the Cabinet des Livres you can admire the famous Book of Hours of the Duc de Berry, a fascinating illuminated manuscript depicting 15th-century life. One of the charms of the collection is that the paintings are hung according to the personal whim of their last owner, the Duke of Aumale.

The palace grounds make a pleasant walk, especially the English Garden behind the Petit Château. Louis XIV was very jealous of the Grand Canal, ponds and waterfalls designed by Le Nôtre and insisted the master gardener do even better in Versailles. You may prefer the more intimate scale of Chantilly.

Horse racing in Chantilly began in 1834. In June, the **Hippodrome** west of the château is host to the prestigious Prix du Jockey Club. But all year round you can visit the monumental 18th-century **Grandes Ecuries**, the stables designed by Jean Aubert which house the **Musée vivant du Cheval et du Poney**, where live horses munch hay next to wooden statues.

Musée Condé: tel. 44.57.08.00 (answers weekdays, 9.30 a.m.– 12.30 p.m.); March to October 10 a.m.–6 p.m., closed Tuesday; November to February 10.30 a.m.–12.45 p.m. and 2–5 p.m.

Musée vivant du Cheval et du Poney: tel. 44.57.13.13. Closed Tuesday. April to October 10.30 a.m.–5.30 p.m.; November to March, weekdays 2–4.30 p.m.; Saturday and Sunday 10.30 a.m.–5.30 p.m.

Skewered

One day in April, 1671, Louis XIV visited Chantilly with 5,000, yes, 5,000 friends for a three-day stay. The Condé family's brilliant but sensitive master chef Vatel went berserk earning his title of "Contrôleur général de la Bouche de Monsieur le Prince" (General Supervisor of the Prince's Mouth). Bad enough on the first night when three tables had to go without their roast. When the fresh fish failed to arrive the next day, Vatel went up to his room and ran himself through with his sword.

CHARTRES Train from Gare d'Austerlitz
One of the most moving experiences on a journey across France is to drive through the wheat fields of the fertile Beauce plain and see, looming suddenly on the horizon, the silhouette of Chartres Cathedral, 85 km south-west of Paris.

This unquestionable masterpiece of French civilization marks the transition in the 12th century from the solid, sober Romanesque style of the Church's beginnings to the more airy, assertive Gothic of its

200

ascendancy. Apart from a few decapitated statues, it came miraculously unscathed through the Wars of Religion and the Revolution. As you face the asymmetrical western façade, the southern tower, **Clocher vieux,** is a supreme expression of Romanesque simplicity, while the taller northern tower, **Clocher neuf,** is lighter, with a slender, more ornate steeple. On the central porch, **Portail royal,** note the stately, deliberately elongated sculptures of Old Testament figures, compared with the freer, more vigorous statues on the northern and southern porches.

You can climb the **Clocher neuf** to admire close-up details of the sculptures, gargoyles and flying buttresses, and for a good view over the town. Visiting times vary according to the weather and on-going services like weddings, funerals or mass, but in principle it's open 10–11.30 a.m. and 2–4.30 p.m. (5.30 p.m. in summer).

Inside, the glory of the church is its 173 12th- and 13th-century **stained-glass windows**, in particular the *Virgin and Child,* the *Annunciation* and the *Visitation* at the end of the choir. That unique "Chartres blue" and deep red bring an ethereal light into the nave, especially from a late afternoon sun through the western rose window, which depicts the Last Judgment. Among the oldest and most famous of the windows, on the southern side of the choir, is an enthroned Mary with Jesus on her lap, *Notre-Dame de la Belle Verrière.* The church is dedicated to Mary, representing her 175 times in the various sculptures and windows.

In the paving of the nave's central aisle, you'll notice a large circular labyrinth. Medieval worshippers traced its path from the circumference to the centre as part of a mystic spiritual excerise.

The choir is enclosed by a sculpted ensemble by Jehan de Beauce (1514), in Renaissance style. The 11th-century crypt can be entered from an outside door, on the south side. Guided tours at 11 a.m., 2.15, 3.30, 4.30 and (in summer) 5.15 p.m.

To explore the old town, leave the cathedral by the Jardin de l'Evêché at the rear, where a stairway and path take you down to a bridge over the Eure river. Follow Rue de la Tannerie along the river, and cross back over the Bouju bridge, which opens onto the most picturesque old streets leading up the cathedral.

COMPIÈGNE   Train from Gare du Nord

On the edge of one of the most beautiful forests of the Paris region, 80 km north of Paris, Compiègne was another favourite residence of the kings of France.

On the site of a 9th-century Carolingian castle, the **château** was completely remodelled by Louis XV in 1738 and completed by Louis

XVI who lived there from 1785. You can visit several royal bedrooms: the **grand appartement du roi**, the **nouvel appartement de Marie-Antoinette**, and the **grands appartements de l'impératrice** (the Empress being Marie-Louise in 1800 and Eugénie during the Second Empire). Eugénie and Napoleon III's memorabilia constitute the **Musée du Second Empire**.

Also in the palace is a fascinating **Musée de la Voiture**, displaying all kinds of vehicles from the 18th and 19th centuries, from the coach that carried Napoleon to and from Moscow in 1812 to a splendid 1900 4-horsepower Renault.

In the town itself, note the Gothic **Hôtel de Ville**, where an equestrian Louis XII on the façade is flanked by St Denis, St Louis, Charles the Bald, Joan of Arc, a cardinal born in Compiègne, and Charlemagne. The **Musée de la Figurine historique** in the hotel next door displays a large collection of tin soldiers and other little figures showing the evolution of period costume and illustrating historic events.

The Forest of Compiègne offers plenty of good walks. You can hire a horse at the village of Saint-Jean-aux-Bois. Take the Avenue des Beaux-Monts to the **Clairière de l'Armistice,** where the Germans signed the peace treaty ending World War I in the private train coach that served as Maréchal Foch's HQ. A replica of the original coach can be seen in the Musée de l'Armistice.

Château (royal apartments, Second-Empire museum and car museum): tel. 44.40.02.02. 9.30 a.m.–noon and 1.30–5 p.m. Free admission for anyone under 18. Guided tours only.

Musée de la Figurine historique, Hôtel de Ville: 9 a.m.–noon and 2–6 p.m. (5 p.m. in winter). Guided tours only, by arrangement with the Compiègne tourist office, tel. 44.40.01.00.

Musée de l'Armistice, Clairière de l'Armistice: tel. 44.40.09.27. 9 a.m.–noon and 2–5.30 p.m., closed Tuesday.

DEAUVILLE AND HONFLEUR SNCF Gare Saint-Lazare

When the Parisians feel like a trip to the seaside, they drive up to Deauville, 170 km north-west of Paris on the English Channel. It's the most prosperous of Normandy's resorts, and also the most expensive. The white sandy beach, with its colourful canvas sun shelters, is a delight, and the swimming is perfectly good, but most people spend their time watching the parade of pretty girls along the celebrated beach boardwalk, the **Promenade des Planches**. The casino, racecourse and golfcourse are the right places to be seen, but at night the atmosphere in the bars and restaurants round the harbour is very relaxed and lively.

Honfleur, 10 km east of Deauville, on the Seine estuary, is a mecca for sailing enthusiasts. The sheltered yachting harbour of the **Vieux Bassin** inspired many painters at the beginning of the century. Explore the old shipbuilder's district along Rue Haute, running north-west from the Lieutenance, 16th-century remains of the royal governor's house at the harbour mouth.

FONTAINEBLEAU

Train from Gare de Lyon, then shuttle bus to château

The great forest of Fontainebleau, 70 km south-east of Paris, was a popular hunting ground for François I and Henri IV. Their **château** became the artistic centre of the French Renaissance—the rich interior decorations are due mainly to Italian, French and Flemish Mannerist painters, known as the school of Fontainebleau. Napoleon cherished it as a place for reflection, and it was there that he abdicated in 1814 to go into exile on the Isle of Elba. Allegorical paintings in the **Galerie de François Ier** bear testimony to the king's preoccupation with war and death, and also to the sanctity of kingship. Napoleon's apartments are still decorated with the furnishings of his empire. A Napoleonic museum has been installed in the Louis XV wing.

Save most of your time for the majestic **forest**, 25,000 ha of oak, beech, silver birch, chestnut, hornbeam and pine. Apart from lovely walks and lengthy hikes over well-marked paths, a great attraction is the miniature "mountain range" of sheer rocks and cliffs, much appreciated by amateur rock-climbers for trying out their equipment and technique before tackling the Alps. The most popular are the rugged Gorges de Franchard, due west of the palace.
Château: tel. 64.22.27.40/64.22.34.39. 9.30 a.m.–12.30 and 2–5 p.m., closed Tuesday. Admission free for anyone under 18.

GIVERNY

Train from Gare Saint-Lazare to Vernon

From Vernon, take a taxi or rent a bicycle for the 7 km to Claude Monet's home, which has been lavishly restored with brand new furnishings, artefacts from his studio and the collection of Japanese prints that provided some of his inspiration. The main attraction is the beautiful garden, complete with the Japanese bridge, water lilies and rose bowers that were among the Impressionist master's favourite subjects.
Musée Claude Monet; tel. 32.51.28.21. April to October, weekdays (except Monday) 10 a.m.–noon and 2–4 p.m.; Saturday and Sunday 10 a.m.–6 p.m. Gardens daily 10 a.m.–6 p.m.

CONSULATES

Contact the consulate of your home country if things go *seriously* wrong—for example, if you lose your passport, get in trouble with the police, or have an accident. The Consul can issue emergency passports, give advice on obtaining money from home, provide a list of lawyers, interpreters and doctors. He cannot pay your bills, lend you money, find you a job or obtain a work permit for you.

Australia	4, rue Jean-Rey (15th); tel. 40.59.33.00
Canada	35, avenue Montaigne (8th); tel. 47.23.01.01
Eire	12, avenue Foch (enter from 4, rue Rude) (16th); tel. 45.00.87/45.00.89.43
Great Britain	35, rue du Faubourg Saint-Honoré (8th); tel. 42.66.91.42
New Zealand	7 ter, rue Léonard-de-Vinci (16th); tel. 45.00.24.11
South Africa	59, quai d'Orsay (7th); tel. 45.55.92.37
U.S.A.	2, avenue Gabriel (8th); tel. 42.96.12.02

LOCAL TRANSPORT

204

Bus. Local buses cover Paris and the outskirts, and can be useful outside rush hour—and show you more of Paris than the métro. Most buses run from 7 a.m. to 8.30 p.m., some until half past midnight.

Métro. This is the most efficient way of getting round town. You can't get lost. In each station there's a huge map—just press the button next to the station you want to go to, and the route lights up. To change trains, follow the signs for "Correspondance". The way out is "Sortie". The métro functions between 5.30 a.m. and half past midnight. RER lines *(Réseau Express Régional)* run into the suburbs.

Tickets. They are sold singly or in booklets *(carnets)* of 10 (1st and 2nd class), and are valid in the métro and the bus. In the métro, one ticket is valid for one journey, with no limit on time or distance. The RER ticket is the same price as the métro for the urban district, but for the outskirts, the further you go, the more you pay. As for the bus, each line is divided into several sections, and one ticket is valid for one or two sections only. Children under 10 pay half price; under 4, they travel free.

Several special tickets permit unlimited travel on Paris transport; prices vary according to the number of zones you want to include. Zone 1 is Paris, the other four correspond to circles radiating outside the city into the furthest suburbs. They are available from métro ticket offices (where you can also pick up free maps of métro and bus networks); or phone the RATP information centre on 43.46.14.14, open daily 6 a.m.—9 p.m. **Formule 1** is a day ticket, valid 24 hours. **Paris-Visite** is valid three or five consecutive days. The **Carte orange,** a weekly *(hebdomadaire)* or monthly *(mensuelle)* pass is worth buying for long stays and lots of travel (you'll need a passport photo).

Taxis. You can hail one in the street, or go to a taxi stand. Or call a radio-taxi, though they charge meter fare for the trip to pick you up. Prices are indicated on the meter, but you might have to pay extra charges—for luggage, for example—according to the rates posted on the cab window.

MONEY MATTERS

The French franc is divided into 100 centimes. Coins: 5, 10, 20, 50 ct; 1, 2, 5, 10, 20 F. Banknotes: 20, 50, 100, 200, 500 F.

The currency exchange offices at Orly and Roissy airports, those at the Austerlitz, Lyon and Nord railway stations, and the one at 154, avenue des Champs-Elysées, are open every day. You can also change money in any bank (open Monday to Friday, 9 a.m. to 4 p.m.). If you're stuck, your hotel might come to the rescue, though you'll get a less favourable rate of exchange. The same applies to foreign currency or traveller's cheques cashed in shops or restaurants. Always take your identity card or passport along when you change money or cash traveller's cheques.

205

Credit cards are accepted in most hotels, restaurants and department stores.

POST AND TELEPHONE

You can recognize post offices *(Poste et Télécommunications,* or *PTT)* by the stylized blue bird on the sign. Letter boxes are yellow, and usually set into a wall, as are stamp machines. Stamps can also be bought at the post office, from tobacconists, or from wherever you buy your postcards.

Post offices open Monday to Friday from 8 a.m. to 7 p.m., and Saturday from 8 a.m. to noon (but see also page 68).

Long-distance and international calls can be made from any phone box, but if you need assistance, go to the post office. There are two types of pay phones—those that take coins, and *publiphones,* for which you'll need a *télécarte,* a phone card sold at post offices, tobacconists, railway ticket offices or certain shops. They cost 40 F for 50 units and 96 F for 120 units. The instructions for use are clearly displayed in each phone booth.

Telegrams can be sent from the PTT offices, or phone 42.33.21.11 for the English service. Other services include telex and telefax.

A note on French answering machines—recorded messages are almost invariably in French (in this book we have mentioned whenever the message is in English), and sometimes in very garbled French. Occasionally the text stops in the middle with a loud beep, and sometimes you'll hear *"Ce service n'est pas opérationnel"*. That doesn't mean that the number has changed, just that there is no message recorded at that moment. Try again later.

TOURIST OFFICES

Before your trip, you might like to gather more information from a French tourist office. Some addresses:

Australia	French Tourist Bureau, Kindersley House, 33 Bligh Street, Sydney NSW 2000; tel. (2) 231-5244.
Canada	French Government Tourist Office, 1, Dundas Street W., Suite 2405, P.O. Box 8, Toronto, Ont. M5G 1Z3; tel. (416) 593-4717.
Great Britain	French Government Tourist Office, 178 Piccadilly, London W1V 0AL; tel. (01) 493-6594.
U.S.A.	French Government Tourist Office, 610 Fifth Avenue, Suite 222, New York, NY 10020-2452; tel. (212) 757-1125.

The main Tourist Information Office in Paris provides heaps of brochures and leaflets on current events, and has a currency exchange. For a selection of the principal weekly events, call 47.20.88.98 (recorded message in English).

Office de tourisme de Paris: 127, avenue des Champs-Elysées (8th); tel. 47.23.61.72.

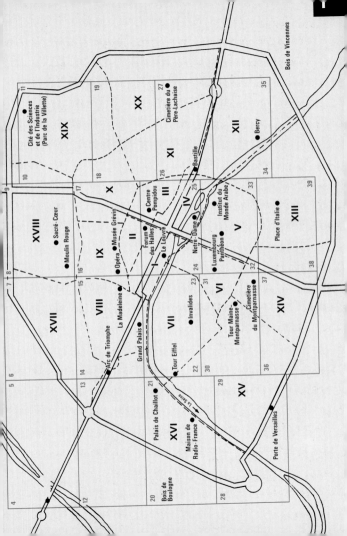

XIX
Cité des Sciences et de l'Industrie (Parc de la Villette)

XVIII
Sacré-Cœur
Moulin Rouge

XX
Cimetière du Père-Lachaise

XVII
Arc de Triomphe

VIII
La Madeleine

IX
Opéra
Musée Grévin

II

I
Forum des Halles
Le Louvre

X
Centre Pompidou

III

XI

XII
Bercy

IV
Notre-Dame

V
Institut du Monde Arabe
Luxembourg
Panthéon

Bastille

XIII
Place d'Italie

VII
Invalides
Grand Palais

VI
Tour Maine Montparnasse
Cimetière du Montparnasse

XIV

XVI
Palais de Chaillot
Maison de Radio-France

Tour Eiffel

La Seine

XV

Porte de Versailles

Bois de Boulogne

Bois de Vincennes

4 5 6 7 8 9 10 11
12 13 14 15 16 17 18 19
20 21 22 23 24 25 26 27
28 29 30 31 32 33 34 35
36 37 38 39

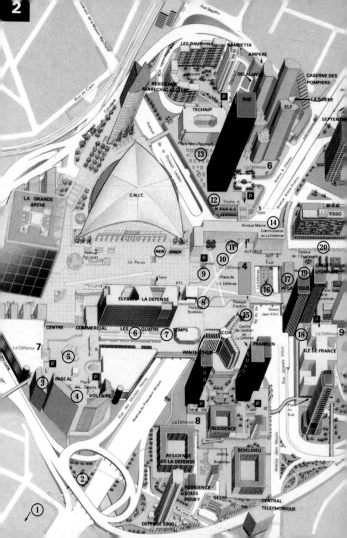

LAVOISIER

DESCARTES

JEAN MONNET

La Défense **5**

CECA

C.E.S.

ECOLE A. MALRAUX

DAMIERS DE DAUPHINE

DAMIERS DE CHAMPAGNE

DAMIERS DE BRETAGNE

NEPTUNE

La Défense **3**

Avenue d'Alsace

Place Dominé

Galeries des Damiers

Auchan

EUROPE

AMERICAN INTERNATIONAL

E.D.F. G.D.F.

BUREAU VERITAS

MANHATTAN

AURORE

RANK XEROX

La Défense **33** LES MIROIRS

GAN

L'ANCRE

La Défense **1**

ASSUR

Allée des Maisons

DAMIERS D'ANJOU

ORION

HARMONIE

CARTEL

NOVOTE

IBIS

Square Vivaldi

EAGLE STAR

EUROPE

VISION 80 **25**

Allée des Corolles

Reflets

22

23

Square des Corolles

25

VISION 80

LORRAINE

ILE

Esplanade

24

26

LES PLATANES

27

MANHATTAN SQUARE

La Défense **2**

Place de l'Iris

32

NEUILLY DEFENSE

Vue sur Bassins

Boulevard de Neuilly

ROUSSEL-HOECHST

28

TOTAL

du

THOMSON

Allée de

31

SOFITEL

Gaulle

EDF DFP

PFA

34

Terrasse Bellini

La Défense **10**

La Défense

29 TOFACE **30**

ATOCHEM

Allée des Sculpteurs

La Défense **11**

Rue Bellini

MINERVE

ALTIANZ

ECOLE DE LA ROTONDE

Rue Arago

Rue Paul Lafargue

Rue Pellini

Quai Gaz Dion Bouton

LA DÉFENSE

PUTEAUX

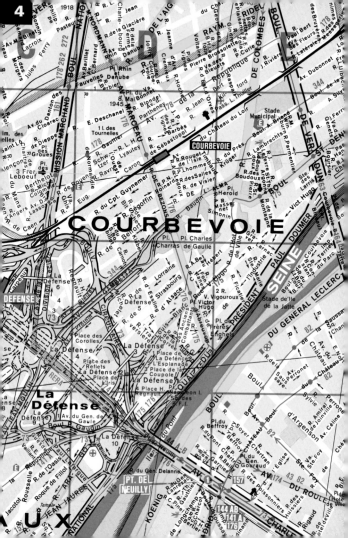

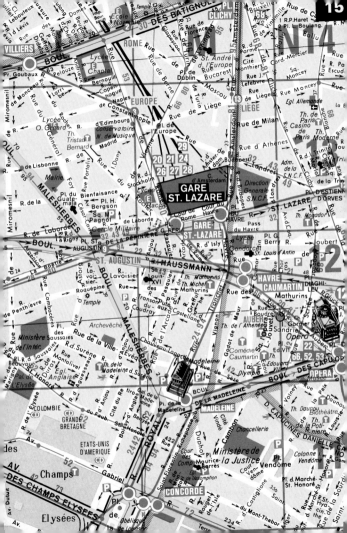

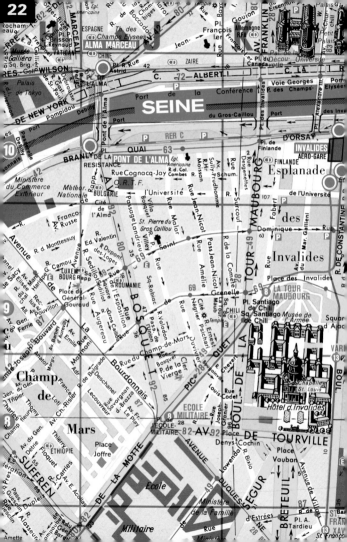

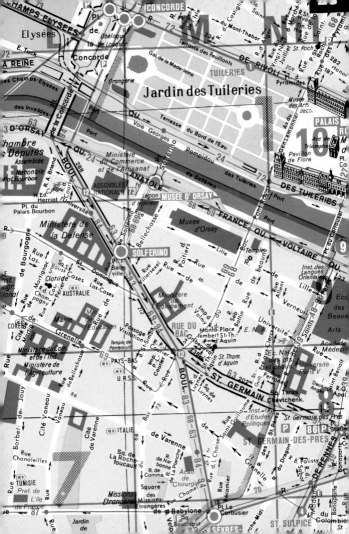

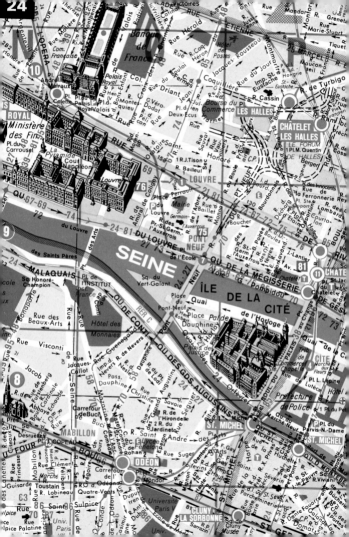

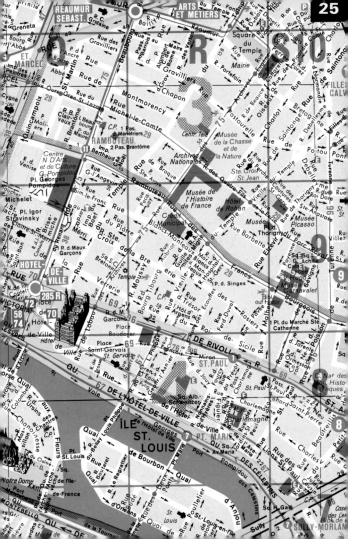

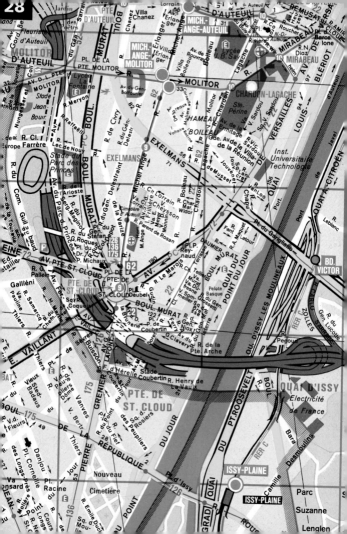

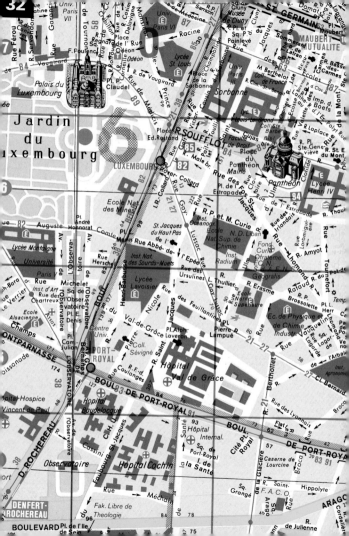

34

GARE DE LYON

Cour L.
Armand

Inst
Médica-legal

Pont d'Austerlitz

QUAI

BOULEVARD

Cour L. Cour
Armand Rue de Chalon

Denis

Pass.
Moulin

Guilla

DAUMESNIL

Pass. Brunol

R van Gogh

Régie Autonome
des Transports
Parisiens

Pass. Raguinot
R. A. C
Passage
Chalon

Gatbois

CHALON

Docks

PL
Valhubert

GARE D'AUSTERLITZ

QUAI

Cour de
l'arrivée

DE LA RAPÉE

d'Austerlitz

D'AUSTERLITZ

QUAI DE BERCY

de la Rapée

Port d'Austerlitz

Ateliers

Messagerie
Départ

Villiot

Allée de Ginkgo
Cour de Bercy

Ministère
1. Cour de Narbonne
des Finances

BERCY

Pl. du
Pacifique

Bat. du

BERC

87

Rue Fulton

Rue Ed. Flamand

Rue de Bellièvre

Kard

Pont de Bercy

BOUL.

QUAI

Palais
Omnisports
de Paris-Bercy

Pl. de
Bercy

Port

4 R. d. Sauternes

Entrepôts
Bassac

R. de Bercy

Cour de
Cour de
Cour de
Port Voyen

DE

R. de Ma-

con

Julien
L. Prou

AURIOL

QUAI
QU.
DE LA
GARE

SEINE

GARE AUX

de Bercy

du R.

R. Bruant
Bruant

CHEVALERET

VINCENT

Rue

81

148

MARCHANDISES

107

Sq.
Dunois

Rue

R.M.
et L. de Bioglie

Rue Louise Weiss

Clisson

Imp.
Baudoin

R. Duchefdelaville

Paris
Pierre-Gourdault

13

R.
Duchefdelaville

155

Panhard

de Tolbiac

Pl. de Tolbiac

2

93

Rue Clisson

JEANNE

D'ARC

Imp.
Clisson

R. de
Navarre

Ville

A. Bianqui

Chevaleret

PL. JEANNE
D'ARC

Notre Dame
de la Gare

R. C. PL.
Souham

57

71

Lahire

R. C. d.
Rentiers
du Dr.
Navarre
R. Renard

Dunois

Rue
Xaintrailles

Sq. F.

46

Charcot

de Domrémy

1 R. de Vimoutiers

U. Trélat

DE TOLBIAC

DE LA GARE

RUE

RUE

Magasins
Generaux
de Paris